CONFLICT AND CONTINUITY
AT ØM ABBEY

OPUSCULA GRAECOLATINA
(Supplementa *Musei Tusculani*)
Edenda curavit Ivan Boserup
Vol. 8

Brian Patrick McGuire

CONFLICT AND CONTINUITY AT ØM ABBEY

A Cistercian Experience
in Medieval Denmark

Museum Tusculanum
Copenhagen 1976

Copyright 1976 by Museum Tusculanum
Printed in Denmark by Special-Trykkeriet, Viborg

TABLE OF CONTENTS

FOREWORD 7
ABBREVIATIONS 8
1. THE COMING OF THE CISTERCIANS TO DENMARK 9
2. THE ØM ABBEY CHRONICLE: A UNIQUE AND FRUSTRATING SOURCE 20
3. THE OPENING OF THE EXORDIUM 1: CISTERCIAN POLISH VS. REAL PROBLEMS . . . 27
4. FAILURE AT KALVØ - SUCCESS AT ØM 35
5. THE ROLE OF BISHOP SVEN 43
6. THE ABBOT LIST (1165-1246) AND THE MIDDLE YEARS (1207-1246) 54
   A. The Earliest Abbots 54
   B. The Need for Practical Abbots 56
7. THE BEGINNINGS OF THE CONFLICT: 1246-1262 63
8. THE FIRST PART OF THE CONTROVERSY - TO SUMMER, 1263 76
   A. The Background of the Monks' Account 76
   B. The First Tremors 77
   C. The Thirteenth Century Process of Definition 82
   D. The Dispute Intensifies 86
9. THE OUTCOME OF THE CONTROVERSY 1263-1268 93
   A. The Aborted Compromise, 1264 93
   B. The Coming of Guido 96
   C. The Lübeck Declaration and its Sorry Aftermath - November, 1266 . 99
10. THE AFTERMATH OF THE DISPUTE 108
   A. Øm and its Sisters 108
   B. The Life of Bishop Gunner 110
   C. The Tradition of Biography at Øm 114
11. THE FOURTEENTH CENTURY: ECONOMIC REVIVAL AND DECLINE 125
12. THE REFORMATION BOOK LIST AT ØM: CULTURAL REVIVAL 128
BIBLIOGRAPHY 137
INDEX 142
MAPS 149
PLAN OF ØM ABBEY 152
PLATES 1-7

FOREWORD

The activity of the Cistercian Order in Denmark has left a collection of literary sources whose contents and importance have until now largely been unknown to medievalists outside Denmark. The literature concerning the Cistercians in Scandinavia contains many excellent articles and books, but the language barrier has made it impossible for non-Scandinavians to appreciate the richness of the medieval culture that came after the Viking Age and before the Reformation.

It is a privilege and a joy for me to be able to bring a small but significant part of the Scandinavian medieval experience to the attention of an international audience. The years since the Second World War have witnessed unflagging efforts among Danish historians, archaeologists, and art historians to reevaluate the medieval centuries in the light of their European context. At the same time the history of the Cistercian Order in many European countries has been studied more closely than ever before. It has been my aim in this book to combime the best of both worlds: to show the reader my heavy debt to my Danish colleagues, and at the same time to show my Danish readers how their history is inextricably bound up in a common European culture and a dynamic religious order.

The Øm Abbey Chronicle has been carefully looked at from almost every possible angle in earlier studies, and it has not been my object to come with a startling new revelation concerning its contents. I have only tried to show the Chronicle as a reflection of the attitudes, hopes, dreams, and disappointments of a Cistercian community during the twelfth and thirteenth centuries.

The people who have contributed to this book deserve to be mentioned, for without their support and criticism I would never have been able to have the peace of mind and the sense of perspective that such a work requires: Niels Skyum-Nielsen, Aksel E. Christensen, Jens Erik Skydsgaard, Inga Floto, Jan Pinborg, Birgitte Bentzon, Graham Caie, Ivan Boserup, Kai Hørby, Anne Riising, Olga Bartholdy, Esben Albrectsen, Hannah Krogh Hansen, Holger Garner, Karen Glente, John Baldwin, and R. W. Southern. To all these people and to the Institute for History at Copenhagen University, which sheltered and guided me as a kandidatstipendiat in the years 1972-74, and to my students, I owe my heartfelt thanks.

Skamstrup, January 1976.

ABBREVIATIONS

Canivez = J.M. Canivez, *Statuta Capitulorum Generalium Ordinis Cisterciensis* (Bibliothèque de la Revue d'Histoire Ecclésiastique 9-14B, Louvain, 1933-41).

DD = *Diplomatarium Danicum* (Det Danske Sprog- og Litteraturselskab, Copenhagen, 1938-   ).

DAM = *Diplomatarium Arna-Magnæanum* I, ed. G. Thorkelin (Cpn., 1786).

PL = *Patrologiae Latinae cursus completus*, ed. J. P. Migne (Paris).

Saxo = *Saxonis Gesta Danorum* I, ed. J. Olrik and H. Ræder (Cpn., 1931).

SM = *Scriptores Minores Historiae Danicae Medii Aevi* I-II, ed. M. Cl. Gertz (Selskabet for Udgivelse af Kilder til dansk Historie, 1918-22, photographic reprint, 197o).

SRD = *Scriptores Rerum Danicarum Medii Aevi* I-IX, ed. J. Langebek and P. F. Suhm (1772-1878).

ÆA = *De ældste danske Archivregistraturer* I, ed. T. A. Becker (Cpn., 1854).

1.
THE COMING OF THE CISTERCIANS TO DENMARK

Like Christianity itself, the Cistercian Order came relatively late to Denmark. The mother abbey of Citeaux sent out in 1144 a delegation of monks to Herrisvad in Skåne.[1] There is a tradition that Archbishop Eskil of Lund gave property to this new foundation and himself consecrated the monastery in 1150. There is no documentary support for this assertion,[2] but we at least can assume that Eskil was instrumental in bringing the monks to Skåne. Herrisvad was in his diocese, and so his cooperation was essential. We know from the great collection of early Cistercian history, the *Exordium Magnum ordinis Cisterciensis*, that Eskil was considered responsible for the foundations of both Herrisvad and Esrum.[3]

---

1) *Annales Colbazenses*, 1144: "Conventus missus est in Herivadum". The same source gives 1143 for the foundations of Alvastra and Nydala, the two first Swedish abbeys. Ellen Jørgensen, *Annales Danici Medii Aevi* (abbreviation - AD). Selskabet for udgivelse af kilder til dansk historie (Copenhagen, 1920), p. 43. See also *Annales Lundenses* and *Annales Ryenses*, p. 77. For the provenance of these chronicles, see Anne K.G. Kristensen, *Danmarks Ældste Annalistik* (Skrifter udgivet at Det historiske Institut ved Københavns Universitet) bind III, 1969.
2) See for example the unpublished typescript of Edvard Ortved on Herrisvad at the Royal Library, Copenhagen - Ny. kgl. S. 2o43 2o, II. Ortved did admit, however, that he could not find any sources for the traditional dating for Eskil's consecration of the abbey - 1 July 1150.
3) I have used the excerpts from the *Exordium Magnum* concerning Eskil printed by M.Cl. Gertz in *Scriptores Minores Historiae Danicae* (abbreviation - SM), Vol. II (photographic reprint, Copenhagen, 1970), pp. 428-442. The text can also be found in Migne, *Patrologia Latina* (PL) 185, col. 1085-88. As with much of early Cistercian writings, the language here is highly metaphorical, but the author still makes it clear that Eskil is to be held responsible for two Cistercian houses in Denmark, one under Citeaux and the other under Clairvaux. These would naturally be Herrisvad and Esrum: Nactus igitur oportunitatem de remotis Galliarum partibus, ubi fontem religionis esse cognoverat non solum quinque sed eciam plures spiritalis professionis conventus evocare curavit, inter quas eciam Cysterciensis ordinis duos conventus obtinuit, unum scilicet de ipsa domo Cystercii et alterum de Claravalle, quosque in optimis terre sue locis tamquam vites fructiferas, vinum iusticie germinantes, pastinavit." (SM II, 434). Note however that the writer does not use the verb *fundare*. If the author is Conrad of Eberbach and was at Clairvaux in the beginning of the 1180's as a monk,

A great deal has been written about Eskil's role in the Danish church and the way he used the Cistercians to back him up in his disputes with the king,[4] but recent historians have tended to dismiss this point of view as shallow and speculative.[5] But even if Eskil's political use of the Cistercians remains a question mark for us, and even if he did not give land to Herrisvad, Cistercian monks both at home in Denmark and abroad in France considered him responsible for the spread of the Order to the North. He became a living legend at the mother abbey of Esrum, Clairvaux. Stories of his boyhood sickness, his vision and cure, all were readily incorporated into the *Exordium Magnum* and also into the first biography of Bernard, the *Vita Prima*.[6] Eskil emerges here as a much loved and respected man who not only brought the Cistercians to Denmark but also assured the final defeat of "pagan rites".[7] Just as Absalon emerges as a giant from the memorable narrations of Saxo, so too Eskil is made into a larger-than-life phenomenon in early Cistercian literature.

Eskil seems to have been only too glad to spread the word about his indispensability to the Cistercians, not only by telling tall tales to the Clairvaux monks, but also by composing a privilege that describes the foundation and endowment of Esrum.[8] It is impossible to date the year when Cistercian monks

---

then he would have been able to know Eskil personally there. (SM II, 428). The Danish Cistercian tradition that Eskil founded Esrum and Herrisvad can be found in the first part of the Øm Abbey Chronicle (from 12o7 or soon after), SM II, 169 - "Ipse eduxit duos conventus, unum de Cistercio, alterum de Claravalle, et *fundavit* duo monasteria, Herivadum in Scania et Esrum in Selandia...."

4) Hal Koch, "De ældste danske klostres stilling i kirke og samfund indtil 1221", *Historisk Tidsskrift* (HT) 1o. Række, 3 Bind (1936), p. 526, n. 2. Reprinted in *Danmarks Kirke i den begyndende højmiddelalder*. Det historiske Institut ved Københavns Universitet, Historiske Afhandlinger Bind 8 (1972).

5) Niels Skyum-Nielsen, *Kvinde og Slave* (Cpn., 1971), p. 122. See also Sv. E. Green-Pedersen, "Studier over de danske cistercienserklostres forhold til ordenens internationale styrelse og til den danske kirke og det danske samfund indtil ca. 134o. Speciale (Cpn., 1969 - unprinted), p. 48. I was unable at the time of writing to acquire a copy of this dissertation, which was instrumental in shaping many of the views put forth on the Danish Cistercians in *Kvinde og Slave*.
Gina Gertrud Smith, "De danske nonneklostre indtil ca. 125o", *Kirkehistoriske Samlinger* 1973, pp. 19-2o, also criticizes the assertions of Hal Koch.

6) SM II, 431-433. The *Exordium Magnum* apparently lifted the description from the *Liber Miraculorum* of Herbert of Clairvaux, who apparently had heard the story from Eskil himself. Lauritz Weibull, "En samtida berättelse från Clairvaux om ärkebiskop Eskil av Lund", *Scandia* IV (1931), 27o-29o. See also my section on the possible sources for the Life of Bishop Gunner of Viborg.

7) SM II, 434 - "Dabat eciam operam paganitatis ritus, quibus adhuc ex magna parte terra illa inbuta erat, radicitus exstirpare...."

8) *Diplomatarium Danicum* (DD) Række I, Bind 2, nr. 126 - "...ac ne Cisterciensis ordinis fratres nobis deessent, ad beatissimum Claravallensis cenobii

first came to Esrum. Our chronicle gives 1153, while we already have a papal bull to Esrum from the end of 1151.[9] This fact was once explained by the assumption (without any real evidence) that Esrum was first a Benedictine house and later became Cistercian. The only possible resolution to this contradiction is to push back the initial foundation of a Cistercian monastery at Esrum to 1151 or slightly earlier and to conclude that a supplementary group of monks came from Clairvaux in 1153.[10] Whatever the exact circumstances may be, we can be sure that Eskil not only brought these monks with him from Clairvaux in that year but also endowed the new house with land that he himself possessed.

Soon after the initial donation, there was trouble. The ensuing dispute is indicative of the history of the Danish Cistercians. When they had a powerful bishop or king behind them, they inevitably won their case.[11] This is what happened at Esrum in the 1150's. The monks could profit not only from a strong archbishop on their side, but also from a newly unified monarchy after decades of chaos and uncertainty.

Although Eskil deserves recognition as something of a northern Bernard carrying on the work of the new reform order, our documentary sources only allow us to view his role at scattered moments and usually from a distance. It is different with Absalon, bishop of Roskilde and successor to the archbishopric of Lund after Eskil retired to Clairvaux in 1177. Absalon is the man responsible for giving an economic foundation to the Cistercian houses of Esrum and Sorø on Zealand and for safeguarding the continuing existence of a Cistercian nunnery at Roskilde. Absalon founded Cistercian Sorø in 1161 as a family monastery to replace the Benedictine abbey there, whose days were numbered and which may well have been totally abandoned by the time the new monks arrived from Esrum.[12] We have no idea of how many monks the mother house sent, but the traditional number for starting a monastery would be twelve, plus the abbot and an undefined number of lay brothers to do the physical labour.[13] Sorø grew up to become by the end of the 1100's the richest Danish Cistercian

---

patrem dominum Bernardum quamvis multo labore et sumptu pervenimus. de cuius filiis semen unde seges postera fidelium animarum pululare (posset) nobiscum in terram nostram adduximus."

9) AD, p. 43 (*Annales Colbazenses*); p. 79 (*Annales Lundenses* and *Annales Ryenses*) DD I, 2, 1o6-1151 29 December.
1o) See *Kvinde og Slave*, p. 12o.
11) For details, see my article "Property and Politics at Esrum Abbey, 1151-1251", *Mediaeval Scandinavia* 6, 1973, pp. 138-9.
12) For Absalon and Sorø, my article "Patrons, privileges and property - Sorø Abbey's first half-century", *Kirkehistoriske Samlinger* (KS) 1974, 11-25. Note that Anne K.G. Kristensen, *op.cit.* on the basis of *Annales Colbazenses* gives 1162 as the date of founding (pp. 112-113).
13) Edvard Ortved, *Cistercieordenen og dens klostre i Norden*: Bind 1 - *Cistercieordenen Overhovedet*, p. 64.

foundation, but it was still only Esrum's daughter, and liable to visitation from the mother abbot.

Theoretically no new Cistercian houses should have been founded after 1152, when a decree by the General Chapter in Citeaux forbade them. We can at least detect a short pause between Esrum's foundation and the beginning of the 116o's that may well have been due to this decree. We can also notice that it was just at this time that the French abbey of Prémontré founded a daughter house in Skåne, Tommerup, and thus began the Premonstratensian Order in Denmark. It is possible and even likely that this new house in Eskil's diocese belongs to the Premonstratensians and not to the Cistercians because the Archbishop was implementing the decision of the General Chapter.[14]

Sorø was not the first new Cistercian house after the pause of the early 115o's. A foundation was already made in 1158 on the eastern shore of Limfjord in northwest Jutland.[15] King Valdemar I founded the monastery as an offering of thanks after the defeat of his enemies. Thus from the very first at least one Cistercian house was tied to the triumphant royal family, a connection that later royal documents for Vitskøl would often mention. The monks who settled here came from Varnhem in central Sweden, from where they had been driven by a jealous queen, Christina.[16] In a short narration about these events, we are told how Christina molested the hapless monks. Once again we stumble upon the pitfalls and difficulties involved in starting a Cistercian house in Scandinavia. Just as at Esrum, local people did not always welcome the foreign monks with open arms. At Varnhem Christina succeeded so well in arousing the local population to hatred for the monks that women came inside the abbey complex in order to urinate and defecate.[17] One Palm Sunday when the brothers were going in procession around the cloister, the women left behind their outer garments and appeared before the monks in their underwear. Naturally the Lord could not stand for such treatment and saw to it that the house of the local priest, where the women had left their clothes, was burned down.

---

14) Tommerup was founded in 1155 or shortly before with help from Eskil - DD I, 2, 116. R.W. Southern shows like other historians that the 1152 prohibition was soon ignored, but his figures indicate that in the first years, it was generally obeyed. It is precisely in these years that Eskil helped founding Tommerup. *Western Society and the Church in the Middle Ages* (Pelican History of the Church, 197o), p. 254.
15) DD I, 2, 12o.
16) SM II, 138-142 - "Narratiuncula de Fundatione Monasterii Vitaescholae in Cimbria".
17) SM II, 139 - "Statimque exemplo regine omne vulgus in circuitu illorum pessimo odio oderunt illos, ita ut mulieres ad purgandos ventres suos abbatie terminos intrarent impudenter." Similar local resistance to Cistercian abbey foundation at Øm, SM II, 176.

Varnhem was a daughter of Alvastra. Although not far off as the crow flies, it was separated from the mother house by the great lake known as Vättern. In the summer time a crossing could be made without difficulty, but in winter ice and hurricane winds must have made this a treacherous affair. The consequent isolation of Varnhem and the demands of Queen Christina finally made it necessary for Abbot Henrik to look for another site for his monks.[18] On his way through Denmark and presumably bound for the General Chapter at Citeaux, Henrik stopped at Roskilde and there conferred with Eskil, who convinced him to bring his monks to Denmark. Henrik was French and had first been a monk at Clairvaux, then emigrated to Alvastra with a group in 1143, and later in the 1140's was sent to Ludrö in Venern to found a daughter abbey. Because of a bad location, he tried another spot, Lugnås, and finally moved thirty kilometres to the south to Varnhem in 1150,[19] only to be driven away a few years later.

In these movements, we can begin to understand what it meant to be a Cistercian in twelfth century Scandinavia. The monks were among the first victims of shifting political, social, and personal arrangements. By the time Henrik and his monks settled at Vitskøl in 1158 they were moving for the fifth time. Our account says that twenty-two monks and many lay brothers came south, with chalices, books, silver, clothes, and cattle. Of this number "many – and the better ones" eventually returned to Varnhem.[20] This parenthetical remark indicates that our chronicler is a monk at Varnhem who symphathizes with the reasons for abandoning the abbey but looks upon the Vitskøl foundation as only an emergency solution.

One of our Clairvaux sources contains an anecdote drawn from Vitskøl that puts us for a moment right into the centre of these monks' world.[21] A demon came to Vitskøl in the form of a young man and served the monks for three years. He was much appreciated for his helpfulness and for the way he always seemed to know what the monks wanted and needed. One day the brothers were on an errand at a nearby village. While they were sitting together in a house, the young man rose up and said, "Listen, there is a thunderstorm in Greenland." A little while later he announced that it had gotten to Iceland, and soon that it had reached Norway. He was terrified and fled towards the nearby water, with the brothers running after him, but before they came to the beach, he had been struck by lightning from the very thunderstorm he had been running from.

---

18) SM II, 139. Tandem denique regina per nuncium suum abbati Henrico precepit, ut domum magnam quandam, in qua abbas ipse libros missales scribere solebat, destrueret et ad locum alium, quo ipsa mandaverat, transferri faceret.
19) Ortved, *Cistercieordenen* II: *Sveriges Klostre*, p. 225.
20) SM II, 141.
21) Ellen Jørgensen, "Djævelen i Vitskøl Kloster", *Danske Studier* 1912, pp. 15-17.

All the brothers immediately realized that he was a demon and that none of them could remember his ever entering the church or showing any sign of being a Christian. As Ellen Jørgensen pointed out in 1912, this story is based on the pagan myth of the troll who is terrified of lightning. The total lack of a Christian background inherent in such a tale shows us that even at a place like Vitskøl, the pagan past was still very evident, even if it could easily be clothed in Christian dress.[22]

But men like Eskil and Absalon after him apparently did everything they could to solidify Christian myths and practices in Denmark. Eskil wisely saw to it that the new house at Vitskøl came under the rule of Esrum instead of the now impossible distant Alvastra.[23] This move can be contrasted with the inconvenient situation of the Norwegian Cistercian houses at Lyse near Bergen and Hovedøya in Oslo fjord. They were founded by monks from respectively Fountains in Yorkshire and Kirkstead in Lincolnshire, and contacts were so limited that finally they had to be put under a Swedish abbey.[24] It might seem natural that after all these years of movement and conflict our Vitskøl community would have settled down for a few years of well-earned concentration on the construction of their new home. But the pioneering spirit - and perhaps a certain restlessness - was still with them. Some of the monks returned to Varnhem, while others were sent out to found a new house to the south in Mid-Jutland's mild and beautiful Lake District.

As we shall see in the narration by the monks' themselves, they first settled in 1165-66 at Sminge on Gudenå near Silkeborg, but the property was too small and limited in its resources for a monastery. From there they came to Veng, which had until then been a Benedictine house, but were more or less forcibly removed by yet another angry woman. They settled for a time on Kalvø on Skanderborg Lake but were too isolated there. Finally in the spring of 1172 they came to a spot between Guden Lake and Moss Lake which they named *Cara*

---

22) A more famous story of a devil in a Danish Cistercian abbey is that of Brother Rus in Esrum, who managed to seduce the whole community with his superb cooking and ability for finding sexual temptations. Although this story is late medieval and speaks more of popular resentment to the monks, it might actually tell us something about the monks themselves. See *Broder Russes Historie*, Chr. Bruun (Cpn., 1868) for editions and text.
23) SM II, 141. Our Varnhem narrator is like his Clairvaux brethren quite attached to the memory of Eskil.
24) *Statuta Capitulorum Generalium Ordinis Cisterciensis*, ed. J.M. Canivez (Louvain 1933) 121o, nr. 33, 35, 1211, nr. 41. 1213, nr. 11. Bibliothèque de la Revue d'histoire Ecclésiastique, fasc. 9-14B. I shall cite Canivez according to the year of the General Chapter and the number of the decision. This new arrangement did not work either, probably because distances were still great, and finally Lyse was placed under Clairvaux directly, with the abbots of Fountains and Kirkstead ordered to visit the house - 1214, nr. 24.

Insula or Øm. Thus some of the brothers who finally made a permanent home at Øm in this year had been travelling with only short interruptions for almost thirty years from the time they left Clairvaux in 1143 to the time they arrived at Øm. They had lived in nine different places before they could come to their final destination.

We can summarize the series of emigrations to Øm thus:
Clairvaux (1143) - Alvastra (1143) - Ludrö (1148?) - Lugnås (1149?) - Varnhem (1150) - Vitskøl (1158) - Sminge (1165-66) - Veng (1166-68) - Kalvø (1168-1172) - Øm (1172).

The series of moves which finally brought a group of monks to Øm makes our most dramatic scenario for the early Danish Cistercians. But all the time new houses were being founded. Herrisvad's first daughter was Tvis on Storeå near Holstebro (1162).[25] Its founder, Duke Buris Henriksen, recorded his desires in a charter whose Danish translation from the 1500's has come down to us. In a forested area on Southern Funen, with the same combination of lakes and rolling landscape that typifies the rich countryside around Sorø, Holme abbey was founded in 1172.[26] We know nothing about the circumstances behind this particular foundation, for we have almost no medieval records from here. Nevertheless we can be certain that like other Cistercian houses it soon began to acquire considerable stretches of land in the surrounding area.

The final daughter of Herrisvad, and the only one known to us through abundant records, was Løgum, *Locus Dei*, in Southern Jutland. Cistercians were first sent to the church at Seem near Ribe, which had been a Benedictine abbey but was reformed in about 1170. The founders included Bishop Radulf of Ribe, Archbishop Eskil, and Herrisvad's former abbot Stefan, who succeded Radulf as bishop of Ribe.[27] In 1173 the abbey was moved south to Løgum, another richly forested area. Once again we see the need for isolation. Seem was just a few miles outside one of the most important episcopal seats and trading centres in twelfth century Denmark, Ribe, and so was not suited to the needs of the monks.

The transfer of Seem to Løgum in 1173 marks the end of the first and greatest period of Cistercian expansion in Denmark. One historian has suggested

---

25) *Annales Colbazenses* (AD, 43) has 1162 as the date, while the foundation charter has 1163 24 March (DD II, 1, 152).
26) AD 43, 87.
27) Jürgen A. Wissing. *Das Kloster Lögum im Rückblick*. Schriften der Heimatkundlichen Arbeitsgemeinschaft für Nordschleswig. Heft 21, p. 30. AD 206 (Petrus Olai): "1173 Conventus missus est de Herivado in Seem. 4 Idus Decembris. Et 1175 translatus est idem conventus de Seem in Locum Dei. Alibi 1173." For a very fine introduction to Løgum Abbey, as well as the Cistercians in general, see Olga Bartholdy's *Munkeliv i Løgum Kloster* (Løgumkloster, 1973).

that we deal with monastic foundation in terms of waves,[28] and with this concept in mind we can say that by now the first waves of monks from both Citeaux and Clairvaux had spent themselves. The thrust of further developments centres on the foundation of "granddaughter" and even "great granddaughter" houses to the French abbeys. Løgum and Tvis are examples, and if we return to the Esrum line, we can see an even bolder initiative. In 1172 Esrum monks founded a house at Dargun in Meklenburg, and a few years later this new house was able to send out a colony of its own to Colbaz, southeast of Stettin (1174 or 1175).[29] Although it is difficult to establish the exact relations between Esrum and its non-Danish daughters, we have at least some inklings of the presence and activity of the Esrum abbot Walbert in this part of the world.[30] The Danish conquest of Rügen in 1169 meant that the Wendish lands along the southern coast of the Baltic were open to Danish power politics and colonization, and even though evidence is meagre, it looks as though the Danish Cistercians went along gladly with royal policies and perhaps with the encouragement of the militant and ambitious Archbishop Absalon made their own stakes in this new frontier land.[31]

The 1170's also saw the founding of Cistercian convents, whose importance to the life of the Order should not be underestimated. A Cistercian nunnery was functioning at the Roskilde church of Our Lady prior to 1177.[32] The nuns were under the supervision and guardianship of the Sorø abbot, while the convent at Slangerup (founded before 1200, but possible as early as the 1170's) was under the abbot of Esrum. Thus the two most powerful and influential monasteries in Cistercian Denmark came to care for the only two Danish nunneries. As Ortved has already pointed out, Denmark came to have many more Cistercian monasteries than Sweden, while the opposite was the case with nunneries. The best explanation for this lies in the relative political unity of Denmark after 1158, while Sweden was still fragmented.[33] Denmark was a country whose magnates possessed an expendable surplus of lands and even money, so it was relatively easy for them to found monasteries. The newly established royal

---

28) Tore Nyberg, "Lists of monasteries in some thirteenth century wills. Monastic history and historical method: a contribution." *Mediaeval Scandinavia* 5 (1972), p. 53.
29) AD 43, *Annales Colbazenses*: 1172, "Conventus venit in Dargon de Esrom.... 1174 Conventus venit in Colbas." Also *Annales Essenbecenses*, p. 145, with same information.
30) DD I, 5, nr. 163.
31) *Kvinde og Slave*, p. 187.
32) Gina G. Smith, *op.cit*.., pp.6-7.
33) Ortved, Vol. II, p. 13. Landsarkivar, dr. phil. Anne Riising has pointed out to me that convents also cost money to endow, but I still think the foundation of a monastery would have entailed greater expenses than the foundation of a convent at this time.

house provided the main impulse, while the episcopacy also showed consistent support. The split between Eskil and Valdemar because of opposing popes in the 1160's does not seem to have affected the Cistercian advance in Denmark, for by now the king's loyal Absalon was also backing the Order. The Cistercians were attractive because they possessed a reform tradition, and so Danish magnates could feel that in establishing such an Order, they were guaranteeing their own salvation. With nunneries the impulse came from another motive: the need to provide for daughters who were not to be married off. But here there was already a good and increasing supply of Benedictine houses that could continue to receive the influx, and so there was no need for a Cistercian nunnery a few miles away from every new Cistercian monastery.

The rest of the century saw a continuing but less hectic Cistercian expansion. The Roskilde nuns apparently sent some of their members to start a convent in Bergen on the island of Rügen in 1193.[34] After a scandal at St. Michael's double monastery in Slesvig, Bishop Valdemar reorganized the monks as Cistercians and founded Guldholm in 1190-91, together with a delegation of monks from Esrum.[35] Once again as with Vitskøl Esrum shows involvement and energy in implicating itself in a foundation in another part of the country. The abbot at this time in Esrum was probably Walbert, who appears as signator in many documents from 1170 to 1193,[36] and was the kind of active and even dynamic monk who typifies a transition from Cistercian expansion made possible through assistance from men like Eskil and Absalon to Cistercian growth stimulated by the abbots themselves. It is a sign of this continuing vitality that Bishop Valdemar at the end of the twelfth century, just as Absalon at Sorø in 1161, turned to the Cistercians and to Esrum for its reformed and reforming monks to put things in order. The foundation of Guldholm was not so easy, however, as that of the earlier monasteries. After quarrels and even physical attacks on the monks, they had to move in about 1210 to Ryd, now Glücksborg on the south side of Flensborg Fjord.[37] These troubles were already manifesting themselves in the early 1190's, but they did not keep Sorø from founding its own daughter house at Ås in Halland on lands already owned by the

---

34) Gina G. Smith, *op. cit.*, p. 8.
35) AD 93 (*Annales Ryenses*) gives 1192, as well as *Annales Essenbecenses* (p. 145) but the date has to be 1191 - see SM II, 150.
36) In my article on Esrum, *op. cit.* p. 128, I wrongly stated that Walbert is first mentioned as abbot in November, 1178. He is already named as such as one of the signators for Archbishop Eskil's foundation privileges for the Premonstratensian abbey of Væ in Skåne, which Niels Skyum-Nielsen has dated to about 25 June, 1170, and placed at the important church meeting at Ringsted. *Scandia* 21 (1951), p. 21, "De ældste privilegier for klostret i Væ".
37) SM II, 151. H.N. Garner, *Atlas over danske klostre* (Cpn., 1968), p. 88.

Zealand house.[38] This was destined to be the last new foundation in Cistercian Denmark for almost one and a half centuries, and when the urge to spread the Order again manifested itself in the fourteenth century, the results were catastrophic. The twelfth century brought almost unlimited opportunities for the Cistercian Order in Denmark, while in the fourteenth they had to do their best just to hold on to what they had acquired.

In the course of half a century the Cistercians had made their mark on Scandinavia, starting in the most Christianized areas in central and southern Sweden and Zealand and eventually spilling over into northern and central Jutland, Funen, Slesvig, and Pomerania. It is easy to think of these monks in terms of superstition and neuroticism, and yet their very myths and compulsions made it possible for them to hold together in the midst of a culture whose members - for the most part - were probably indifferent or even openly hostile to the purposes and methods of the monks. These men and women were not devoting themselves to spreading the gospel, and yet their very presence helped to deepen and strengthen fragile Christian roots in Danish soil.

It is fashionable nowadays to look upon monasticism as yet another upper class movement which succeeded in maintaining social exploitation in the name of religion. Only a few decades ago another interpretation was prominent: the monks were seldom willing to live up to the demands of their Rule and often were a debauched and corrupt lot. Thus one popular moralizing judgment has given way to another, despite the efforts of men like David Knowles in England and Hal Koch in Denmark to show the valuable cultural contributions the monks were able to make. In the face of the Marxist criticism of pre-capitalistic society, the present-day historian trained in critical methods can perhaps feel at a loss to say anything at all, for he is immediately labelled as being for or against one *ism* or another. Likewise in the face of the thoroughly necessary but at times ruthless criticism of the few sources we have for medieval Denmark, the historian can easily come to feel that the beautifully written and coherent presentations of men like Knowles and Koch are no longer possible. On the one hand we have the Scylla of a fully formulated theoretical basis for all human history, which makes it irrelevant to write about monks. On the other the Charybdis of neo-positivism, which captures the historians with its promises of truth but often gives only a deadening aridity. What can one do in response to these contradictory demands and constant accusations? My answer is to go back to the sources, to evaluate them as well as possible, to compare,

---

38) AD 93 (*Annales Lundenses*), 1194. Same date in *Annales Essenbecenses*, p. 146. Vilhelm Lorenzen, *De danske Cistercienserklostres Bygningshistorie* (Cpn., 1943) p. 243. Bishop Valdemar of Slesvig is also supposed to have endowed Ås - see *Dansk Biografisk Lexikon*, C.F. Bricka (1904) XVIII, p.193.

contrast, and to look for the human beings behind them. Such an analysis is necessarily influenced by the historian's training, political beliefs, and by the age in which he lives. But necessary baggage can also be useful. Let us see what we can do.

2.

THE ØM ABBEY CHRONICLE:
A UNIQUE AND FRUSTRATING SOURCE

In order to see the Cistercians in medieval Denmark as they were, as living, feeling human beings, we cannot avoid the eloquent witness of the Øm Book, better known as the Øm Abbey Chronicle. For a unique instant in our sources, the monks speak to us about their problems and concerns and thus tell us how they felt as a community in society. Moreover, we are fortunate enough to have the original manuscript preserved, so that we even can speculate about when each of the segments of the Øm Book was written.[39] We can look at the handwriting, the spelling, the omissions, the oversights, and at one and the same time get a physical and a psychological grasp of the monks.

And yet the Øm Book has not fared well on the battlefields of nineteenth and twentieth century history writing. Only once has an historian tried to treat it as a whole, taking the section written in 1207 concerning the foundation of Øm, the *Exordium Monasterii Carae Insulae*, together with the abbot list that follows, and finally the monks' account of their dispute with Bishop Tyge of Århus, written in 1268 or soon after. This historian, G. Buchwald, published his results in 1878, in the aftermath of Denmark's defeat to the newly constituted German Empire.[40] In his arrogant prose and lust for debunking just about everything the monks say, Buchwald misuses the apparatus of critical rationalism and could even be accused of nationalistic prejudices. Unfortunately the reply of A. D. Jørgensen to Buchwald that already came in the following year was harshly nationalistic and did not include a careful analysis of Buchwald's charges.[41] Even though the Danish writer had some help-

---

39) Copenhagen Kgl. Bibl. MS E donatione variorum nr 135, 4°. Published by M.Cl. Gertz in SM II, pp. 158-278. Photographic reissue, 1970. Gertz's preface, pp. 154-7, was the first systematic investigation of the parts of the manuscript. Many of his conclusions were criticized by C.A. Christensen in his preface to a facsimile edition of the Øm Book in *Corpus Codicum Danicorum Medii Aevi*, II (Cpn., 1960).
40) G.v. Buchwald, "Die Gründungsgeschichte von Øm und die Dänischen Cistercienser," *Zeitschrift der Gesellschaft für Schleswig-Holstein-Lauenburgische Geschichte* 8, 1878, 1-121.
41) A.D. Jørgensen, "Striden mellem Biskop Tyge og Øm kloster", *Årbøger for Nordisk Oldkyndighed og Historie*, 1879, pp. 110-153.

ful intuitive remarks about the Øm Book, Buchwald remained its supreme interpreter.

When other historians turned their attention to the manuscript, they were caught almost solely by the dispute with the bishops of Århus in the 1250's and 1260's. The first such example is an article by Henry Petersen in 1870. There the initial section, the *Exordium* proper, was only used to illuminate points in the thirteenth century controversy between the monks and Bishop Tyge.[42] The same can be said about the abbot list in the Øm Book, even though it contains some frank and sharply perceptive perceptions about the men who headed Øm. Finally, the last segment of the Øm Book, the biography of Gunner, abbot at Øm from 1216 to 1221 and then bishop of Viborg from 1222 until his death in 1251, has been either largely ignored or else taken by itself in isolation from the other segments of the Book.[43] This is unfortunate, for the *Vita Gunneri* is the one genuine description of a person we have from the Danish medieval period. Despite its brevity it at moments reaches the level of awareness of a human being that we find in such central biographies as Walter Daniel's life of Abbot Ailred of Rievaulx in Yorkshire.[44]

I should like to provide a treatment of the Øm Book as a wholeness. By respecting its various authors as prejudiced but understandable human beings who were caught up in the survival of their abbey, I shall try to get some feeling for the quality and tenor of life at Øm. We can see how things looked from the monks' point of view. Fully admitting their narrowness and limitations, we can still give them a chance to spread their own message and speak directly to us.

Our first problem is to determine what type of source we are dealing with. The entire manuscript has been labelled *Exordium Monasterii Carae Insulae*, but the real Exordium or account of the monastery's beginnings only takes up

---

42) K.N. Henry Petersen, "Øm klosters feide med bispen af Aarhus i midten af det 13 århundrede", *Historisk Archiv*, I, 1870. Similar approach in Erik Schalling, "Kanonisk eller nationell rätt? Ett bidrag till diskussionen om 1200-talets danska immunitetsstrider", *Kyrkohistorisk Årsskrift*, 1937 (38 årgang), Uppsala, pp. 103-34. Also Niels Knud Andersen, "Striden mellem Øm kloster og Aarhusbisperne: Et Forsøg på en ny Forståelse," *Dansk Teologisk Tidsskrift* 1939, pp. 129-146. Similarly, Niels Skyum-Nielsen, *Kirkekampen i Danmark* 1241-1290 pp. 183-197, 238-244.
43) A few remarks in Hans Olrik's translation, *Viborg Bispen Gunners Levned* (Selskabet for Historiske Kildeskrifters Oversættelse, 1892). Reprinted recently by Scripta in Århus (no date given). Ellen Jørgensen, *Historieforskningen og Historieskrivningen i Danmark indtil Aar 1800* (Cpn., photographic reprint) p. 24. Henning Høirup, "Gunner af Viborg", *Fra Viborg Amt*, Årbog udgivet af Historisk Samfund for Viborg Amt, 1961, pp. 32-59.
44) Sir Maurice Powicke, trans. and ed., *The Life of Ailred of Rievaulx*, Nelson Medieval Texts (Edinburgh, 1950).

one of four very different sections. We will call it the Exordium 1.[45] This account of the foundation of Øm is by no means a simple narrative. It is liberally spiced with privileges from popes, kings, and bishops and at times incorporates their charters without the slightest comment. But at times the narrative does take over completely, as in the chapter describing one of the central figures in Øm's early history, Bishop Sven of Århus.[46] The foundation narrative is followed by a list of abbots (pp. 192-2o6), apparently started by the same author who wrote the first section, but continued by others and continuing right up to the beginning of the 13oo's. Thirdly (pp. 2o6-263) there is a narrative of the dispute between the monks and the bishops of Århus, especially Tyge, in the 125o's and 126o's. This we can call the Exordium 2. Here the commentary, personal remarks, and general description of events once again are often subordinated to the documents. Fourthly (pp.265-278) there is the short biography of Bishop Gunner of Viborg, who had been abbot at Øm until 1221.

Although we ultimately have to rely on internal evidence in order to establish the purpose for writing the Øm Chronicle, we can at the outset obtain some help form Cistercian literature in general. The Øm monks were likely to have been acquainted with the narratives describing the origins of their Order, first the *Exordium Parvum*, a brief account of the Cistercians' earliest days, and second the already mentioned *Exordium Magnum*, with its collection of rambling stories about the spread of Cistercian houses all over Europe. Since the latter belongs to the 118o's, the Øm monks had ample time to get acquainted with the work during the intervening quarter of a century before they started on their own Exordium. The very repetition of the word *Exordium* indicates that Øm monks were setting out to give their own local version of the Order's great chronicle. We know that at least at the Reformation, the Øm monks had a copy of the *Exordium Magnum* in their library.[47] It would be absurd to assume from this fact that they already owned a copy in the thirteenth century, but the entry in the Reformation book list at least shows that a later generation of Øm monks could have known the account well. Finally we cannot neglect the likelihood that Øm monks were present at the General Chapters of the Cistercian Order in the 118o's and 119o's, even though we have no direct evidence. But they were expected to come at least occasionally, for in 1215 they were ordered to show up in the following year, despite their excuses about the dangers of war, and when they did not appear there in 1216, they were punished.[48]

---

45) SM II, pp. 158-192.
46) SM II,ch.31,pp.186-9: "De moribus domni Svenonis episcopi." Also ch. 35, pp. 191-192: "De fine vite domini Svenonis episcopi".
47) See my section on the Øm Library.
48) Canivez, *op.cit.*, 1215, nr. 19; 1216, nr. 14.

This evidence, inconclusive as it must be, points to the probability that the Øm monks were aware that the mother house at Citeaux and its most distinguished daughter, Clairvaux, were eager to use narratives in order to defend their claims. The *Exordium Magnum* came into being at the same time as the pace of Cistercian foundations was beginning to slow considerably and when the first open criticism of the Order began to issue forth from other quarters.[49] Similarly the Exordium 1 of Øm was written at the very time when Cistercian prerogatives in Denmark began to be challenged. One recent writer on Øm, Svend Green-Pedersen, has tried to focus the writing of the Exordium 1 on a single dispute: the problem with the payment of tithes on lands owned by the Cistercians.[50] He has pointed out that the Exordium contains several papal bulls dealing with this exemption and reasserting it. The dispute over the payment of tithes at Øm was noticed by Hal Koch in 1936,[51] and it certainly was a matter causing friction between the Århus bishop and the Øm monks until the Fourth Lateran Council in 1215, which dealt with the problem in a semi-decisive way. Nevertheless, I cannot agree that this conflict can be localized as the central one motivating the writing of the Exordium 1.

If we look at the preface to the Exordium 1 we find a general warning to the evil and encouragement to the good. The language is similar to that of numberless privileges and chronicles from Cistercian and other monastic houses. In the very banality of the formulae, however, we stumble upon a convincing motivation for such a literary production: the preservation of the rights and prerogatives that the monks had gained since the time of foundation. Our author, anonymous but certainly an Øm monk, says that anyone who wants to challenge the monks' holdings or claims will certainly have to back away once he has "realized the veracity of the foundation and the dignity of the founders."[52] Finally the man who helps the monks instead of harming them can look forward to gaining eternal salvation through their merits and the prayers "of the whole order."

The potential enemy is thus undefined, and it could be the bishop of Århus just as well as local landowners who are making trouble. It was precisely in these years after 1200 that the death of Absalon marked the end of the Cistercian Order's golden age in Denmark, when the monks almost always could count

---

49) See for example David Knowles *The Monastic Order in England* (Cambridge, 1966) pp. 663-74, on Gerald of Wales and some of the other late twelfth century critics.
50) Sv. E. Green-Pedersen, "Øm klosters grundlæggelse og dets forhold til Bisp Sven af Århus", *Århus Stifts Årbøger* (Historisk Samfund for Århus Stift), 47, 1964, pp. 183-4.
51) Hal Koch, *op. cit.*, p.555.
52) SM II, 158: "...cognita veritate fundationis et reverentia fundatorum...".

on the bishops to defend their rights. It was at this time that both Sorø and Esrum initiated some of their fiercest land disputes with local families, and some of these altercations lasted for decades.[53]

If we look into the internal situation at Øm, we discover that the monastery in the years 1197-99 had an abbot, Niels, who was considered too spiritual to take care of the daily needs of the monks.[54] The following abbot, Thorkil (1199-1216), under whom the Exordium 1 was written, was considered to be the exact opposite type, someone who tired himself out with secular affairs for the sake of the monks.[55] We can thus look upon the Exordium 1 as a reflection of a period when the Øm monks felt endangered from many sides and had just experienced the shock of an incompetent abbot. The composition of the account may well be the result of an attempt by Abbot Thorkil to clarify the rights and privileges of the monastery, to establish their historical foundation, and to give his successors a thorough background for their claims.

It is probably no accident that the great English Cistercian chronicle, the *Narratio de Fundatione Monasterii de Fontibus*, is almost contemporary with the Øm Exordium 1. Its composition has been dated between c. 1205/6 and c. 1226, with the bulk of the work done on it after 1212.[56] Political factors were different in England from those in Denmark, but Cistercian houses in both countries felt the need because of open and more subtle hostilities to "record the circumstances of foundation, and whether implicitly or explicitly, to justify them."[57]

If we turn to the account of the dispute with the bishops of Århus, our Exordium 2, it might seem much easier to explain why the work was written. The abbey felt its very survival endangered, and so it used every weapon it could to defend itself. The monks wrote out of desperation. Already Green-Pedersen and before him a delightful amateur historian, C. Luplau Janssen, have concluded that the account is meant as a legal document, in which "the histo-

---

53) Poul Nørlund, "Klostret og dets Gods", pp. 63-65, contained in *Sorø: Klostret, Skolen, Akademiet gennem Tiderne* I (Cpn., 1924). For Esrum see for example the 1246 document in which Saxe Torbernsen handed over Nødebo village, "non obstante controversia, que inter me et monasterium...sepe fuerat agitata". *Codex Esromensis*, ed. O. Nielsen (Cpn., 1880-81), nr. 100. This dispute could well go back to the beginning of the century.
54) SM II, 193: "vir innocens et nimie simplicitatis."
55) *Ibid.*, "qui multos labores et magnas fatigationes in seculari adhuc habitu constitutus sepissime pro fratribus sustinuit." After he became a monk and then abbot, Thorkil kept up this routine, "ne fratribus aliquid deesset".
56) L.G.D. Baker, "The Genesis of English Cistercian Chronicles. The foundation History of Fountains Abbey I", *Analecta Cisterciensia* 25, 1969, pp. 39-40.
57) *Ibid.*, p. 27.

rical material in the book is almost parenthetical padding."[58] This position is a bit oversimplified, for even if at times the documents crowd out the narrative, the latter adds an extra and important dimension to the dispute by showing us what the monks felt about the affair. The Exordium 2 can perhaps best be seen as a logical continuation of Exordium 1 and the intervening abbot list. In the Exordium 2 narrative and documents are integrated in order to assert the claims of the monks. The central difference from Exordium 1 is that this time the problem is much narrower and apparently much more immediate.

One way of approaching the problem of composition is by asking who was meant to read Exordium 2. There is no preface to help us this time, but there is one fascinating passage which comes after two bulls of Alexander IV have been cited: "Of these letters we have one sealed with wax (*bullatam*), but we have not yet come into possession of the other, except for a transcript from Clairvaux."[59] The author here seems to be assuming that his audience is primarily interested in the legal arguments involved and that they will be demanding not just evidence for the monks' assertions but also the documents themselves. The readers of the account are thus expected to have a legal background so that they can deal with claims and counter-claims. The groups or institutions in Danish and European society which would have such a background and could be implicated in the dispute, are the following: the pope and his chancery; the papal legate Guido; the mother abbey of Clairvaux and her abbot; the Cistercian General Chapter at Citeaux; the court of King Erik Glipping and especially his mother, Margrethe Sprænghest, and her advisors; the Danish Cistercian abbots, especially the abbot of Vitskøl, the mother abbey of Øm; the Danish bishops. We know from the content of the Exordium 2 that all these authorities were at least notified of what was happening, and many of them became actively involved in the events.

In November 1266, Abbot Ture of Øm made an appeal to church leaders at a synod in Lübeck in which he outlined the offences of Bishop Tyge and asked for help.[60] Either before or afterwards, he wrote it down in a form that was incorporated into the Exordium 2. After the inclusion of this document there is very little left to narrate in the Exordium. There are no more documents, only an implicit admission of defeat, as we shall see. There is a good chance that the Exordium 2 was completed shortly after this appeal was made. By this time the unhappy fate of the Øm monks was sealed, and they lived in daily fear

---

58) Green-Pedersen, *op. cit.*, p. 182.
59) SM II, 213: "Harum litterarum unam habuimus bullatam, sed alteram nondum habueramus, nisi transcriptum de Claravalle."
60) SM II, 247-252. The appeal is called a *libellus* in the Øm Book.

of a final royal action on behalf of Bishop Tyge (as the monks themselves tell it in the last chapter of the narration). We can thus look at the Exordium 2, completed in the form which has come down to us, as a last desperate attempt to get all the legal and emotional threads together in order to back up the claims of the monastery against bishop Tyge. It was meant for anyone and everyone who might be able to help the monks, but as the work neared its final stages and the controversy became more violent, it became ever more obvious that there was no hope left. And so the writer simply ended by describing the sorry state of the monastery and without telling us what the king actually did.

The Exordium 2 was thus probably never used for the purpose for which it originally was intended: a general appeal to all who might have some influence in the matter. It reflects a community on the verge of hysteria and dissolution, and it is this tone that prompted one historian to call it the monks' "manifesto of revenge" against Bishop Tyge.[61] The Exordium 2 is both more and less than such a polemic: it is more because the monks are trying not just to defeat Bishop Tyge but to maintain the rights they feel they have as an exempt Cistercian house. It is less because the monks have practically lost all hope of salvaging their dignity and even their lives. Revenge implies hope in the possibility of reprisals, a hope that is all but dead in the last chapters of Exordium 2.

With these purposes and intentions in mind, we can begin a review of the contents of the Øm Book.

---

61) *Kirkekampen*, p. 191.

3.
THE OPENING OF THE EXORDIUM 1: CISTERCIAN POLISH VS. REAL PROBLEMS

The first chapter of the Exordium 1 illuminates the founding of Øm in the same way as Newton shed light on Nature's laws in Pope's famous lines. In a flash everything is revealed:

> Nature and Nature's laws lay hid in Night.
> God said, Let Newton be! and all was Light.

The chapter is entitled, "When and from which persons this monastery began".[62] We are told that the brothers first came to Sminge, which is in the Gudenå valley north of Silkeborg, that Bishop Eskil of Århus prepared this place for them, and that it was inadequate, for it had only a single farm. Consequently the abbot at Vitskøl, Henrik, went to Eskil's successor at Århus, Sven, and asked him to look after Christ's "tiny flock". Sven was not responsive at first, for he resented the "generosity" of his predecessor. But during a storm at sea he changed his mind. A Cistercian brother on the ship encouraged him to found an abbey if he survived. On returning home, he and Abbot Henrik went together to King Valdemar and told him they wanted to transfer the Sminge brothers to Veng, where a Benedictine community was in decline because of its members' neglect. Jens, abbot at Veng, voluntarily gave up his post and became a monk at Vitskøl. And so, as we read both here and in a papal privilege confirming the move, the master at Veng became a disciple at Vitskøl.[63] Following the Cistercian ideal, the reformed Jens is supposed to have spent the rest of his days in tears and penance for his sins. Finally he returned to Veng and there died.

In this single chapter we meet the partisan mentality of the Cistercians, which is just as pronounced here as in writings of English or French members of the Order. The monks consider themselves to be superior to their Benedictine predecessors. The latter are in moral retreat, and it is time for the new flock of Christ to take over the choicest grazing lands. We have a similar instance of a Cistercian assertion of superiority in a Sorø account of the

---

62) SM II, 16o-161.
63) SM II, 163-164.

monastery's period as a Benedictine house before 1161.[64] But unlike at Sorø, we have an alternative monastic figure to balance the incompetent Benedictine abbot. This is Henrik of Vitskøl, who is said to have been loved by all. He is described as a man with a light in his face and a honeyed voice. In the Sorø account the central figure is not a monk, but a bishop, Absalon. Together with Esbern Snare, he is too much a man of the world to be described in such language redolent of Cistercian spirituality. Our Øm chronicler would probably have liked at this point to raise Sven of Århus to the same level of hero bishop, but unfortunately Sven at first was none too enthusiastic about the monks. This is admitted, but we notice how Sven's wrong attitude is quickly rectified by his meeting with divine will. Afterwards Sven will be allowed to grow into a heroic figure, a founder bigger than life, but for the moment he is something of an embarrassment!

We thus can reach a first conclusion about the Cistercian mentality: its need to fasten onto a great man who embodies and realizes the divine will. At Sorø it is easy to find such an individual, but at Øm there is a split. This split becomes more obvious after we leave the mellifluous phrases and Cistercian sheep images of the first chapter and penetrate into some of the confusion about the origins of Øm. In the end we will find that the first chapter of the Exordium 1 is a carefully balanced literary product that idealizes the founding in order to increase the respect of later generations for the abbey.

The nagging question remains: how much truth is there in this idealized portrait? Buchwald wanted to throw out the promise by Sven at sea to found an abbey.[65] He saw a Cistercian tradition for such stories and rightly pointed to the narration about the origin of Vitskøl itself. More recently, Sven Green-Pedersen thought it entirely possible in the medieval world, with its belief in divine intervention, that Sven did make such a promise.[66] I can only agree. We know from the French sources what a high opinion the Cistercians had of themselves, and their confidence must have been impressive to all who came into contact with them.[67] The Order was already by now firmly en-

---

64) *Scriptores rerum Danicarum medii aevi* (SRD), ed. J. Langebek and P.F. Suhm (I-IX, Hafniae, 1772-1878), IV, pp. 466-67.
65) Buchwald, *op. cit.*, pp. 24-28.
66) Sv. Green-Pedersen, *op. cit.*, pp. 173-246, 2o2. This is a very helpful and thorough article, which has done much of the groundwork without which my treatment would be poorer. But the polemic against Niels Skyum-Nielsen is unfortunate and limiting.
67) The language of the *Carta Caritatis* and *Exordium Parvum*, with their assertion of a return to strict Benedictine monasticism, in themselves show us how the Cistercians considered themselves unique and essential to the Church. Text in *Nomasticon cisterciense*, R.P.D. Julian (Solesmes, 1892), pp. 62-63, 68-73. Also the *Vita Prima*, on the impression made on travellers by the loneliness of Clairvaux - PL 185, col. 248.

trenched in Denmark, at Herrisvad, Esrum, Sorø, and Vitskøl itself, and the work of archbishop Eskil to bring the Cistercians to the North was only a few years in the past.

The monks knew how to penetrate the minds of people whose help they needed. Later on in the Exordium 1 we hear of a peasant named Apé who at first refused to sell his land to the monks when they moved to Øm but after an impressive and frightening dream gave in.[68] Consciously or unconsciously, the monks at Øm managed to convince Apé and others like him that they represented the vanguard of salvation. Because of such powers, the Danish Cistercians in the twelfth century often could turn their wishes into realities.

Aside from the storm and promise episode, there is nothing supernatural in the opening of the Exordium. The author tries to limit himself to assertions that can be proven by the documents he supplies. For the repentance of the Benedictine abbot Jens at Veng, however, we have only our Cistercian writer's word for it. The Veng episode has been used by historians such as Poul Rasmussen to show that early Cistercians in Denmark often took over former Benedictine foundations so that they could get rid of their competitors.[69] But our writer tells us there were only three monks at Veng, so we can hardly think of the Cistercians as destroyers of healthy houses. Likewise there hardly seems to have been any competition at Kalvø, where only two monks lived. In the case of Sorø, our only source, admittedly a Cistercian one, describes the Benedictine foundation as practically abandoned by the time the Cistercians came.[70] Finally at Esrum, there was no Benedictine forerunner at all, as has already been shown.

In returning to the Exordium 1, we find that the nice phrases of the first chapter are followed by the almost apologetic information in the next one that the brothers, "so that they could obtain a more favourable attitude" from the bishop, gave him Sminge.[71] Even though there are one or two instances in Sorø's dealings with Absalon in which he appears to get the benefit of a land transaction, there is no such instance of such a "pacification gift" as this one. Once again the writer speaks openly of the bishop's initial bad will towards the monks, with the phrase about "the bitterness of his anger" appa-

---

68) SM II, 176-7 - ch. 2o.
69) Buchwald, p. 24, first pointed out rivalry, while Rasmussen wrote directly about attempts to extricate Benedictines: *Den katolske Kirkes Jordegods i Århus Stift III: Herreklostrenes Jordegods i det 16. Århundrede og dets Historie* (Østjydsk Hjemstavnsforening, Cpn., 1957), p. 54. Green-Pedersen gave this idea prominence, p. 197.
7o) SRD IV, 467: "...et desolatus factus est locus quoniam dispositione divina locandus erat aliis agricolis, qui facerent fructum."
71) SM II,162: "Quod fratres, ut maiorem gratiam haberent electi sui, concesserunt ei Smaheng".

rently referring to his vexation with the monks for getting the Sminge property from Bishop Eskil.[72] A further explanation given is that the bishopric could not really afford to make such a gift at the time, for it was very poor. But this excuse is far from adequate, for our writer has also told us that it was only a single farm that the monks received in Sminge, and when we compare this with the lands given at foundation to Esrum or Sorø, or the Benedictine Næstved for that matter, Sminge's endowment under Bishop Eskil was ridiculously small for starting a new monastery.

The only possible conclusion we can make from this account of Sven's anger and initial resistance to the Cistercians is that he in the beginning simply had no attachment to them. He may well have feared having monks with exempt status inside his diocese. Even after he changed his mind and helped with the transfer to Veng, the monks felt so insecure with him that they tried to buy his good will through the very object that originally had vexed him, the Sminge property. Thus the beautiful, idealized story of the first chapter has taken on a dark side, and we can already see that Øm had a precarious beginning. The monks were dependent not only on a hostile bishop but also feared the attitude of local priests. This is probably why the writer carefully points out that Sven gave the monks only what he had from his own patrimony or what was left over from his episcopal incomes. The Cistercians are anticipating possible criticism that Sven had plundered his bishopric in order to give to their Order.[73]

This defensive attitude can be explained by the probability that when the Exordium 1 was begun in 1207, the monastery was under attack for its freedoms and privileges, especially for its exemption from the payment of the tithe on lands already under cultivation that the abbey came to acquire, the so-called praedial tithe.[74] Other writers on Øm have gone into this subject more thoroughly,[75] so it is only necessary to add here that the Exordium 1 was born in an atmosphere of uncertainty and perhaps even crisis not resolved until the Fourth Lateran Council declared that the monks would have to pay praedial tithes on lands acquired after 1215. This situation explains why the work is much more a collection of documents with a brief commentary than the full-fledged monastic narrative that we might have hoped for. It was necessary to

---

72) SM II, 162: "amaritudinem indignationis sue."
73) A similar instance of self-defence against possible accusations from secular clergy can be seen at Sorø where the chronicle points out that Absalon's gifts of land to the abbey were almost never from the Roskilde bishopric but came from his own patrimony, SRD IV, 470.
74) Hal Koch, *op. cit.*, pp. 555-6.
75) Green-Pedersen, pp. 203-4.

make not a leisurely exposition of the abbey's early history but a sober collection of facts and proofs. Still, the monks' feelings break through this legalistic surface and reveal anxieties and worries that the monks do their best to hide.

This emotional background is very much present in the third chapter, where our picture of life at Benedictine Veng is supplemented by the news that when the Cistercian abbot, Brienne, lodged there, he was treated without respect. Abbot Jens had Brienne's servants bound and tied when he learned they had stolen corn from the granary to feed their horses. But it was the Benedictines who were at fault, for they were not satisfactorily caring for their guests' horses. As a result of accusations Jens resigned and became a Cistercian.[76] The story here ignores the statement given in the first chapter that Veng was dissolved because the Benedictines had neglected their Rule. Here a single incident is supposed to bring the dissolution. The bad treatment of horses and boys may have simply brought the situation to a head and given Brienne a pretext for having Jens removed. But what is central here is the way that the ideal Cistercian world of polished phrases so evident in the first chapter breaks down upon closer examination into an insecure everyday reality.

The new occupants of Veng must have had some pangs of conscience about the Benedictine break-up. Or they at least were afraid for their own Cistercian future, for Abbot Brienne headed for Rome to get papal confirmation of the transfer from Sminge. The author claims that the pope gladly granted permission, for he was interested in the progress and prosperity of the Cistercian order.[77] This looks like Cistercian propaganda. There might have been a tradition at Øm that Brienne was well received at Rome, but it is more likely that our writer used such language about papal favouritism because he wanted his audience to have greater respect for the foundation and its rights.

We find in the next chapter the text of Alexander III's letter to King Valdemar concerning the removal to Veng. This document has become quite central in Danish medieval history, for the pope also asks Valdemar to receive back his exiled archbishop, Eskil, and to protect and defend his rights and lands.[78] This letter has been dated 1165-66 and immediately precedes Eskil's actual return to Denmark. The centrality of the Cistercians in the spiritual and political life of the period emerges form these lines. Brienne returns to Valdemar not just as a papal messenger concerning the abbey but also as a diplomat pleading the cause of Eskil. Already in their first years in Denmark

---

76) SM II, p. 162 - ch.3.
77) SM II, 163 - ch. 3.
78) SM II, 163 - ch. 4. Also DD I, 2, nr. 167.

the Cistercians willingly identified themselves with the leading prelates of the Church. In the twelfth century this was wise and politic, while in the thirteenth it could become foolish and fatal, as we shall see.

After a similar letter to the bishops of the kingdom, our writer inserted a privilege of King Valdemar to the monastery and brothers of Veng. Like most documents in the Exordium 1, and in contrast to those in the Exordium 2, this privilege has no date. We are given the text alone, without signatures.[79] Valdemar exempts the Veng brothers from the payment of leding, a military tax, by the monastery's labourers. The wording is uncompromising and concrete, and we should think that the Cistercians, so early after their arrival at Veng, must have been glad to get such a privilege. But the experts have concluded that this document was drawn up in Valdemar's name not for Cistercian Veng, but for the Benedictine foundation, thus sometime between Valdemar's 1157 takeover and 1164, the date of the Benedictine dissolution. Why have the Cistercians placed this privilege so innocently and convincingly at this juncture in their account? Probably they wanted to claim that what was in force for the Benedictines at Veng automatically applied for them. The insertion of such a privilege without comment but with the obvious implication that it applies for the Cistercians adds one more detail to our revision of the first chapter's harmony and perfection. The Cistercians obviously intended to get all the advantages possible, and they were willing to skip over careful explanation in doing so!

Our writer seems to be aware of the bundle of problems he has given us since the first chapter, for in chapters 7 through 1o, he skips back to the pre-1165 Sminge situation. Once again we are forced to add detail and qualification to the picture of a monastery founded by a hero. "We should not pass over in silence what we should have written in the beginning," he starts. The chapter is entitled: "That this house in its outset was not begun without a (sufficient) foundation."[80] Now at last, we hear that the original founder, Bishop Eskil, had been "defiled by schism", for he had supported the antipope Victor against Alexander. But the situation was not as bad as it seems, for the true pope wrote to Abbot Henrik of Vitskøl concerning the place which Bishop Eskil had offered as the site of a Cistercian abbey.

This letter has been dated to 1164, when Alexander was in exile at Sens.[81] Archbishop Eskil was with him at the beginning of this year, and so the origins

---

79) SM II, 165-6. DD I, 2, nr. 123.
8o) SM II, 166: "Quod domus hec in exordio suo non sit sine fundamento fundata." "Non est silendum, quod in primis scripsisse debueramus..."
81) DD I, 2 157 - SM II, 166-7 - ch. 8.

of Øm, as those of Esrum a decade earlier, are linked to Eskil. Our chronicler does not speak now of Eskil: he will be celebrated later on.

These pages in the Øm chronicle allow us to conclude that in the 116o's, just as in the 126o's, the affairs of the abbey were intimately caught up in the relations between royal and ecclesiastical personalities. Øm's early years are overshadowed by the papal schism and its resulting conflict between Valdemar and Eskil, while Øm's later years are made infinitely complicated by the fact that the great authority on which the monks depended, the archbishop of Lund, was at odds with the king. The great difference for Øm between the two disputes is that the first one is much less intense and immediate for the monks than the second.

The 1164 papal letter says that the monks have given up a "less favourable place" in order to live in a better one. Our writer explains in the following chapter that the first spot was Sabro, which Bishop Eskil of Århus subsequently took back and instead gave Sminge. Thus the list of places which led to the final foundation at Øm becomes even longer, but the important fact for our writer is that the Alexander III letter gives a stamp of legitimacy to all the early events of the abbey. Once again we see the early thirteenth century concern for making the first years exemplary and legal so that present day challenges could not break through. History at Øm abbey is thus a necessary defence against the challenges and accusations of the time. But this defence is ill-organized and sometimes even contradictory. The Exordium 1's constant backtracking and lack of chronology points to a writer of limited talents who did not organize his materials well. He strives for the ideal portrait, but all his qualifications and explanations reveal an inability to reconcile Cistercian idealism with the historical facts.

Losing completely the thread of the narrative, the writer goes on in the tenth chapter to tell us about Sabro's later history. The monks, who like their colleagues elsewhere seldom gave up for good on a lost possession, regained Sabro under King Knud.[82] The text of his privilege is given, and we can date it between 1193 and 12o2. This is the gift of Sabro to Knud's chaplain Emer, who the writer says gave the land five years before his death "to Mary and the brothers of Øm". The writer also tells us that Knud had obtained Sabro in an exchange with Bishop Sven. We are thus given full details of the transaction, so that in the couse of a few chapters we have been on a zigzag chronological tour, starting in 1165, going on to 1166-67 with the Veng confirmation, then back to 1164, with the papal confirmation of Sminge, and now

---

82) SM II, 167-8. To be included in the as yet unpublished DD I,3.

advancing into the 119o's. In the next chapter we will doubleback to the transfer of the monastery from Veng to Kalvø on Skanderborg Lake, which came in the 116o's.

Why such chronological chaos? Aside from speculating about our writer's limited abilities and the insecurity of his period, we can say to his favour that he is trying to achieve something very difficult. He is taking the Cistercian spirituality found in narrations about the early days of the Order, such as the *Exordium Parvum* and the *Vita Prima* of Saint Bernard, and combining it with a powerful defence of the Øm monks' rights and privileges. In the end, the second purpose wins over the first, for there is a much greater need to protect the reputation and claims of the monks than to delve into the Cistercian ideal of piety and brotherly love. As almost always happens in Cistercian history, Bernard's message is sacrificed to the daily demands of survival in a world that by 12oo is becoming ever more complex and structured. Bernard himself had to go out into this world in order to protect the interests he felt vital and in the process compromised himself. So it is no surprise that the fragile beginnings of the Øm Cistercians have to be defended by documents and legalistic assertions.

Despite these mitigating circumstances, there is something deeply dissatisfying in the content of the Exordium 1. There is a lack of boldness here. Perhaps this is unavoidable for any institution that at first was favoured by powerful interests and subsequently had to make it on its own. But this attitude of self-protection and lack of concern for other segments of society, except insofar as they threaten or help the monks, becomes one of the strongest factors contributing to the repulsive and tragic dispute with the bishops of Århus later in the century.

4.

FAILURE AT KALVØ - SUCCESS AT ØM

From the twelfth chapter onwards in the *Exordium 1*, we achieve a sense of chronological narrative and follow the monks through the transfer to Kalvø and the final move to Øm. Archbishop Eskil again becomes an important person for the Øm monks. Abbot Brienne went to Rome a second time in 1167, and on the way stopped at Clairvaux, where he found Eskil, who later the same year would return home. Eskil is mentioned here as a man who already is a legend, responsible for the foundations of Herrisvad and Esrum, for sending many monks to Denmark, and for himself ending as a monk at Clairvaux and there being buried under marble. All this information can readily be found elsewhere, and Eskil is too distant a figure to take on the heroic but fatherly proportions of Abbot Henrik, who was known personally to the monks. Nevertheless, our writer is more than glad to add Eskil to the list of distinguished persons who helped Øm on its way and says almost apologetically that the monks had not previously received any privileges from Eskil only because they had not before asked for them![83]

It is fairly clear from the text of this privilege that Eskil was not only benefiting the monks' cause but also his own, for he says he is confirming the translation of the monks from Veng to Kalvø at the request of King Valdemar, and the bishops Absalon of Roskilde and Sven of Århus. To these people, he claims, "we can deny nothing."[84] This phrase, cliché as it is, still seems to have some meaning and probably reflects Eskil's desire to acquire Valdemar's favour. Once again the Cistercians, just because of their penchant for travelling up and down Europe, are implicating themselves in royal-episcopal relations.

Eskil also says that the monks are to keep all their Veng property, from which they have moved because they were forced to do so. Our writer has already explained what is meant by this phrase. The Lady Margrethe, sister of

---

83) SM II, 169 - ch. 12 - Iste archiepiscopus Eskillus semper et ubique edificationi et confirmationi huius domus intendit et devotus fuit, licet ante privilegium suum non dederit, quia prius non petebatur.
84) SM II, 17o - ch. 13: "...quibus nichil negare possumus..."

Count Eric, who is named as one of the founders of the abbey, made life miserable for the Veng Cistercians between 1165 and 1168. The monks finally exchanged lands with Valdemar by which they gave him two-thirds of Veng, worth 20 marks gold, and received land in Harlev, Framlev herred, valued at 21 marks gold.[85] The monks thus made a slight profit, but there is no question here of a royal donation. This new piece of property was not fit for an abbey, and so the brothers instead moved south to Kalvø, where there was a Benedictine abbey that could only claim two members.[86] This can hardly be looked upon as an attempt by the Cistercians to enrich themselves at the expense of a competitor. The Cistercians only took over the island itself, while the rest of the Benedictine property probably was transferred to the nunnery at Ring, south of the Lake.[87]

The narration makes quite clear that the move was made only because of dire necessity and not out of any feeling that life would be easier at Kalvø, another reason for rejecting any theory about the Cistercians' intentions to kill off competition. The monks simply had to get out of Veng as fast as possible. During these years, the role of King Valdemar in the fate of the Cistercian community seems to have been important, even though our writer never says anything directly. First of all, Abbot Brienne obtained at Rome not only a papal letter of confirmation addressed to his community, one to Absalon of Roskilde, and one to Sven of Århus, but also a letter to Valdemar saying that the king had confirmed the removal of the monks to Kalvø and that the village of Veng had been legitimately exchanged.[88] Also, in the letter to the brothers themselves, the pope said that the transfer had been made under the authority of Archbishop Eskil, and with the assent of King Valdemar. Eskil is placed first, but Valdemar's role is recognized.[89]

Green-Pedersen has considered Valdemar's relationship to Øm more closely and concluded that he was far more active and influential during these years than the Exordium 1 indicates.[90] The chronicle does tell us, however, that

---

85) SM II, 169 - ch. 12.
86) *Ibid.*: Quod postquam factum est, omnes fratres simul congregati, assumptis reliquiis et ossibus fundatorum, Eskilli videlicet episcopi et Erici comitis et aliorum, cum consilio et auxilio regis et episcopi se et omnia sua ad insulam, que vocatur Calve, transtulerunt, locum dantibus eorum adventui nigris monachis, qui prius ibi habitabant. Et notandum, quod in Weng non fuerunt monachi nigri nisi tres tantum cum abbate, in Calve vero non plus quam duo, quando ordo Cisterciensis ea suscepit.
87) Poul Rasmussen, *op. cit.*, p. 51.
88) SM II, 171 - ch. 14 - DD I,2, 178, dated 1167-68.
89) SM II, 172-3 - ch. 16 - DD I, 2, nr. 177.
90) Green-Pedersen, 194-5.

Valdemar did not favour the monks when he had to choose between the Lady Margrethe and the Cistercians.[91] Rather bitterly, our writer describes how Margrethe wanted to use the Veng property to found her own convent. She begged the king for his share. Apparently she had owned the last third of Veng all along and thus had been in a position to harass the monks. To the Queen she offered gold rings and a chasuble filled with gold, so heavy that it only could be folded in a certain way. Other presents, which she had seized from the church of Veng, she also offered the Queen.

Once again we are confronted with the problem of the narrative's veracity. The monks had good reason to hate Margrethe, for she had made it necessary for them to move a second time, so it would be no wonder if our writer is transmitting an oral tradition on court gossip and the community's exaggeration of it. But the fact that this story is accepted so totally by our chronicler once again points to Cistercian impatience with all who do not favour the order and have other plans or purposes in life. Margrethe, even as described by her enemies, was not an avaricious women out to impoverish the monks, but merely a determined lady with projects of her own based on her concept of piety.

Whatever Margrethe may have done, the brothers went to the King to plead their case. They were represented by two *familiares*, which seems to indicate friends or allies who would be likely to have influence at court. The monks gave them lands in Mesing, Hjelmslev herred, to a value of 1o marks silver, to encourage them to be eloquent. But to no avail. Even though the King did give the brothers back their two-thirds of Veng, they had to give up other possessions, two of which, Sminge and Vole, Valdemar on his deathbed gave to his concubine! There is something shady in all these negotiations, for even if Lady Margrethe was primitive in her methods, the brothers' payments of property to these men show that pure business sense, and perhaps even a touch of bribery, motivated these "allies". Our writer does not hide the fact that the lands were given up in this way. But he grieves that despite papal letters the community had not to the present day (12o7) been able to get anything back that Margrethe had stolen, including the monks' land in Kollens, Hjelmslev herred.

In defence of the monastic claims, we are given the text of a papal letter to Valdemar concerning the possessions of the Veng church which Margrethe is supposed to have stolen, together with the property of Kollens.[92] This letter, dated between 1167-72, reveals how little the pope could do for conditions in a Danish abbey. Even though it may have been personally acquired by Abbot

---

91) SM II, 173-4 - ch. 17-18.
92) SM II, 174-5 - ch. 18; DD I, 2, 182.

Brienne on a third trip to Italy in 1169, the bull was apparently insufficient to convince Valdemar to change his policy. Our writer says that nothing could be done, for the woman was his near relative, so he "did not want to make her unhappy while she lived."[93]

The monks also claim that she had promised the third part of Veng to them and then refused to give it up. In view of her attitude, such a promise seems preposterous, but the matter was never clarified, for the king's delay lasted until his sudden death. The brothers do not tell us directly even here that Margrethe was the rightful owner of the last third of Veng. We have to draw this conclusion out of the text, and once more we can see how they arrange facts in their own favour and leave out unpleasant conclusions.

But there is one unpleasantness that they emphasize to the skies:

> ...the brothers, as always, complained and today complain and will not cease complaining, until justice is done for those things unjustly taken away from them.[94]

This remark sets the tone not only for the Exordium 1 but for the entire Øm Book, apart from the Life of Bishop Gunner.[95] What started out as a calm, idealistic Cistercian work has decisively changed into an aggressively defensive plaint over the evil ways of the world against the Øm monks. We often think of the twelfth century in Western Europe as a time when society was open to new forms and expressions of life, when expansionistic tendencies gave unlimited opportunities for new religious orders and intellectual systems.[96] But in this unhappy episode with Margrethe, this serious clash between a secular person and the monastery, we realize how delicate the balance was between prosperity and ruin. So long as the Øm monks are favoured by the scions of the ruling class, they have no worries, but the moment one powerful and determined person turns against them, they are in for trouble.

If King Valdemar had taken the monks' side, the last decades of the century would have been much less troublesome for the monks. But he preferred the family of his own flesh to the spiritual family of the Cistercians. We can already detect the centrality of royal power in the success or failure of a Cistercian foundation. Even when the king holds himself benevolently neutral in a dispute, the monks are lost. There is no other power sufficient to move

---

93) SM II, 175 - "...eo quod rex propter cognationem tenere diligebat mulierem nec volebat eam contristare in vita sua..."
94) SM II, 175 - "unde fratres, sicut semper conquesti sunt et adhuc hodie conqueruntur nec cessabunt conqueri, donec eis iusticia de iniuste sibi ablatis fiat." Notice the dexterity of language here.
95) The importance of this remark was already noted by Niels Skyum-Nielsen, *Kirkekampen*, p. 183.
96) One of the best expositions of this idea is in Friedrich Heer, *Mittelalter* (1961). Eng. trans. *The Medieval World* (Mentor, New York, 1963). *passim*

the advantage to the monks. Our writer tells us of the uselessness of papal letters in resolving the matter, and such will also be the case with Bishop Tyge in the 126o's.[97] Green-Pedersen has pointed out that in this matter we hear nothing from Bishop Sven, who by the 117o's was becoming more favourable to the monks.[98] This may well be because Sven realized the hopelessness of any intervention so long as Valdemar refused to go against a relative's interests.

From the Margrethe problem we return to the wanderings of the monks, this time from Kalvø to Øm, where they finally were able to settle for good.[99] The reasons given for leaving Kalvø are credible: the crossing over was difficult. Sometimes for a week, sometimes a fortnight, no one could come or go, either the weather or the ice impeding them, and a bridge could not be built. While Sminge had been too poor and Veng too troublesome, Kalvø was too isolated.[1oo] Similarly Abbot William, the French Augustinian firebrand, moved from Eskilsø in Roskilde Fjord to Æbelholt on the plains of northern Zealand at about the same time.[1o1] An island could never be the site of a thriving monastery, for the need for running water and good connections with the outside world made all but the largest islands better suited for hermits than for monastic communities.[1o2] At Sorø, the island of Soer, the need for a freely flowing water supply led to the building of a massive canal system connecting the monastery with Tuel Lake. Otherwise it is possible that even the monks of this rich foundation sooner or later would have had to pull up stakes.[1o3]

This time the monks put the utmost care into their preparations. They must have been nearly exhausted by conflicts and problems and perhaps felt that this

---

97) SM II, 175 - "Tot et tantis domini apostolici litteris missis nullam ex eis fratres, ut diximus, restitucionem consecuti sunt..."
98) Green-Pedersen, p. 2o2.
99) SM II, 175-6 - ch. 19.
1oo) Cistercian isolation was not desirable when it meant an economic burden and transport problems. H.N. Garner of Øm Kloster Museum has kindly pointed out to me that even though Kalvø lies very close to a neck of land jutting into Skanderborg Lake, this peninsula would not have made an adequate landing place for the monks because of the marshiness of the land. The monks would have had to row or sail to a more distant landing place.
1o1) The move was made in about 1175 - see *Æbelholt Klostermuseum Vejledning* (Nationalmuseet, 1969), p. 8.
1o2) The two Scandinavian exceptions to this general rule about not placing Cistercian abbeys on islands are in Norway, with Hovedø in Oslo fjord and Tautra in Trondheim fjord. Both islands are of sufficient size to provide fresh water, but the main explanation for such a location for Cistercian abbeys may well lie in the milder winter climate afforded by such a spot in such a northerly area. The best introduction to the Norwegian Cistercians is still Christian Lange, *De Norske Klostres Historie i Middelalderen* (Christiania, 1858).
1o3) The Sorø Book mentions the construction of the canals, SRD IV, 475.

was their last chance to move.[104] They chose Øm after they found that the level of the lake to the south of the site, Mossø, was slightly above that of the lake immediately to the north, Gudensø. It was one of the community's own monks, Martin, who made this calculation and thus showed a degree of technical proficiency among Danish Cistercians which also is evidenced by one of Abbot William's letters. He asked the Esrum abbot if he could borrow a monk for a few more days in order to finish laying water pipes.[105] The talents of Martin do not seem to have been a unique phenomenon. Once it was determined that the monks could dig a canal between the two lakes and thus have their essential running water, "they rejoiced at their find", sold their scattered possessions, and exchanged them for the territory around Øm. We do not know the names of more than a few of the monks' holdings during this period, but they were very scattered and far from each other, going as far north as Essenbæk near Randers.[106]

These holdings the monks had probably taken over from the Veng Benedictines, for until this time they seem to hav gotten very little from Bishop Sven of Århus. The move to Øm in the spring of 1172 can be looked upon as a last ditch attempt to make the monastery function, after almost a decade of troubles and defeats. It is no wonder that the monks gave the site the name of *Cara Insula*, the beloved isle. Here they had to find their home.

If we look at Øm on our map and compare its location with that of other religious foundations, it does not seem to be so well situated. Mossø had already attracted two Benedictine foundations, Vissing convent and Vor monastery. Although we lack early records for these houses, they were probably founded before 1170.[107] Various sources from the later Middle Ages point to disputes and controversies over fishing privileges in the lake, and it seems to have been difficult to establish exactly which parts of the lake "belonged" to which house.[108] Fish was an essential part of the monastic diet, and another reason for locating the monastery on a lake, so we can imagine that there was sharp competition at times.

---

104) SM II, 176 - ch. 19.
105) SRD VI, 54 - William says that only Brother Stephen of Esrum can carry out the project: "Sed ad hoc quis idoneus nisi frater Stephanus?"
106) For Øm's pre-1180 holdings, see Poul Rasmussen, pp. 51-2.
107) Poul Rasmussen, p. 10.
108) Such as in 1324 from the Archbishop of Lund, forbidding anyone to fish in Vor abbey's territory on Mossø: Skanderborg Register (1606) B 10 in *De ældste danske Archivregistraturer*, vol. I, 182 (abbreviation: ÆA). In 1930 was found a fish weir in the part of Gudenå that connects Mossø with Gudensø a few kilometres west of Øm. C. Asschenfeldt Birkebæk has in a brilliant article in *Århus Stifts Årbøger* 56 (1963), pp. 41-58, determined that the two fish weirs now located here belonged to Øm and Vissing and are the same as the "Vosgård" mentioned in a fifteenth century dispute between Vor and Øm: "Mossø-klostrenes omstridte fiskegårde ved Vosgård."

The records we have for Vor indicate that even if its holdings were not so large as those of Øm, they were very substantial.[109] Mostly centred in the good farmland south of Mossø, the Vor lands cut off the Øm monks from an obvious and nearby area for expansion. Another house whose presence constricted Øm was the convent of Ring on the south edge of Skanderborg Lake. Perhaps once a double monastery with the defunct Kalvø Benedictine monastery, Ring convent had substantial holdings in the area.[110] Finally, the area around Skanderborg itself seems to have even in this period made up a royal holding which never was alienated, even in part, to any of the nearby monasteries.[111] During the disturbances of the 1240's and 1250's, Skanderborg symbolized for the monks the threat of attack and destruction. To the south and east, then, the Øm monks had only limited possibilities for expansion, while in the west, the area around Himmelbjerg was probably too heavily forested and hilly for the setting up of any large farms.

Apparently the monks followed nature and logic and during this first period got what they could from the lands immediately to the east of Øm, in Dover and Illerup parishes.[112] They also formed a grange at the strategically placed Tåning, between Skanderborg and Moss lakes and on the road to Horsens. But Øm would never have become a substantial foundation if it had not been for the donations in Djursland by Bishop Sven, and yet these very holdings contributed greatly to the vexations and miseries of the monks. Never would they get a nicely constricted, geographically defined central block of holdings such as Esrum had. There were too many established interests in the immediate vicinity of Øm, and unlike at Sorø, there was no great family to take the monks under their wing and protect them for two or three generations. The monks were exposed to the vicissitudes of the world, and their only real champions were favourable bishops, such as their own Gunner of Viborg, or Sven of Århus and one of his successors, Peder Elavsen, who died in 1246 and was buried at Øm.[113] Not until this line of protectors died out did the monks get into the terrible trouble that nearly brought the total destruction of their house.

It is essential to remember that while Vitskøl, Esrum, and Sorø got started

---

109) Poul Rasmussen, pp. 85ff... See especially the map, p. 88, where Vor's holdings are concentrated south and west of Mossø.
110) Poul Rasmussen, pp. 97ff. Map p. 99.
111) SM II, 197. It was from Skanderborg that Queen Jutta, wife of Erik Plowpenny, set out to plunder the Øm grange at Tåning. The monks feared that her men would ravage the abbey and transport its goods on the monastery's ships to Skanderborg. Even Ring abbey on Skanderborg Lake acquired almost no property in Skanderborg parish during the medieval period - the area seems to have been almost totally closed to monastic expansion.
112) Poul Rasmussen, p. 53.
113) SM II, 98.

in the 1150's and 1160's, Øm did not get underway until the 1170's. The earlier foundations were all more or less able to get control of large blocks of land thanks to generous donors, while the Øm monks had to sell what they had and then convinced the peasants of the district to sell their holdings to them. The Exordium 1 shows us how difficult this could be with the story of Apé the peasants's dream. Apé was only one of a group of richer peasants who refused to sell his land to the monks, until one night he dreamed he saw a church of great size and beauty, with a choir and a tower pushing into the sky in the place where the monastery came to be built.[114] Mary herself threatened him with a swift death if he did not make it possible for the monks to go ahead with their plans. When he awoke and told others about his vision, they ridiculed him for it. Still, he sold his land. It is fascinating that Apé saw in his dream church a high tower and that our writer reports this, despite the strict Cistercian prohibition against towers attached to their churches.

Geographically, the monks had come to the wrong part of the country to start a monastery. In western Zealand, great families dominated, and so it was relatively easy for a favoured foundation to get sufficient property for a solid economic base.[115] In mid-Jutland, peasant holdings of various sizes seem to have been much more common. The entire picture would have been altered if King Valdemar had given a royal farm, as he had done with Vitskøl, but perhaps the bitterness of the dispute with Margrethe made him hold back, so Skanderborg, which would have been a real prize, remained in royal hands.

This time, as before, the monks were going to take no risks, and the abbot Brienne took off for his final trip to Italy.[116] Significantly, the bull he brought back does not emphasize the removal to Øm, but the fact that the monks still held the properties of Veng and Kalvø.[117] Again we see the monks' fear of Margrethe.

---

114) SM II, 176-7 - ch. 2o.
115) See Poul Nørlund's "Jorddrotter på Valdemarstiden", *Festskrift for Kristian Erslev* (Cpn., 1927), especially the section "Hviderne og Sorøegnen".
116) The Øm Book says that this trip was Brienne's third to Rome, but this may actually have been his fourth. He got a papal privilege for Kalvø in 1167-68 (DD I, 2, 177), but we have his name mentioned in connection with Archbishop Stephen of Uppsala at Benevento in 1169 (DD I, 2, 189). Skyum-Nielsen indicates that these were probably separate trips to Italy and is not surprised at this because of the "lively" communication between the Danish Cistercians and the papal court in these years. All these trips strengthen our impression of Brienne individually and the Øm community in general as being extremely eager to do everything possible to guarantee their position and strengthen their privileges.
117) SM II, 177 - ch. 21.

5.

THE ROLE OF BISHOP SVEN

By this time Amilius had taken over the abbacy from Brienne.[118] We might expect the Exordium 1 to end here, after more than twenty chapters and many papal privileges and royal confirmations. But we are only two-thirds finished, for even though we have seen how Øm began, we have not seen how it could survive with the limited properties it had. And here enters decisively the personality of Bishop Sven. He has been with us from the beginning, but it is only after 1172 that our writer is able to point to examples of his generosity and favouritism of the monks. Buchwald called this section the "Sueno vita" and rejected its characterization of Sven as a piece of monkish propaganda.[119] Fortunately Green-Pedersen has shown the weaknesses in Buchwald's attempt to dispose of Sven by contrasting the portrait of him with the much more down-to-earth and practical description of Bishop Gunner of Viborg.[120] Buchwald thought he could reject the earlier "vita" on the basis of the later one's style and content, but he gave no attention to the fact that the two biographies belong to two different periods in the abbey's history. But his suspicions at least remind us that we are presented here with a saintly figure who probably was not as consistently good and generous as he is made out to be. Our writer admitted at the opening of the Exordium 1 that Sven was initially opposed to the monks. His explanation for this resistance was inadequate, as we have seen. It may well be that Sven's earlier behaviour made it necessary to sanctify him, for the Sven that emerges here is a plastic idol, placed on the monastic altar of history as a talisman against the attacks of the evil and the unsympathetic. And they woould be legion.

We are told at the very beginning of this segment that Sven would have become a monk if he could have done so but that the Øm abbot told him he would

---

118) According to the abbot list, SM II, 192, Amilius held office from c. 1173-1180.
119) Buchwald, pp. 32ff.
120) Green-Pedersen, pp. 2oo-2o2.

obtain greater glory if he remained a bishop and protected the house.[121] The language used here is effusive and full of metaphors about walls against the world and ships at sea. But beneath the showy surface the Øm abbot was pointing to an undeniably necessary fact. Sven could do much more for Øm as bishop of Århus than as a humble monk. Buchwald's suspicions about the two papal letters, which are separated by a space of several years and both give Sven permission to become a monk, lead us nowhere. The greatest obstacle to Sven's profession seems to have been the practical-minded Øm monks themselves.

Our writer says that Sven gave the monks "whatever he could, and I do not say, whatever he wished, for he wished to give them everything, if it had been possible."[122] His purpose was to see that the monks could "serve God in peace and quiet without anxieties and cares", and this seems to be an accurate description of his work. To illustrate his innumerable gifts, the properties in Djursland are named, first in an undated testament. The document belongs to 1177-78, thus a good five years after the brothers came to Øm.[123] There are a number of reservations and escape clauses in the testament, so that these properties only go to the monks after Sven's death once his other debts and claims are settled. Other writers on Øm have not paid particular attention to these conditions, but the presence of these clauses may indicate that Sven is still not completely won over by the monks and does not want to endanger his estate's legal situation after his death because of promises to the monks.

In the dated testament, 1183, these conditions have been dropped.[124] Sven says here that the Djursland properties are on the sea and exposed to the attacks of pirates. But this was far from the worst of it. The holdings were more than eighty kilometres from Øm, a phenomenal distance considering the roads of the time and the relatively nearby possessions held by monasteries

---

121) SM II, 178 - ch. 22: Quod profecto opere adimplesset, si domnus abbas non obstitisset, affirmans maioris esse meriti ad promerendam eterne felicitatis gloriam, si se opponeret murum pro domo domini contra malignantium incursiones et servos dei sub alis sue defensionis protegeret atque foveret, ut ex hoc multi possent in pacis tranquillitate viventes deo servire et pro eo copiosius orare, quam si ipse solus in terra claustralis quietis residens dominicam naviculam absciso fune inter fluctus huius seculi conquassandam relinqueret ad multorum scandalum et perturbationem. Notice that even if our writer piles metaphors atop each other, the language is still dignified and balanced. Once again it is obvious that our writer has both talent and training, even if he is overambitious.
122) SM II, 178 - "..quicquid potuit (non dico: voluit; totum enim vellet, si possibile esset), conferret monasterio." The contrast between *posse* and *velle* is cleverly worked out, showing a solid grasp of style enabling the expression of subtle thoughts.
123) SM II, 179 - ch. 23. For dating, see DD I, 3 (unpublished).
124) SM II, 180 - ch. 24.

like Esrum and Sorø.[125] In true Cistercian style, the Øm monks did not refuse the gift, but it is hard to imagine their being overjoyed. Poul Rasmussen has said the monks took the lands because there were valuable chalk quarries in Rosmos and Hoed parishes, part of the donation.[126] Chalk quarries or not, it is hard to imagine the monks turning down any gift, no matter how distant or inconvenient. But these same properties would be a source of trouble for the monks, both in the 126o's and later. In a fourteenth century notation in the Øm Book, the exact boundaries of these holdings are given together with a warning of anathema to anyone who might violate them.[127] None of the abbey's other holdings are delineated so exactly in the Øm Book, so it is likely that at this late date, the monks were still having trouble.

We have a number of royal and episcopal confirmations of Sven's will, but the most significant reflection of his favouritism towards the monastery is the fact that he twice sent messengers to Rome "at great cost" to get the donations confirmed.[128] This act has helped convince Green-Pedersen that Sven's positive actions for Øm outweigh his negative ones,[129] for by getting papal confirmations not only of his donations but also of all Øm properties, Sven saw to it that they were exempted from paying the episcopal tithe, thus losing potential income for himself. The Øm writer says that he does not think it necessary to include all these papal confirmations "because they can be held for a long time without renewal."[130] In this innocent remark we can sense some of the twelfth century confidence in the thriving of the abbey that must have still predominated in the years after 12o7. Granted, our writer does give us a few of the papal privileges, as he says, to make the memory of Sven sweet, but there is no compulsion here, as in the 126o's, to lay out all the documents, even the ones that had no value at all. Despite what has been said about the complaining Øm monks, their pessimism is balanced in this period by a feeling that even if things can be tough, they will be able to survive.

The two papal letters which the writer does include, however, show that there was trouble with the monastic exemption from the payment of tithes. If

---

125) Although the Djursland holdings' distance from the abbey are a record for Denmark, Cistercian houses in other countires occasionally had granges at an even greater distance, such as Himmerod in Southern Germany. See Carl Wilkes, *Die Zisterzienserabtei Himmerode im 12. und 13. Jahrh.*, Beiträge zur Geschichte des alten Mönchtums, Hft. 1o-12 (1924), p. 153.
126) Poul Rasmussen, p. 54.
127) SM II, 263-4.
128) SM II, 184 - "magnis sumptibus et expensis".
129) Green-Pedersen, p. 2o5.
130) SM II, 184 - "...que quia longo tempore sine renovatione possunt custodiri, non ea iudicavimus hic inserenda."

we are going to understand this problem, it would be well to glance ahead at
the documents we have for Århus cathedral for the 1190's, after Sven's death.
During this period we find papal admissions of indulgences to those who contribute to the building of a cathedral of stone at Århus.[131] It is possible
that the burden imposed on parish priests and parishioners for the construction of St. Clement's cathedral brought a financial squeeze that led to resistance to the monks' exemptions. But the problem was already there in the
1170's, when Bishop Sven first obtained a papal exemption for Øm from paying
the tithes on its lands.[132] With Apé and his fellow peasants, we saw how
unwelcome the demands of the monks could be, and here we find that the same
could be the case with local parish priests.

One of the final chapters of the Exordium 1 provides the longest piece
of uninterrupted narration in the entire section. It deals with the character
of Sven.[133] In this way Sven is given more attention and detail than any of
the abbots. Through his sanctification he could become in death just as much
a protector for the Øm monks as he had been in life, and perhaps warn future
bishops of Århus that they had a tradition to live up to.

We are told that whenever anyone even named the Cistercians in Sven's
presence, he would become happy. His servants knew this and if he was upset
would say to him, "As far as we can make out from a distance, a monk or a lay
brother is coming down the road." Such words worked wonders.[134] The tender,
humorous tone of this anecdote is similar to that found in the biography of
Bishop Gunner. Despite the differences between the two descriptions, already
emphasized by Buchwald, there is a common ground of fond remembrance. This
similarity points to a basic continuity of life and attitudes between the two
centuries. Also the gently humorous tone hints at the mildness of everyday
existence, something that otherwise is totally lost to us in our property
records and crisis narrations.

Sven is depicted as a man who wanted to give the monks everything he could,
but the abbot and brothers often resisted him. We are not told the reason
why; perhaps it was out of self-respect. But this behaviour is supposed to
have been "very hurtful" to him. When the abbot refused his gifts, he said

---

131) G. Thorkelin, *Diplomatarium Arna-Magnæanum* (DAM) I (Cpn., 1786), p. 69.
132) This papal bull cannot be dated more precisely than sometime between 1166-81 - SM II, 184-5, ch. 29 - DD I, 2, 173. I should think that it belongs to the end of the 1170's, when Sven first made his testament for the monks, but there is no reason why it could not have been issued earlier.
133) SM II, 186-9 ch. 31.
134) SM II, 187 "Quantum possumus a longe discernere, monachus vel conversus venit per viam." Ad quorum voces ita gaudens et iocundus reddebatur, ac si nichil indignationis animo concepisset."

that some day the abbot would be glad for such gifts, for there would be no one to give them. Our writer reflects sadly that this prediction has come true.[135] This may be just a literary device, but it is more likely that the writer of the Exordium 1, in comparing the tradition of Sven's works with the situation of his own time, really does find a substantial difference and longs for the good old days. This theme is only parenthetically mentioned, but it is implied in the entire chapter. Later on, in the 1250's and 1260's, it will become of primary importance.

The composer of the Exordium 1 strikes a fine balance between the material endowments of Sven and his spiritual attributes. When the abbot had to sell an unusable altar chalice, Sven saw to it that the monks had several chalices made, which in 1207 were still being used. He wanted the brothers to have a generous supply of whatever they needed, for he could not tolerate the thought of lay people discovering that the brothers were in need. So he not only replenished their grain supplies but saw to it that the brothers' lay labourers were paid.[136] If there was to be any trouble with money, then it was to be a matter between the bishop and the monks, for it would be embarrassing and humiliating for the community to be unable to pay its debts. These very material considerations are followed by illustrations of Sven's attitude towards the monks: his respect in visiting the monastery by leaving his horses at the gate; his practice, if he ran into the brothers outside the monastery, of holding himself back so they could go ahead. It was wrong to cross their path, for "among them the angels of God walked to guard them."[137] But if he could not avoid meeting them, he would get off his horse, and all who were with him would do the same and stand humbly until the brothers had passed.[138]

---

135) SM II, 187: Aliquando optulit abbati animalia et queque alia, et nolebat accipere; et ille leniter subridens dixit (*quod postea experimento didicimus*) quod scilicet abbas libenter vellet accipere, quando nullus ei aliquid offeret.
136) If I read the latin *nec* correctly, then the paying of wages to the monastery's labourers was considered the lowest priority of all. Sven is said to have taken care of all the things that the monastery needed so that he would not allow even the wages of the labourers to be in default - ita ut *nec* mercedes mercennariorum pateretur deesse." SM II, 188. Here for once I think we can legitimately utilize the Marxist apparatus of class conflict and the idea that a privileged class is exploiting an unprivileged one, for at least the attitude of discrimination and superiority seems to be present in this remark.
137) SM II, 188 - "Si forte occurrisset conventui eunti ad laborem vel inde redeunti, retrahebat se, dicens indignum se esse obviare eis, cum quibus semper et inter quos affirmabat angelos dei ad custodiam deambulare." Whether or not Sven really said this and used this image is unimportant compared to the fact that the monks remembered him as doing such.
138) Apparently bishops who got off their horses were the exception rather than the rule in the twelfth century. Bishop Hugh of Lincoln is praised because

Much of this sounds like a chronic case of Cistercian wish fulfillment, and we could assert with a critical eye that our author is composing his account more than fifteen years after Sven's death. But a monastery was an excellent place for such stories to be told and retold, so even though we may find a great deal of literary embroidery here, I think we are getting an essentially believable account of the way Sven impressed the monks in later years, during the 1180's when he had completely given himself over to the Cistercians. The memory is probably all the sharper because of the changed situation after Sven's death. As our author says, so long as Sven was bishop, the monks never had to defend their rights at secular courts. Either he looked after such matters, or else laymen respected and feared him so much that they did not dare bring the matters to court. Whatever the reason, our monk and author is obviously looking back with yearning at a better, less controversial period, when the monks could feel looked after and protected. The anecdotes given are sentimental but not unlikely. Sven's behaviour would be completely understandable to us today if it was centred not on an institution but on a person.

The chapter closes with a description of the books that Sven gave the monastery so that the monks would not only be "guarded on the outside but refreshed on the inside." We find in these lines some of the most polished and able writing by any Danish religious in the medieval period. Our author continues the metaphor of nourishment by saying that the first "course" given by Sven was Gregory's *Moralia in Job*, which is a commentary on the Book of Job emphasizing various levels of interpretation. Our writer claims that this book "is sweeter and nourishes the soul more than all other readings." The word *dulcis* in all its forms is one of the key cultural words of the twelfth century,[139] and we feel here, just as with the early thirteenth century Danish romanesque style, that we are still steeped in a period that England, France, and the Low Countries had left decades before.

---

he did not insist on confirming children while he was sitting in the saddle. See *The Life of St. Hugh of Lincoln*, ed. D.L. Douie and H. Farmer (Nelson Medieval Classics) 1, 127-8. Also R.W. Southern, *Western Society and the Church in the Middle Ages* (Pelican History of the Church 2), p. 187: "Virtue takes many forms, but it is hard to evoke the situation in which it was a notable virtue in a bishop to refuse to lay hands on the children from his saddle..."

139) Such a statement is almost impossible to document, but the word abounds in Cistercian literature, especially in passages having to do with tears and strong emotions. A good example can be found in the Life of Ailred of Rievaulx, *op. cit.*, p. 35. Ailred has just had a vision about the death of a wayward monk. In the morning this monk appears back at the monastery, and Ailred goes down to meet him, kissing him tenderly and weeping over him: "Quem, ut vidit, osculatus est dulciter et de visione cogitans flevit super eum valde suaviter."

Sven apparently considered his role at Øm as more than that of benefactor, for he would give any volume "which could edify morals" and always managed to get hold of what he wanted. He even had certain stories written out, but this at the suggestion of the abbot, and he supplied Øm richly with scribes and parchment. Our writer explains that the gold lettering to be found in Øm books, even if against the Cistercian rule, was not a breach for the monks because they did not make it themselves. Here as elsewhere he seems to be almost apologizing for the generosity of Sven and insisting that the gifts did not lead the monks away from the right practices of the Order. Nevertheless, Sven in his love affair with Øm was very much caught up in the *things* the monks could possess (even though he also wanted the monks to make good use of them). Like so many benefactors, he could best express his affection by transferring his material riches to the monks. But in so doing he deprived them of the very poverty and simplicity that Bernard had so much insisted on. It is strange how often in history idealistic poverty attracts idealistic wealth, while common garden variety poverty only propagates itself.

Even if Sven emerges from these chapters as a saint, he does have human touches, about as believable as we can find in almost any twelfth century description of a person. Even if the factual information of this account has been manipulated, the very manipulation brings us to the heart of the Cistercian life dream: the projection of a person or persons who will take the monks to their heart, accept them totally, spoil them, and be infinitely good to them. Our monastic writer is expressing here nothing more or less than the human need to love and feel cared for.

We are fortunate enough to have one source for our knowledge of Sven, Saxo's *Gesta Danorum*. It is only with fear and trembling that I take up Saxo's work, because more than any other source in Scandinavian medieval history, Saxo has been exposed to ruthless criticism and analysis.[140] But in what follows I am solely interested in Saxo's attitude to Sven and not in whether or not the technical details of his description are correct. The first instance in which we meet Sven is at the unsuccessful attempt to colonize Volgast.[141] During the campaign against the Wends in Pomerania in the beginning of the 1160's, King Valdemar wanted a contingent to stay behind in the town of Volgast. He wanted to make Absalon and Sven colonizers in the city. But when he asked them to find others who would stay with them, only Absalon could get promises of support. In this instance Sven is sharply contrasted

---

140) The masterpiece of modern Saxo criticism is Curt Weibull's *Saxo*: Kritiska Undersökninger i Danmarks Historia från Sven Estridsens Död till Knut VI (Lund, 1915). Fortunately Skyum-Nielsen's *Kvinde og Slave* attempts to combine Saxo with the documentary evidence, and the work of Inge Skovgaard-Petersen may further this new attempt. See also *Saxostudier*, ed. Ivan Boserup (Cpn., 1975).

141) *Saxonis Gesta Danorum* I, J. Olrik and H. Ræder (Cpn., 1931), p. 551.

with Absalon: the latter is surrounded by a circle of loyalty, while the former is unable to muster the same reaction in his men.

After the taking of Arkona in 1169, Karenz, which is also on the island of Rügen, surrendered.[142] Absalon arrived with only thirty of his own men to receive the city's surrender. All the city' soldiers - six thousand according to Saxo - came out to meet him. At the sight of them Bishop Sven was struck with fear and asked why the enemy marched in such a way towards them. But Absalon told him not to be afraid: if they had been up to no good, it would have been much better for them to stay inside the city. Once again we have a contrast, this time even more direct, between *stupentem Suenonem rogantemque*, a stupified and questioning Sven, and *Absalon metu carere praecepit*, an Absalon who is ordering Sven not to be afraid.[143] Absalon then went ahead with having the town's idols cut down and dragged out of the city. As usual, Absalon knows exactly what to do and how to go about it. Later on, we see Sven in a new context. He wanted to teach the people of Karenz a lesson about the powerlessness of their idols and so stood on one of them as it was being dragged out of the city.[144] This is a marvellous picture which has given vent to romantic nationalism in Danish art,[145] but even in this tableau Sven is still a secondary figure, only able to show his bravado because of the careful and wise actions of Absalon.

In the mid-1170's when one of the king's relatives refused the job of guarding the Danish and Rügen fishermen against the Wends and the King called on Absalon, he gladly consented to help, saying that he would not think of abandoning Valdemar at this point.[146] Absalon asked some of his West Zealand allies and relatives for help in the matter, and Saxo mentions Sune Ebbesen and Esbern Snare, the very same men who according to the Sorø Book sold or deeded their lands to the monastery. Saxo claims that Absalon's very presence created order and peace in the area, for the Wends did not dare to attack now. Then, almost as a footnote to this hearty description, he adds that Bishop Sven of Århus and some men of Jutland were also there. Once again Absalon had captured Saxo' imagination, while Sven is just the sidekick and secondary ally.

Only once does Saxo show Bishop Sven acting independently, and in this instance he interprets such behaviour unfavourably.[147] After a rising in Skåne, which seems to have been primarily directed against Absalon, Valdemar went there in order to pacify the population. The King was apparently furious with the thankless way the people were handling his beloved Absalon. In the midst of this, Bishop Sven embraced the King and begged him "not to do anything harsh

---

142) Saxo I, 473-476.
143) Saxo I, 474.
144) Saxo I, 476.
145) See the illustration in Green-Pedersen, p. 2o1.
146) Saxo I, 49o.
147) Saxo I, 527-8.

against the people". Saxo's description of the King's reaction puts the final touch on the Absalon-Sven opposition:

> Pietas illi an metus hunc ausum praestiterit, incertum est.
> Sed apud regis animum, continua Absalonis caritate flagrare solitum, venientis amici pericula complectentis precibus praeponderabant.

Saxo undermines here any positive interpretation of Sven's action. By saying that it was uncertain whether he acted out of piety or of fear, Saxo obliterates what in a hagiographer would have been a clear indication of saintliness. Sven has to be knocked down, for Saxo wants to emphasize the King's total devotion to Absalon in this moment of danger. Once again Absalon is asserted at the expense of Sven.

It may be rather naive to point out, example by example, this tendency to heroize Absalon, which every serious reader of Saxo will notice. But the story of Absalon and his expoits forms the emotional core for the last section of the *Gesta Danorum*. Only by being aware of this tendency can we realize that Saxo's portrait of Sven is just as prejudiced and distorted as the Øm writer's. The latter at least had good reason to capture something of the character of Sven, to make him into a person whose memory would live on, while for Saxo Sven is a puppet to be manipulated in accordance with his desire to praise Absalon. Green-Pedersen, after a brief review of the sources for Sven in Saxo, concluded that their picture of the bishop does not necessarily invalidate that of the Exordium 1, for the two narratives show Sven in different contexts.[148] I would go further and say that the two descriptions have almost nothing at all to do with each other. Only in Saxo's final scene with Sven, with the bishop begging the King to be merciful, do we for an instant catch something of the same gentle, impressionable, and very emotional personality that emerges from the Exordium 1. Despite Saxo's negative conclusion, the rash and undiplomatic embrace of Valdemar at such a moment of crisis corresponds to the portrait of the changeable but basically devout man we see through Cistercian eyes.

We can look back upon the last ten or fifteen years of Sven's life as a unique period of happiness for Øm. Aside from disputes over tithes and difficulties with the Lady Margrethe, the Øm monks, settled into their new life, were probably at last fairly comfortable, both in terms of material and emotional security. The impression given by the careful and beautiful hand that wrote the Exordium 1,[149] together with frequent Biblical citations skilfully woven into the text, is of life at Øm as something complete and almost polished.

---

148) Green-Pedersen, pp. 199-2oo.
149) Gertz in his introduction to the Exordium (SM II, 155) commented on the beauty of the hand responsible for the Exordium 1.

As historians we have penetrated the myth of the foundation and have seen the problems that the text had half hidden, and even if the finished composition is badly organized and even confusing in its structure, the work as a whole points to a monastery that could afford to look back and be thankful for what it had.

During the years up to 119o Øm received up to half of the properties that it possessed at its dissolution.[150] By the time the Exordium 1 was written, the monks thus had a solid economic base. Despite other nearby foundations, there was still physical and psychological room in which to manoeuvre, to grow and even to flourish.

But the monastery had two built-in weaknesses. First, as previously shown, its properties were far too scattered and distant from each other. About twenty percent of the monastery's holdings were on Djursland. This meant constant travel back and forth by the monks in order to administer their lands. Second, and even more seriously, the monks were all to dependent on the good will of the Århus bishop. After Sven died in 1191, Peder Vognsen became bishop. He was succeeded by his brother Skjalm Vognsen in 12o4. These two men came from the group of families in West Zealand that later historians came to call the Whites. Not only were many of them emotionally attached to Sorø's Cistercian house. The grandparents of the Vognsens had been decisive in the early development of the abbey. Peder Torstensen had married Cecilie, the daughter of Skjalm Hvide, the half-legendary founder of the clan, and the sister of Absalon's father, Asser Rig. Peder and Cecilie lived at Pedersborg just north of Sorø, and Peder made much trouble for the monks.[151] Cecilie tried to make up for this, and the grandsons seem to have inherited her attitude.[152] In any case, the Vognsen's roots were in West Zealand and not in the Skanderborg area. Peder Vognsen used his inheritance and other properties to found the cathedral chapter at Århus, while Skjalm increased the chapter's income and continued with the building of the cathedral. Both of them were buried at Sorø, but Peder's body was later moved to Århus.

The Vognsen bishops of Århus start a new period, in which the bishop's primal interest is to build up his own diocese and not to support a monastic order. This was only natural. The unusual situation had been under Sven, when monks were favoured and there apparently were no canons at Århus, incredible as this may seem. In such a new world the Øm monks had to walk softly, for

---

15o) Poul Rasmussen, p. 32.
151) SRD IV, 474-5.
152) As in the land gift to Sorø by Skjalm Vognsen (12o7-1215: DD I, 4, 13o), so that the monks could have pittances (festive meals) twice yearly. We have no evidence of any similar gifts by the Vognsens to the Øm monks.

they no longer were seen with the angels of God in their midst and were but one more religious foundation.

By the end of the 11oo's the Danish Cistercians seem to have lost much of their initial attraction to prominent members of the lay and ecclesiastical upper class. There was a nasty controversy between Benedictines and Cistercians that perhaps can help account for the growing tendency to group Cistercian houses with those of other orders and not consider them anything special.

Benedictine and Cistercian houses in southern Slesvig lashed out at each other through the 119o's, and finally the crusty William of Æbelholt was called in to negotiate.[153] Eskil was dead, and Absalon would soon die. The great age of foundations and phenomenal growth was over, and in twenty years or so, the first friars would arrive in Denmark. In such a changing world, the Cistercians no longer could expect preference. They had to work hard to keep what they had and to add a little. It is understandable that just at the time when all the confident assumptions of the past were being undermined, the monks of Øm wrote down the story of their first difficult but rewarding years.

---

153) Abbot William's letters on the subject, scattered through the troublesome collection we have of his writings (SRD VI, 1-79), deserve further analysis. See also the lines in the account on the foundation of Guldholm, SM II, 151: "Armati enim monachi nec non famuli eorum nostros quam sepius invaserunt eosque spoliaverunt et verberibus affecerunt; calumniabantur eciam se iniuste et violenter eiectos esse de monasterio suo, dicentes se non consensisse episcopo in mutacione loci nec locum aliquatenus resignasse..."

6.

THE ABBOT LIST (1165 - 1246) AND THE MIDDLE YEARS (1207-1246)

The primary source for this period is the list of abbots that is given in the Øm Book after the Exordium 1.[154] The record of the first five abbots, from 1165-1199, is written with the same hand as the Exordium itself. Gertz, in his introduction, claimed that the account of Abbot Thorkil, 1199-1216, was written in a second hand, while Skyum-Nielsen showed that this was the same hand.[155] After 1216 we find very many different hands, but there is a long stretch from 1235 to 1257 for which one hand seems to be responsible.[156] The following section backtracks to 1255 and then goes right up to 1320.[157] But this part of the list is not nearly so full as the preceding, and as we move along in the century, especially after 1268 or so, the information gets more sparse. It is as if the monks no longer were so much interested in recording the history of their house. But another explanation may be the existence of an independent list of abbots that was composed in the monastery and which has not survived to our day. If this is so, then there was no good reason to continue a second abbot list.[158]

A. The Earliest Abbots

Before we go over to the years after 1207, it might be helpful to summarize the accounts of the early abbots so that we can compare them with their successors. Brienne, 1165-73, we have already met. Like some of the twelfth

---

154) SM II, 192-206.
155) DD I, 5, 197.
156) See C.A. Christensen's preface to his facsimile of the Øm Book, p. XIII.
157) SM II, 202-206.
158) See Gertz's notes: SM II, 202. I agree with him that the account referred to here of Abbot Asgot's mores, his cheerfulness and generosity, cannot be fount in the Øm Book. Gertz thinks that this lost account is the same as the "cronica nostra et acta temporum" (SM II, 199) mentioned in the Øm Book, but this title indicates the type of brief chronicle of political and ecclesiastical events that we associate with other Danish Cistercian houses, such as the Ryd Annals. The account of Abbot Asgot may well have been included in an unknown third narrative composed by the Øm monks.

century abbots at Sorø and Esrum, he was English. His successor, Amilius, 1173-80, was German, and then came William, 1180-93, who is called a Norman. Only then do we find a Dane, Brandan, 1193-97. Just as at Sorø, the twelfth century at Cistercian Øm is dominated by foreign abbots. We know hat Eskil brought monks from Clairvaux to Esrum in 1153, and it may well be that there were similar migrations from England to Denmark by Cistercians.[159] It looks as if the Order blossomed so quickly in the North precisely because of foreign imports. It was a good half century before native Danes predominated in the monasteries.

This possibility opens an even more exciting, even if provisional, way of looking at the period. It seems that by 1150, the Benedictine houses in Denmark were in decline, and this may have been due to a failure to attract native Danes.[160] The Cistercian accounts of Sorø, Veng, and Kalvø under Benedictine rule, when we take away all their moral prejudice, point to foundations with very few members on the way to abandonment. Only with the coming of a foreign element, the Cistercians, does monastic life take on a new attraction. But once this influx came, the problems with recruitment seem to have disappeared. If we accept the number twenty-two for the monks who came from Varnhem to Vitskøl in 1158 and then assume that seven years later the minimum number of twelve monks plus the new abbot headed for the Silkeborg area (while others returned to refound Varnhem at about the same time), then the French monks must have been supplemented in the meantime by Danish novices. Likewise the Esrum expansions into Pomerania and the daughters of Herrisvad necessitated a sufficiency of numbers that almost had to come through Danish recruitment. And so the signs of monastic decline in Denmark were halted by the Cistercian immigration after 1144, which in turn seems to have provoked a new wave of native monasticism in the last third of the century.

All the foreign twelfth-century abbots at Øm share one characteristic: they are remembered as spiritual men more than businessmen.[161] Even the industrious and much travelled Brienne, noted for being loved by laymen and appreciated at the Roman curia, is primarily described ad a "wise man of learned speech". Amilius fits even better into the Cistercian pattern of spirituality, for he was "intent on prayers and readings with tears". Despite their spiritual penchants, however, all these men are described as being capable in the external pursuits of the monastery. They are able to balance prayers with secular problems.

---

159) We do know of Yorkshire migration to Norway. See David Knowles, *The Monastic Order in England*, 940-1216 (Cambridge, 1966), p. 248.
160) This Benedictine decline seems to have been a European phenomenon. See Southern, p. 234.
161) SM II, 192-3.

The first native abbot, Brandan, was not remembered for his prayers and learning at all, but for his strictness in following the discipline of the Rule and in keeping his promises. There is a change of emphasis here, much more marked with the account of Niels, 1197-99, who is unfavourably judged for his "excessive simplicity". Thorkil, 1199-1216, under whom Exordium 1 was written, is called "very learned in worldly matters", and the writer emphasizes how tiring the tasks and activities he engaged in for the monastery could be. Thorkil was the first to have been brought up among the monks from boyhood and was involved from the very beginning with lay affairs.

Thus far only one abbot has been unfavourably mentioned, Niels, but the drift of the account has been away from spiritual concerns and over to secular matters. The descriptions are too short and vague to tell us exactly what the abbots did, but in the lines about Thorkil we can see the insecurity of the monks that we already have mentioned in connection with the writing of the Exordium 1. Men like Thorkil are necessary for the monastery to function. Even though he also may have devoted time to prayers and tears, what is important and what is mentioned here is that he was a good administrator. With Thorkil the transition is complete from the myth of French Cistercian spirituality symbolized in legendary abbots to the need for practical, worldly, native Danish abbots who have grown up with the monastery and know the lay of the land.

B. The Need for Practical Abbots

With Gunner, 1216-21, we achieve a balance between spiritual and secular abilities, while his follower, Jens I, 1222-29, is said to have been suitable in the internal affairs of the house but less fitted in external matters.[162] Like his twelfth century predecessors, he wanted "peace and quiet in all things", so much so that he eventually gave up his post to become prior again. Niels II, 1229-33, was so well known for his cleverness in business matters that he was promoted to abbot of the mother house at Vitskøl. A number of other Øm abbots eventually became abbots at Vitskøl, just as Sorø abbots during this period went to Esrum, and it is clear that this was considered a reward for good service.

We can see the demands of secular business in the record of Magnus of Viborg, 1233-35, who had first been a monk at Vitskøl. He was so repelled by his duties and especially by his obligation to take part in lay courts of law that in the last meeting, he had such a difficult time that he asked God for

---

162) SM II, 194.

quick deliverance from the burden. The same day he was stricken with illness and brought back to the monastery, where he soon died:

> Et quia minus videbatur exercitatus forinsecus ad secularia placita (dederat enim ei deus magis cor ad precepta sua et legem vite et discipline), in ultimo colloquio, quod habuit cum secularibus, contra se satis durum et asperum, in toto corde suo rogavit dominum, ut cito ab huiusmodi angustiis liberaretur. Et exaudivit dominus vocem ipsius; placita enim erat deo anima eius. Unde correptus infirmitate in ipso colloquio, adductus est ad claustrum.... (SM II, 195)

Even if we remove the element of the supernatural from this tale, and this is the last time in the Øm Book that the writer speaks of direct divine intervention, Magnus apparently was unable to find the will or the stamina to persevere in the secular duties of the abbacy.

With this account of Magnus ends the part of the abbot list containing only short notices and summaries of lives, and we go over to Michael, 1235-46. The criteria for describing Michael are completely different from those used with the twelfth century abbots. They were wrapped in their sanctity and at the same time competent with the monastery's affairs. They may not have been so tearful as they are made out to be here, but this at least is the way our early thirteenth century writer thought of them. His successors in writing the list were more concerned with whether or not the abbots could properly look after the financial, legal, and agricultural interests of the house. We have entered an age when it is not good enough for an abbot to be simply good. He must also be clever!

Still, there is a certain sympathy for abbots like Magnus who could not stand all the duties and details. Naiveté is not wanted, but it can still be understood. But an abbot like Michael is the necessary response to the challenge of the new age. Adapting a Biblical image already used in describing the helpless Niels, our author says that Michael had both the shrewdness of a serpent against the display of secular power and the simplicity of a dove towards those who were obedient.[163] Far from being a stringent disciplinarian, he was gentle and patient with renegade brothers so that he could bring them back to the ways of salvation. This passage had the spirit of an earlier monastic age, as described in Eadmer's Life of Saint Anselm. As abbot of Bec, Anselm tried to reform delinquent brothers by reasoning with them instead of whipping them.[164]

We can perhaps get a glimpse of the reality behind these words in the 1240 and 1241 mentions at the Cistercian General Chapter of the monks of Herrisvad,

---

163) SM II, 193, 196.
164) *The Life of Saint Anselm* by Eadmer, ed. and trans. by R.W. Southern, Oxford Medieval Texts (1972), pp. 37-40.

Tvis, and Øm.¹⁶⁵ During their travels they one night went to a tavern and remained there until midnight. Their behaviour scandalized the abbess of Het-Münster, near Ruremund in the diocese of Köln. The exact words of the 1241 decision are:

> ...post coenam et intraverunt tabernam ubi minus honeste et in scandalum ordinis se habuerunt usque ad mediam noctem.

The response of the General Chapter was apparently so harsh because the abbess complained and thus made a scandal. Although Skyum-Nielsen has used this incident to contribute to his thesis about moral decline at Øm in the years before the dispute with Bishop Tyge, I cannot for myself look upon the event as anything more than a minor, even if scandalous, episode.¹⁶⁶ The demand that the Cistercians attend regularly the General Chapter imposed much travelling on them, and it is no wonder that once in a while out on the road the temptations of the world to gaiety and self-indulgence got the better of them.

Despite such incidents and the increasing burden of business on the abbots, the years up to the middle of the 1240's seem to have been fairly quiet at Øm. The monks did not get many new properties, but they could on the other hand feel secure under the protection of their former abbot, now Bishop Gunner of Viborg, who lived until 1251. The biography of Gunner really tells us more about the attitudes of the 1260's, which were a time when Gunner needed to be remembered as a comfort and consolation in time of trouble, than about the state of the monastery in the 1230's. Nevertheless we do find out that there was frequent communication between Viborg and Øm, that the monks could always count on being well received by Gunner, and even being feted, and that whenever he came to visit them, he would show his respect for them and for their abbot.¹⁶⁷ Moreover, some of the Øm monks seem to have spent most of their time at Viborg, including perhaps the author of the biography. He speaks glowingly of the advancement in spirituality and learning that daily contact with Gunner brought.¹⁶⁸ Of all the Danish Cistercians from this period, Gunner is the only one whom we definitely know had gone to Paris and completed his studies there. Just as in the rest of Europe, Cistercians were beginning to feel that it no longer was enough to concentrate on the writings of the Fathers and on St. Bernard but began to turn, slowly and reluctantly, to the philosophy and theology of Paris. Gunner's experience and interests may indicate an intellectual expansion in Cistercian Denmark.¹⁶⁹ But our author does not look upon Gunner

---

165) Canivez, *Statuta capitulorum*, 1240, nr. 69.
166) *Kirkekampen*, p. 183.
167) SM II, 276-77.
168) SM II, 269-270.
169) The Cistercian college at Paris, College de Chardonnet, was not finished until 1246, but the coming of the friars to Paris in 1217 had already

as an intellectual figure. He is remembered more for his delightful personality, his sense of humour, and his kindness.

In this amazing, relaxed, and confident biography is reflected some of the social stability and harmony among the various power groups in Denmark that seems to have prevailed until the death of Valdemar II in 1241. The very fact that a Cistercian abbot was so readily in 1222 accepted by the Viborg canons as the best candidate for the bishopric shows a fluidity in society that did not exist at the end of the 12oo's. As we have already seen, the Herrisvad abbot had become bishop of Ribe at the beginning of the 117o's, so the idea of a Cistercian bishop in Denmark was hardly new. Still it was an unusual step for the Viborg canons to risk having a bishop who had a loyalty that had nothing to do with them. The relationship between Øm and the chapter at Viborg indicates a confidence and trust that is worlds away from the Øm-Århus mutual suspicion of the 126o's, when the Øm abbot could only come to the cathedral under the guarantees of the noblemen who were seeking a settlement.

The few other mentions we have of Øm during these years up to 1246 contribute little to this picture of general harmony coupled with increasing demands of the monks. In 121o the Cistercian General Chapter had asked the abbots of Øm and Tvis to look after the situation of an abbey which had been transferred, after a catastrophic fire, without the Chapter's consent.[17o] The Danish abbots were to investigate the site, see if it was in order, and discipline the abbot who had acted without permission. In the text the name of the place is "Beer", obviously a misspelling, as so often happens in these records, with all their exotic names from Europe and the Near East.

Another time, the abbots of Øm and Tvis did not appear at the Chapter. In 1215 we hear that they did not come because of the danger of wars, and so the Chapter ordered them to appear the following year, no excuses allowed. But the 1216 General Chapter did not find the Øm abbot present, and so he was ordered to remain outside the abbot's stall in his church's choir and to have only bread and water every Friday until he presented himself at Citeaux at the following Chapter and asked for pardon.[171] In the same year the abbot of Nydala in Sweden received the same punishment. It must have been a hard journey to make, but we can see in these provisions a continuing effort in the Cistercian Order to hold itself together and to consider its Scandinavian houses as subject to the same rules as other abbeys.

---

brought fresh interest in the new learning to the Cistercians, who "became anxious to remove the reproach of ignorance freely hurled against them by the more ambitious and progressive friars." Hastings Rashdall, *The Universities of Europe in the Middle Ages* (Oxford, 1936) I, 5o6.
17o) Canivez 121o, nr. 15.
171) Canivez 1215, nr. 19; 1216, nr. 14.

Although we know little about the monks' efforts to maintain their privileges in these years, we are fortunate to have in the Vatican Registers the text of a confirmation of Øm's holdings at Veng by Honorius III. This document provides a last witness to the dispute with Margrethe.[172] The bull says that the church of Veng was held by the monastery there long before it became Cistercian. In these lines we can trace the desire of the monks to show that their claim to the church was respectably ancient.

During these same years we meet Gunner time and again in the documents and get a fuller picture of him than we do from the biography. In 1216 Pope Innocent III ordered Bishop Ebbe of Århus, together with the Øm abbot and the dean of the cathedral in Viborg to intervene against the citizens of Viborg, who had moved boundaries and issued invalid judgments over the properties of the Viborg canons.[173] Through this document we can perhaps understand a little better why Gunner in 1222 was an obvious choice at Viborg. He also looked after the interests of the chapter in another incident. In 1219 Abbot Gunner settled a problem which for any other Øm abbot would have been virtually impossible to take on: reconciling the interests of the Vitskøl Cistercians on the island of Læsø with those of the Viborg chapter.[174] In the decision Gunner says that he had gone himself to Læsø together with Jens, prefect of Viborg, and Peder, prior of Vitskøl, and personally inspected the various places that were disputed. Finally they had determined where the boundaries were to be. The language of the charter is clear and precise. There can be no doubt about the result, for there is no attempt to leave the solution on the level of vague legal generalities.

At least for the time being, Gunner's decision was satisfactory to both parties. In 1221 Abbot Jens and the monks of Vitskøl confirmed the agreement proposed by Gunner.[175] Niels Skyum-Nielsen has determined that the scribe of the bulk of this charter is none other than the monk who wrote down the text of the Exordium 1 that we have. We thus have an instance in which the abbot of Øm and one of his scribes are cooperating to bring justice to their Vitskøl brethren, but without alienating the canons of Viborg. With or without intent, Gunner was laying the groundwork for his later election as bishop.

How could a man, no matter how clever and thoughtful, reconcile such different interests and not be accused of being partisan? We lack sufficient details, but Gunner must have been an extraordinary man, whose charm and humour went together with a quick legal understanding and a sense of justice. Here

---

172) DD I, 5, 1o5.
173) DD I, 5, 81.
174) DD I, 5, 161.
175) DD I, 5, 197. Note Skyum-Nielsen's commentary.

I think we come to the reason for Øm's success in these years, despite our lack of evidence for support or encouragement from the Århus bishops. Both as abbot of Øm and bishop of Viborg, Gunner created a climate of friendliness, an era of good feeling, that reflected back on the Øm monks and probably protected them from maltreatment.

All in all, this period seems to have been one of cooperation in order to maintain the rights of institutions. In 1238 we find the abbots of Vitskøl, Øm, Tvis, and Holme, together with Ås in Halland, agreeing to a settlement by the bishop of Slesvig concerning a dispute between the Cistercian abbey at Løgum and a certain Ubby Tordsen.[176] The abbot of Øm was Michael. The abbots say that they found out about this settlement when they were at Herrisvad for the purpose of visitation. We know that the abbots of the four eldest Cistercian houses were supposed to visit the mother house, Citeaux, once a year, and here we have an instance of daughter abbeys of Herrisvad, in this case Tvis and Holme, visiting their mother house. It seems odd that the abbots of Vitskøl, Øm, and Ås, who all belonged to the Esrum line, were there too, but we have a similar incident in 1254 when the abbots of Sorø and Ås visit Herrisvad.[177] These crossovers would indicate that the hierarchy of mother-daughter abbeys in Denmark may not have been followed so strictly and that daughters of one mother house could act as visitors for another. In these documents we get a brief but strong impression of the way Danish houses kept in contact with each other through their use of the Order's system of visitation and thus looked after each others' concerns and problems. This solidarity would be tested to the utmost in the 1260's when Øm got into trouble, and it would be shown that mere cooperation was not enough.

If we look back over these documents and privileges to the Exordium 1 itself, we can see how the partly disturbed and insecure atmosphere at Øm in the first decade of the thirteenth century was gradually replaced after 1215 by a period of harmony. Even though our sources for the 1220's, 1230's and first part of the 1240's are much less abundant than they are for the decades before and after, there is enough material to present a picture of calm. In one way we can conclude that this was inevitable, for Denmark itself profited immensely from a ruler like Valdemar II, who despite his foreign adventures, imprisonment and ransom in the 1220's, was able to unify the country and rule without the constant threat of factions and revolts that came to plague the kingdom after his death. In an even larger sense Øm benefited from the general European prosperity that characterizes the first half of the thirteenth century: in-

---

176) SRD VIII, 220 (Løgum abbey's property documents).
177) Canivez 1254, nr. 6.

creasing trade, growth of universities and towns, and generally stable political entities. Nevertheless, the local peace and harmony in central Jutland were probably largely due to the personality of Gunner. As we have seen and as we shall see again when we deal in detail with the content of the biography, Gunner had a profound influence on the people around him. Much more than Eskil, he seems to have succeeded in combining spiritual passion with political wisdom.

7.

THE BEGINNINGS OF THE CONFLICT: 1246 - 1262

The dispute with Bishop Tyge of Århus did not begin until 1262, and even though most writers have given brief attention to what came immediately before, no one has investigated this entire period as a preparation and, indeed, explanation for what came between 1262 and 1268. Skyum-Nielsen has spoken of a decline in *morals*, but we need also to consider a simultaneous decline in *morale* that resulted from an unprecedented series of attacks on the monastery.[178] By the time we come to 1262, the exhaustion of the monks is in itself almost enough to account for their stubborn and foolish behaviour.

From 9 October, 1246 to 6 July 1249, Jens II was abbot at Øm.[179] In his time, says the abbot list, the house had many problems. The most dramatic was an attack on the horses of the abbey kept at Ynes, south of Horsens fjord, where a farm in Glud parish, Bjerge herred, has the name of Jensgård.[180] Our writer attributes this attack by Germans to the general evils that afflicted the country during the disputes between King Eric Plowpenny and his brother Abel, duke of Southern Jutland. For the first time we see Øm as the victim and not beneficiary of political circumstances.

The response of the monks was far from mere passive complaining. Abbot Jens pursued the "barbarians" to get back his horses, was captured and seriously wounded by them in the left shoulder. During the excavations at Øm between the wars by C.M. Smidt, he found the grave of an abbot who had the marks of just such a wound and thus confirmed the story.[181] This is only one instance

---

178) *Kirkekampen*, pp. 183-4.
179) SM II, 196, 2oo.
180) See Jørgen Olrik's translation of the Øm Book, p. 72, n. 126. *Øm Klosters Krønike* (Historisk Samfund for Århus Stift, 1954).
181) C.M. Smidt, *Øm Kloster: Vejledning ved besøg i ruinerne* (Historisk Samfund for Århus Stift, 1968), pp. 3o-32. Smidt's guide, despite its brevity, is still the best introduction to Øm's archaeological history. The excavations begun in the summer of 1975 as a joint project by Historisk Samfund for Århus Stift and the Institute for Medieval Archaeology at Århus University under Professor dr. phil. Olaf Olsen and cand. mag. Rikke Agnete Olsen are already bringing to light much new information about the location and type of conventual buildings there. See "Øm Kloster-Projektet" Nr. 3 (9 August 1975) for details. In the meantime H.N. Garner's

in which archaeology has been able to back up the statements of the Øm Book. Other examples are the story of the canals, traces of which have been found, and especially information about the places where abbots and bishops were buried.[182] We can conclude from these verifications that the various writers of the Øm Book were often concerned with giving precise detail. When we come up with a vital piece of information that cannot be confirmed by such physical evidence, we should at least keep this accuracy in mind. There is of course a great difference between factual information and emotional criticism, but the care of our writers to be exact should encourage us to assume that the monks usually tell the truth, unless good reasons can be found to the contrary.

Jens's short period as abbot can probably be attributed to his wound, which was of a type that would have been very painful.[183] The monastery suffered in these years from Abel's plunderings, as well as from Erik's armies, and the Øm farm at Horsens was completely burned down.[184] Once again we have a distant possession of the monastery made insecure because of the altered political situation. In these years the royal residence at Skanderborg came to play an unhappy role in Øm's fate. Erik Plowpenny's queen, Jutta, resided there and seems to have used it as a base for operations. From there she seized the monks' grange at Tåning and took home what she wanted.[185] She even threatened to harm brother Olav Quiter, who was supervisor of the grange, together with Abbot Jens and the brothers, if they did not give up all their possessions to her will. For the first time the disadvantage of the Djursland property becomes

---

brief guide provides a supplement to Smidt. The work of Garner and of Historisk Samfund for Århus Stift in bringing all aspects of Øm's history before the general public has been invaluable. Their reprints of the Øm Chronicle translated to Danish and Smidt's guide are still available. Also *Århus Stifts Årbøger* since the 1930's has provided a continuing stream of articles about Øm: J. Lind, "Klosterhaven i Øm" 24: 1931, 130-142; Ejler Haugsted, "Benediktinernes Kirke i Venge", 30: 1937, 165-95; Kr. Isager, "Skeletfundene i Øm kloster", 35: 1942, 46-66; Holger G. Nielsen, "Om tamt og vildt ved Øm", 55: 1962, 24-34; Jacob Isager, "Syvogtyve abbeder i Øm", 57: 1964, 133-40; Holger G. Nielsen, "Øm kloster: Cara Insula gennem fire århundreder", 62: 1969, 7-65, a chronology of Øm's history, with a complete literature list and abbot list.

182) Canals - SM II, 197 and Smidt, 12-13. Burial place of Bishop Peder Elavsen, 1246, in the new church in front of the altar of Mary - SM II, 198 - Smidt, 29; Abbot Michael, buried in the new chapter room, where only foundation laid - SM II, 196 - Smidt, 28-29.
183) Smidt, 31-33.
184) SM II, 196.
185) SM II, 197. It is important that the farm at Tåning is still called a grange, even though by this time the grange system seems to have been in decline in Danish Cistercian houses because of a shortage of lay brothers. See Poul Nørlund, "Klostret og dets Gods", *op. cit.* p. 88. For the decline of the grange system on a European level, see Georges Duby, *Rural Economy and Country Life in the Medieval West* (Edward Arnold: London, 1968) pp. 264-5.

concretely clear. Jutta placed ambushes on the route the brothers took in transporting grain from their farms in Djursland back to Øm and stole the grain from them whenever she got the chance.

The monks must have felt acutely their immediate danger when they heard that Vissing, the Benedictine nunnery only a few kilometres away at the west end of Mossø, had been attacked and was totally destroyed by fire, except for the church itself. This time it was Duke Abel's men who were responsible, but in the conflict between Erik and Abel, no monastic foundation in central Jutland seems to have been safe, and the opposing armies plundered them whenever they needed supplies. The monks were so terrified that they blocked their western canal, Åsgård, with pieces of lumber and scrapped their ships, for they feared that Jutta would try to transport the plunder from Øm to Skanderborg by water. The writer does not add that this would have been impossible without a portage, but he seems too caught up in his narration of the monks' perils for such details. Next the monks took their clothes, except those for daily wear, and all their food supplies and hid them in the tower of the new church. Towers were forbidden by the Cistercian rule, but the word *turris* does not necessarily mean anything more than a raised platform for the purpose of fortification,[186] and thus does not have to indicate that the abbey church had an illicit tower. We incidentally learn through this account that the new abbey church was already under construction in 1247.

In these lines, just as much as in the description of the dispute with Bishop Tyge of Århus, we can sense the brothers' pain and consternation and their basic inability to cope with a cruel new world avalanching upon them. Abbot Jens could vainly try to respond to force with force, but the main reaction seems to have been defensive: withdrawal behing the lines formed by the canals, attempt to build a fortress, and a tedious and terrifying wait for the enemy to arrive. By destroying their boats, the monks were hurting their own economic position, but they were willing to do so to make themselves less tempting to Queen Jutta. For one of the first times in Danish history, we can see from the people involved what it must have been like to be caught in the crossfire of civil war.

To add insult to injury, the monks were forced to give up a property during this period because of the demands of the new bishop of Århus, Peder Ugotsen.[187] His predecessor, Peder Elavsen, had died in 1246 and had distinguished himself by being the last Århus bishop to be buried at the abbey. There followed three years, precisely this chaotic period, when there was no bishop at Århus. Elav-

---

186) Du Cange, *Glossarium Mediae et Infimae Latinitatis* 6, 7o5.
187) SM II, 197-8.

sen had given the monks a third of Søldring, which in the medieval period was an island north of the entrance to Randers fjord. The monks also bought a third of it from the bishop and the final third was exchanged with a Jens Judesen for Horndrup in Tåning parish. Once again the monks got a very distant holding and thus broke the general Cistercian practice of exchanging a more distant piece of land for a closer one. But they may have wanted this land because of a need for greater supplies of fish. In any case, our writer tells us in full detail about the transaction and says that "our brothers live there without quarrel and collect all its incomes."[188]

But after Peder Ugotsen became bishop, he tried immediately to get Søldring back, or at least to get rid of the monks there, with the result that they finally gave up the property to Jens Judesen in return for Horndrup. The monks received about a third in value of what they had forfeited. But still the bishop was not satisfied and finally the monks tried to buy his good will by giving him eighty marks. But, says the narrator, we received no decent treatment from him but only sorrows. Abbot Jens was so worn out with these trials and tribulations that he grieved daily and finally died in 1249.

This last section about Søldring is the least satisfactory part of the description of events after 1246. We can understand how the monks felt themselves helpless bystanders and victims in the civil war, but they make no attempt to explain the motives and reasons for Peder Ugotsen's opposing them on Søldring and finally forcing them to give up the property. Here we stumble on one of the great weaknesses of the Øm Book, its one-sidedness. The monks are totally unable to see problems and quarrels from the other party's point of view. They would have us believe that the bishop acted harshly merely out of a desire to harm them, but it is more likely that there was some reasonable motive behind his actions. It could be, for example, that he simply felt his predecessor had been all too generous to the monks and that now it was time to make them pay for their privileges. For seventy-five years the monks had been able to rely either on the benevolence of the Århus bishop or at least on his neutrality and non-interference with their affairs. It must have been a shock for the monks to realize that now there was a bishop who was directly hostile to them, and instead of taking the consequences and trying to compromise with the bishop, the monks appealed to the good old days when they were privileged and preferred. And this failure to adjust to a new situation was their fatal mistake.

---

188) SM II, 198, "...ita quod quinquennio et amplius ante mortem episcopi in ea resideret fratres nostri sine querimonia, omnes usufructus percipientes."

Oluf was Jens's successor and held his post until 1255.[189] The abbey was still under attack from all sides. The southern possessions seem to have been especially exposed, for it was near Horsens that Oluf's "brother in the flesh" Sven and his sister Margrethe were killed. The abbot's bastard son, Sven Pave, drowned at Øm. All these events were only "the beginning of his sorrow". The abbot list has expanded here into something of a national chronicle, for it mentions the death of Erik Plowpenny and blames Abel. The narrator stops, however, in the midst of his moral judgments and says that the interested reader can find fuller detail in the Øm *cronica nostra et acta temporum*, which even though it is lost probably resembled the Ryd or Essenbæk Annals, short, pithy, yearly notations of events.

But our writer cannot help expressing his wrath against Abel, who is "not Abel, but Babel", as opposed to the saintly Eric. Abel is accused of disrespecting the privileges of all church institutions and inflicting many evils, also on Øm. Just for the confirmation of the exemptions from certain payments by the monastery's labourers, which the writer claims were given freely by earlier kings, Abel extracted three hundred marks. This concrete example may well be the full extent of Abel's "harm" against Øm, for it is likely that any physical attacks on the monks would also have been recorded here if they had taken place. We can sense in these lines the monks' sour and disillusioned attitude. Now, after so many free years, they must stoop to buying their privileges.

Just at the time the royal attitude became incorrigibly arrogant, the bishop of Århus also began to treat the monks harshly. Apparently under Bishop Peder Elavsen, as we hear from two 1266 witnesses, there was a tradition that the Århus bishop came to the monastery every Lent for a certain period. The monks looked after his needs and gave him the status of a regular guest in their house.[190] Peder Ugotsen held strictly to this tradition and demanded that for the three years when the episcopacy had been vacant, the monks pay compensation of 19o marks.[191] The writer claims that "he extorted it violently from us", but since the word *violenter* is used so frequently in the next pages in situations where there obviously was no use of physical violence, we can interpret it here as meaning "against our wills".

When the bishop did come to visit, our writer says it was a "trap", for he looked at the books which Peder Elavsen had given the monks and ordered them

---

189) SM II, 198-2oo.
190) SM II, 239-4o. The witnesses were Bishops Esger of Ribe and Niels of Slesvig.
191) SM II, 2oo: "propter apparatus trium annorum, qui restiterant, dum vacaret sedes episcopi, a nobis *extorsit violenter* centum nonaginta marcas denariorum."

to be brought to him in the "house of the bishop" at Øm. He is said to have promised that they would be returned to the monks' library, but instead, "having forgotten the lord God his creator and also his oath", took these books "violently" from the monastery. It has been claimed that the bishop did so because the monks had books that should not have been in their library.[192] But I can find no support for such a theory other than the golden lettering in the books given by Sven, and even if they were a dubious possession for Cistercian monks, they were not in conflict with the Rule, as the author of the Exordium 1 asserted. But the books in question here are those given by Peder Elavsen, and the text indicates that Peder Ugotsen did not select some of them but simply carted them off *en masse*.[193]

In all this description our writer keeps telling us how much things cost, such as the privilege from Abel, and how the books were worth more than two hundred marks. This concentration on figures and money losses is something new in the Øm Book. The monks are grabbing onto concrete facts and figures in order to convince themselves - and others - of their righteousness. The remarks about Peder Ugotsen are excessively harsh, and it is clear that our writer is not able to begin to understand why the bishop acted as he did.

Besides troubles with the bishop, the monks experienced in these years something that brought "infamy to this house and scandal to the whole order."[194] Our writer prefers to pass it over in silence "because it is known to the whole world." This undefined incident has been used as more evidence for moral decline at Øm, a decline which Bishop Tyge in the 1260's is supposed to have had a duty to rectify.[195] It has been assumed that the monks must have kept the

---

192) *Kirkekampen*, 184: "Peder gennemgik klostrets bogsamling og fandt ting, som burde udtages, måske nogle af de pragtbøger, det ikke selv måtte tilvirke."

193) SM II, 2oo: Manens itaque nobiscum, prout sibi placuit, libros nostros omnes in armario conspicatus est; inter quos *vidit etiam libros quos bone memorie predecessor suus, Petrus Elavi filius*, partim ob remedium anime sue *nobis contulerat et quosdam ab ipso in vita sua comparavimus precio competenti*. Videns itaque illius boni viri virtutes et munera et nobis ipsique mortuo invidens, *iussit libros* illos deferri ad domum episcopi. The *libros illos* could only refer to the entire collection of books given by or bought from Peder Ugotsen's predecessor. What seems to have peeved the bishop is thus not anything objectionable in any of the books, but the fact that the monks had books which once belonged to the bishop of Århus. According to Anne Riising, it *could* be a question of books that belonged to the office of the bishop and not to him personally.

194) SM II, 2oo.

195) *Kirkekampen*, pp. 183-4: "når de øverste instanser blev holdt i uvidenhed om svære brud på klosterreglen, var det måske alligevel nærliggende for ham at gribe ind" (referring to the bishop). For support for this assertion, C.R. Cheney, *Episcopal Visitation of Monasteries in the Thirteenth Century* (Manchester University, 1931), pp. 5o-51, is quoted. Cheney however is speaking only of instances in which bishops consulted with the visitors for an exempt order. Concerning the morals of an

THE BEGINNINGS OF THE CONFLICT 69

whole matter from being reported to the General Chapter, for we hear nothing of it from that source during this time. I can only counter that the General Chapter rarely pointed to moral mispractices among the Danish abbeys. It happened perhaps five times in the whole century,[196] and it is entirely likely that there were many other incidents that never were mentioned in the disciplinary decisions of the General Chapter. Especially when a matter was as grave as this one seems to have been, the natural reaction on the part of the Order would have been to settle it out of the public view, and not among the published decrees of the Chapter. Second, the very fact that our writer mentions that something terribly serious had happened shows that he is not participating in an attempt to keep the affair hushed up. It is entirely possible that the affair was mentioned at length in the more complete list of abbots which probably existed at Øm in these years but which has not survived. In the last part of the abbot list there is a mysterious mention of such a fuller account, which the writer makes clear was not meant for anyone except the community itself, at least while those mentioned in it were still alive. This notation was added in 1274, thus after the batttle with Bishop Tyge was over and at a time when the Øm monks must have been very sensitive about their privacy.[197] So without further evidence, I do not think we can accuse our monks of conspiring to hide some grave fault.

Whatever happened, this scandal together with the other defeats was enough to drive Oluf into retirement. His follower Asgot became abbot on 8 June 1255.[198] We have two reports of him, the first and more complete probably composed soon after 1257, the second written later on in the century.[199] In

---

abbey Cheney never indicates that bishops could feel it was natural for them to intervene directly.
196) Instances for moral discipline at General Chapter (Canivez):
   1: Abbots of Øm and Tvis disciplined for not coming to General Chapter - 1215, nr. 11.
   2: Monks of Herrisvad, Tvis, and Øm reprimanded for drinking and making a public scandal - 124o, nr. 69.
   3: Abbots of Sorø and Ås deposed for their unjust deposition of Herrisvad abbot - 1254, nr. 6.
   4: Revolt of Tvis monks against their abbot - 1268, nr. 37.
   5: Abbot of Holme ejected abbot of Herrisvad, who should have visited and did not come to General Chapter - 1269, nr. 7o.
197) SM II, 2o4-2o5 - Ab exordio huius monasterii et usque in presens sunt abbates huius domus numero viginti duo; quorum mores et actus, labores et persecuciones, de omnibus communiter et de singulis singillatim, satis expresse et ex integro habentur, licet ad audientiam communem (minime) pervenerint, necdum tempore quorundam viventium admitti possunt. Jacob Isager, "Syvogtyve abbeder i Øm", *Århus Stifts Årbøger* 57: 1964, 133-4o, has shown that this passage was written in 1274. Another hand in 1281 changed the 22 to 25.
198) SM II, 2oo.
199) The first account ends with the dedication of the new choir in 1257, p. 2o1, while the second forms part of the abbot list written in 1274.

the second, he is described as a man who was generous in his time as abbot and full of joy, "neglecting many things because of his kindness." This description is fundamentally different from the one of Abbot Michael in the 1240's, who was supposed to have been gentle with delinquent brothers so that he could reform them. Asgot is said to have been gentle *to neglect*, and here the assertion of a moral decline at Øm during this period begins to take on substance. First there was the huge scandal under Oluf, and now came an abbot who did not care to know what was going on. It is as if in these troubled years of the 1250's, the monks could not find any man as abbot who could provide the house with consistent, strong leadership. The result, to borrow from the monks' own language, brought interior abuses and exterior chaos.

The longer, earlier passage about Asgot concentrates on his achievement in completing the abbey church, which had been under construction for more than a decade. For a brief, final moment, we are back in the age of expansion and self-confidence, and our writer praises Asgot for his work. First the brothers' dormitory was moved, and there the refectory was placed instead. Smidt in his excavations found that the abbey quadrangle had no south wing, where the refectory normally would have been, and so confirmed this statement about the conversion of the old dormitory into a refectory.[200] It was probably meant as a temporary situation, but in the decades after the 1260's neither the choir of the church nor the abbey buildings were substantially added to,[201] so the brothers apparently kept their temporary refectory for many years. The new dormitory was now on the first floor of the east wing, which was the finest and most complete part of the cloister, also containing the chapter room.[202]

The consecration of the new church in 1257 marks the last proud event in Øm's history before the catastrophes of the 1260's. Dignitaries came from all over, but the bishop of Århus made himself conspicuous by his absence. Our writer does not mention this fact but merely says that the "archdeacon of Århus and many other noble persons, whose names I now do not remember" were present.[203] There was a solemn procession from the old church to the new. Since Smidt has determined that the old choir was on the same site as the new one, the "vetus ecclesia" mentioned here must have been a temporary building.[204]

Almost a half century after Esrum and Sorø had gotten their full and large churches, Øm could lay claim to a half-completed one, with most of the nave

---

200) Smidt, p. 19.
201) The new excavations may, however, unearth later buildings. So far, however, they have confirmed the impression that the building program stopped during and after the disputes. See "Øm kloster Projektet", nr. 3, pp.3-4.
202) Smidt, pp.20-21.
203) SM II, 201.
204) Smidt, p. 17.

missing. As at Løgum and Vitskøl, the nave was never finished, for the extra space was meant for lay brothers, who after 1250 became fewer in number. The church at Øm, with its awkward and graceless shape on Smidt's plan,[205] shows bettter than any written source the difference between the twelfth and thirteenth centuries for the Danish Cistercians. Dreams and plans could be realized completely in the first century, as at Esrum and Sorø, but only halfway in the second, as at Øm and Vitskøl. Løgum remains the great exception, in which the fourteenth century saw the completion of a modified version of the nave.

So far as we know, no serous attempt was ever made to modify or renovate the awkward rectangle at Øm. If we had more sources concerning the abbey in the fourteenth century, we might be able to qualify this interpretation. But from one age to the next, there was definitely a drying up of the sources of piety and religious inspiration. Even if the abbey continued as an institution, it no longer could capture the imagination of rich and powerful men and women. And that is precisely what a monastery, or any institution founded on ideals, had to be able to do in order to grow physically and spiritually. Once an institution was simply there, a part of the landscape, it already had begun to lose its vitality, even if its physical plant and financial situation were intact.

One more event came with the consecration of the new choir in 1257. Olav Quiter, the lay brother and supervisor of the Tåning grange whom we already have met, gave some Djursland properties to the monks. It is quite a revelation to find a lay brother rich enough to make such a donation, and we are warned here against thinking of these men as coming exclusively from a poor background. Olav wanted the income from these properties to be used solely for pittances, or special meals for the brothers. Here we may be seeing something of the slackening of discipline and growing concentration on income as opposed to piety that seems indicative of these years.[206]

At this point our full account of the abbots ends, and the short notices that follow are not very helpful. But the next abbot, Jens III of Dover, who must have held office from 1260-62, is mentioned in greater detail in the introduction to the account of the controversies with the bishops of Århus.[207] It

---

205) Smidt, p. 261.
206) The first Danish Cistercian instances of pittances came at Sorø, which is not surprising, considering the big landowners who endowed the monks there. DD I, 4, 130 (1207-1215) and DD I, 4, 154 (1208-1246). The Øm pittances are unique in that they were given by a lay brother and not a layman or a bishop. This fact may indicate that wealthy men sometimes chose to become lay brothers instead of monks, perhaps because they could not read and preferred supervision of field work to reciting monastic office.
207) SM II, 212, 208.

is possible that from 1257 to 1261 the monks enjoyed a respite from attacks. Bishop Peder Ugotsen died in 1259, and for three years the monks did not have to worry about Lenten visits or unwelcome borrowing from their library. And they could be content with their new buildings.

In these years Øm for the first time since the end of the twelfth century seriously began to acquire new properties. If we look at the tables meticulously put together by Poul Rasmussen, we can see that the number of properties alienated from Øm in the 1230's and 1240's more or less balances off those gained, while in the 1250's none were alienated, and so Olav Quiter's donations made for a net gain of two holdings.[208] Then in the 1260's the monks gained ten properties, a real advance. Skyum-Nielsen has used this fact to undermine the credibility of the monks when they told Bishop Tyge that they could not afford paying procurations because of poverty.[209] But the monks may have had a case here. As far as we can tell from the short notices in the Skanderborg Register, almost all the properties were gained by exchange or purchase, and the great majority of them came during the first part of the decade.[210] Thus by the time the dispute with Tyge had become very serious in 1264, the monks were just ending a period when they had been using up their financial resources in order to get new properties. Also some of these holdings were in Skæring, north of Århus, about halfway between Øm and Djursland. The monks were apparently trying to acquire a bloc of properties here to provide them with a safe stopping place on their trips to and from Djursland.[211] Obviously the monks wanted to avoid staying in or around Århus and subjecting themselves to the whims of the bishop.

This period of growth at the start of the 1260's is not a sign of a new prosperity and does not invalidate the abbot's plea of lack of funds. The number of new territories is very modest in comparison with the gains of the twelfth century. Moreover the monks probably had to pay for almost all of them. Together with the 1250's building expenses, the expansion probably strained the abbey's financial resources. The new holdings would eventually pay their way, but for the first few years they would be more a burden then a source of income.

Another worry was the political situation, which continued to make life dangerous for Øm. The monks' breathing space after 1257 was apparently abruptly

---

208) Poul Rasmussen, p. 146.
209) Kirkekampen, pp. 162-3. SM II, 214.
210) Skanderborg Register (Æ A) L31 (1260, Firgårde, Dover parish). T6 (1261, Skæring). T25 (1262, Skæring). A19 (1264, Purup, Østbirk p.). L13 (1264, Hårby, Veng p.). A9 (1268, Horndrup, Havreballe, near Tåning).
211) The monks had first gotten the Skæring property in 1242 and 1245 - Skanderborg Register, T31 and T11.

ended in the summer of 1261 by King Kristoffer's widow, the regent Margrethe.[212] In her zealous efforts to defeat Erik Abelsen and the Counts of Holstein, she quartered 1600 horsemen at Øm for two nights, together with runners and foot-soldiers.[213] The numbers sound extravagant, but our writer is convinced that this event was a turning point for Øm: "thus from that day the amount of our material possessions began to decrease."[214]

The writer of these lines is the same monk who is out to get the bishop of Århus, and so we have to take them with care and even a bit of skepticism. Nevertheless, it makes sense that a monastic house burdened with building and land costs could hardly have given such an extraordinary payment of hospitality without considerable financial suffering. The breathing space after the attacks and fears of the late 1240's and 1250's was thus short and inadequate. We are told cryptically that Abbot Jens of Dover preferred "to serve God rather than live with the clamour of the world", so he sought frequently to give up his post and finally got his wish.[215] Other abbots had done the same before, such as Magnus who asked God for relief from the burdens of office and got it immediately in 1235.[216] But Magnus and the incompetent Niels (1197-99) gave up office because they as persons could not take the administrative involvement with secular affairs, while this factor does not seem to have been important for Jens of Dover. With him and his even more unsuccessful successor, Bo, we begin to meet abbots who seem fitted enough for their duties of office but still break down from the pressure of developments.

In 1262 when Bo became abbot, the monks were on guard, wary, careful. If they had had narrow possibilities of better times after 1257, these had been smashed in 1261. In such a situation we can perhaps better understand their reaction and even falsity towards Bishop Tyge of Århus. They did not want to be wronged again, and this time they felt that they had to stand up for their rights. Like the dear Bourbons after the upheavals of the French Revolution and Napoleon, they had learned nothing and forgotten nothing. Thus their situation must be seen in much wider terms than those of moral decline. The monks could no longer believe fully in their own sanctity or in the goodness of the world around them. They could no longer expect to be treated well just because they were Cistercians. As always, they yearned for such preferential treatment, but within them there seems to have been growing a deep bitterness against this awful new world.

---

212) Jørgen Olrik, p. 73, n. 168.
213) SM II, 2o8.
214) SM II, 2o8: "...unde ab illo die cepit substancia rerum nostrarum temporalium decrescere et minutari."
215) SM II, 2o8.
216) SM II, 195.

This resentment may have been accompanied by a sense of growing isolation from the other Cistercian houses of the country. They had their own troubles in these years, even if they may not have been as serious as Øm's difficulties. In 1254 the abbot of Sorø was deposed by the Cistercian General Chapter for his attempt to remove the abbot of Herrisvad.[217] A few years earlier almost the whole monastery complex had burned in a great fire.[218] Esrum was caught up through the 1250's in an expensive, frustrating, and ultimately fruitless attempt to reassert its hegemony over Pomeranian abbeys.[219] The mother abbey's rival was the house at Doberan, which asserted that it was the true mother and thus rightful visitor of Dargun. By 1258 the judgment went in Doberan Abbey's favour, and the decision was made not by neighbouring German abbots but by the abbots of Clairvaux and Morimund. The words contained in the statutes of the General Chapter must have been a bitter pill for Esrum. The abbot there was imposed "perpetual silence" in the matter. To make sure that he would never again have legal grounds for any such future complaints, he was ordered to hand over to the Doberan abbot all the documents and papers he had concerning Esrum's relationship with Dargun.

With Esrum and Sorø paralyzed with their own problems, one might think that Øm could turn to its own mother abbey, Vitskøl, but the latter house had good reason for not wanting to get too intimately involved in her daughter's problems. We have for Vitskøl from May, 1263, a privilege from Bishop Niels of Viborg, who was also royal chancellor and on the King's side in the dispute with Archbishop Jakob Erlandsen.[220] Niels makes known that Vitskøl's property should continue to be exempt from the payment of the tithe, *even if* the abbey is forced to use lay labourers instead of lay brothers to cultivate these lands. With the decline of the grange system after about 1250 in Denmark, the Cistercians were forced to turn to local peasants to look after their possessions. Eventually this brought the splitting up of the granges into individual holdings on which the peasants paid rent or service yearly to the abbey. This meant that the monks were no longer working the land "at their own expense", as the papal bulls always had demanded. The monks were thus in immediate danger of giving the local bishops a chance to demand the payment of tithe on lands belonging to the monks that for decades had been exempt. This would have meant a huge financial burden for the Cistercian monasteries, and even ruin. It was paramount to have the exemption from payment adjusted to the new economic situation

---

217) Canivez, 1254, nr. 6.
218) SRD IV, 535.
219) Canivez, 1252, nr. 34; 1254, nr. 21; 1255, nr. 20; DD II, 1, 266 (1258-9); DD II, 1, 260 (1258).
220) DD II, 1, 382.

and so Vitskøl simply could not afford to alienate the affections of its local bishop.

More than anything else, the Øm monks must have felt at the beginning of the 1260's that if they were going to survive, they would have to do so on their own. And they were right. Even if after the controversy with Bishop Tyge became serious, the monks received much moral support from sister houses, this help never did much real good.[22oa]

22oa) The Øm monks may have been partially responsible for a decision at the Cistercian General Chapter in 1261 dealing with procedures to be taken against bishops who harassed Cistercian houses (Canivez, 1261, nr. 5). In general the 1260's are a time of pressure and conflict for the Order, as reflected in these decisions.

8.

THE FIRST PART OF THE CONTROVERSY
- TO SUMMER, 1263

A. The Background of the Monks' Account

Although Bo, who was only abbot from 1262 to 1263, had one of the shortest periods as abbot at Øm, we know more about his two years than any others in all of Øm's history. The account of this period, with its use of direct quotation, intimate and careful details, and sometimes almost vibrant excitement, has frequently been ascribed by historians to Bo's own authorship. This point of view gains strength from the fact that the narration after 1263 is much more condensed and schematic.[221] C.A. Christensen also thought that he could determine from the use of the word *nos* that it was Bo who was speaking for himself here, but Sven Green-Pedersen has countered that this *nos* is used elsewhere when the writer is speaking of the convent as a whole.[222] My own explanation for the good reporting during Bo's years versus the more condensed account up to 1268 lies in the probability that the earlier section reflects a feeling on the part of the monks that they had a chance of winning against Tyge. They added as much detail as possible in order to justify their case. But after 1263 they were forced to admit to themselves that Tyge was ruining them. By 1268 they had run out of steam and gave up finishing their account without indicating how the controversy ended. But they really did not have to do so, for it was clear to them - as it must be to us - that Tyge had won the day. We can thus consider the first section as written in 1263 or soon after, when there was still hope, while the second was composed in 1267 or soon after, when there was no hope.

Even if Bo is not necessarily the author of the entire account, he certainly contributed much to it, as did his follower, Ture, who is mentioned in the later abbot list as being responsible for an account of his "work and sorrows" contained in another segment of the book (*alio quaterno*). The passage does not

---

221) C.A. Christensen xiv; *Kirkekampen*, p. 183.
222) Green-Pedersen, p. 189.

say he wrote it but that it was composed "on his initiative".[223] We can only conclude that Ture at least inspired and encouraged the writing down of the narration and that Bo, who is mentioned as being "not only a good scribe, but also illustrator, and a person skilled in many things," probably composed and possibly also did the physical act of writing down at least the first part of the account of the dispute.

Green-Pedersen speaks of "teamwork" between Bo and Ture,[224] and this is probably as close to the truth as we can come. But he misunderstood the purpose for recording the dispute, as well as for writing the earlier parts of the Øm Book. Using the later abbot list, he took the strange passage which we have already mentioned in which the writer says the lives of the abbots are to be kept secret for the time being.[225] Green-Pedersen thought that these lines applied to the Øm Book itself and so concluded that the monks meant the Øm Book for their own eyes only, plus perhaps a selected few people.[226] But, as we have seen, this passage refers to a much fuller account of the abbots that we do not have.

One final observation about the Exordium 2 before we begin a closer analysis. Gertz noticed how the Exordium 1 is written in a beautiful hand and is obviously a final draft based on a rough text that was corrected and improved. The Exordium 2, however, was never rewritten and is full of mistakes in both spelling and grammar.[227] The sloppy and hasty composition of this part of the Øm Book tells us in itself something invaluable about the quality of life at Øm in the 126o's. There was no time to revise and perfect the narrative, only to get it down quickly on parchment, and once there was time, there was no inspiration left to revise and improve. In the Exordium 1 there are many biblical quotations, skilfully woven into the fabric of the text, while there are only a few in the Exordium 2. Our later writer did not have the chance to meditate on events and to visualize them in terms of biblical images. We are looking in the Exordium 2 at a pressed, haggard community, worn out with cares, and giving up many of the refinements of learned life. These are people under pressure.

B. The First Tremors

A number of years ago, John Kennedy, then senator from Massachusetts, wrote

---

223) SM II, 2o3: "De ingressu ipsius et electione et labore atque dolore multa reperientur in alio quaterno expressius *ex eius industria* exarata."
224) Green-Pedersen, p. 191.
225) SM II, 2o4-2o5. See my footnote nr. 197.
226) Green-Pedersen, 182.
227) SM II, 155-6.

a book called *Profiles in Courage*. Here he coined a phrase which was on the lips of many Americans during the heady but sparse years of that phrase-laden time, the New Frontier: "grace under pressure". In reviewing the account of the monks' and Bishop Tyge's behaviour in the Exordium 2, this phrase has often come to my mind. For if there is anything the two parties did not show, it was grace.

The monks' account actually starts before the time of Bishop Tyge with a kind of historical introduction by describing the demands of Bishop Peder Ugotsen in the time of Asgot's abbacy.[228] The bishop demanded procurations three weeks a year from the monks. He wanted to be able to stay at the monastery together with his attendants for this amount of time at the beginning of Lent. When the brothers countered that they could not afford such a payment, which may have been true, for we are back in the troubled 1250's, the bishop countered that the brothers were privileged enough in that they were exempted from other payments to the diocesan authority. In the end it was decided that these traditional exemptions no longer would apply, but instead the bishop would cease expecting the Lenten procurations. The writer claims that this was a defeat for the monks and complains about injustice, but most historians think the monks got off rather well.[229]

After the death of Peder Ugotsen in 1259, the monks were three years exempt from such payments, so long as the bishopric of Århus was vacant. But when Tyge became bishop, he insisted on the right of procurations. The monks countered that the agreement with his predecessor also applied to him, but here they were on soft ground. Tyge demanded the restoration of the Lenten procurations, and so began the dispute.[230] Our author claims that Tyge had bought his episcopacy at the curia for 600 marks, but the angry tone of the account makes it necessary to be wary in the face of such accusations.[231]

Before the two parties had come into conflict, a number of incidents had apparently already convinced the monks that they had to be unyielding towards Tyge. An attack on a lay brother at the Rosmos farm in Djursland looked as if it was supported or at least approved by Tyge.[232] Other attacks on Øm people

---

228) SM II, 206-7.
229) See, for example, *Kirkekampen*, p. 186.
230) SM II, 209-211.
231) Skyum-Nielsen has already compiled a convincing list of exaggerations and mistakes in this part of the Øm Book (*Kirkekampen*, p. 310, nr. 4) and even though I will deal with some of these separately later on, it should be pointed out from the very start that when it comes to Tyge, our author is always inclined to interpret his actions in the worst possible way and thus to see fault where there may be none - as when Tyge was constituted bishop of Roskilde in the absence of Bishop Peder - SM II, 239.
232) SM II, 209.

followed. A visit by Abbot Bo to Tyge only brought vague declarations that the monks would give the bishop what belonged to him. When Tyge arrived at Øm in the beginning of February, 1263, the monks received him with what they claimed was every sign of respect: a procession and an invitation to come into a warm room. When Tyge entered the room, which was probably located in the building known as the "bishop's house", he was upset that there was only a grease lamp burning and later complained to the king. Our author has a ready explanation for such behaviour: Tyge was on the lookout for a chance to oppose the monks.

This event, like so many recorded in the account, is odd and troublesome. If we believe the monastic writer, then Tyge was simply an enemy from the start and did everything he could to harm the monks. But if we reject our author as too partisan and as a spokesman for a group of people carried off by their own paranoia, then we have to dismiss such accusations as ungrounded. The result of such an approach, however, would be to invalidate the historical worth of the entire account. I think a middle way between total credulity and total rejection is possible if we assume that our author is generally accurate about the actions of Bishop Tyge *that he himself witnessed at Øm*. But the interpretations given to these actions must be looked at carefully.

In this instance we can conclude that Tyge probably did get upset, but there may have been other reasons than the single lamp. The atmosphere was heavy with tension, and Tyge's later behaviour shows that he expected the monks to cheat and fool him whenever they could.[233] Here as elsewhere Tyge acts to defend himself by being aggressive. Whether he is the provoker or the one provoked is not clear, but it is obvious that the monks too are being aggressively defensive. The two similar behaviour patterns reinforce and accentuate each other and lead to a succession of explosive climaxes. The more tense the confrontations become, the more the monks get caught up in Tyge's reactions and the less they notice how they themselves act. They can see only Tyge's irrationality and think of themselves as being rational.

From Tyge's own letters - which we must give the monks credit for including in their narration - we can see that the bishop was not just a creature of whim and rage but could defend his case logically and eloquently. Also we know from Tyge's efforts in the dispute between the king and the archbishop that there was considerably more to him than a bundle of emotions.[234] And

---

233) As Tyge's famous remarks that Øm had writers who easily could falsify documents - SM II, 221.
234) In this context we can almost say that Skyum-Nielsen in *Kirkekampen* did a necessary job of rehabilitating Tyge and showing him as a person and not a monster - p. 186. At times I have thought of Skyum-Nielsen's results on the Øm Book as a kind of anti-memoir for Øm in Tyge's favour. But now that we have both thirteenth century memoir and twentieth century anti-memoir, it is necessary to take the best from them both!

yet we cannot accuse the monks of hiding from us Tyge's true personality, because they in their own distorted and incomplete picture of reality were able only to see one side of the man. Similarly Tyge probably was only capable of seeing one aspect of the monks' claims and charges: the attempt of a privileged and pampered group of people to free themselves of all responsibilities and burdens.

This perspective can hopefully help us in considering one of the decisive turning points in the dispute. The day after his arrival, Tyge went to the chapter house of the monks and, according to our writer, tried to perform a visitation.[235] He asked the monks if they were obeying the rules of their order and if anyone had anything against anyone else. In the Cistercian Order, such a procedure was allowed only for the abbot visitors, and Tyge could not have helped knowing this. Bo told him he was out of place, and Tyge left the chapter room. Although Tyge did not press his attempt, the very fact that he tried tells us a great deal about him as a man who would not stop in an attempt to exercise authority until he was made to do so. This episode calls to mind Cheney's comment on epsicopal visitations, concerning the thirteenth century archbishop of Rouen who tried to define his rights and prerogatives by seeing how far he could go with the monks before they drew the line.[236] In this incident we can give Tyge the benefit of the doubt and assume his intentions were good. But the monks probably did not think so and looked upon the incident as an indication that Tyge would try to get whatever he could out of them.

This defensive attitude explains what happened at the meeting that followed between Bo and the brothers. He told them he was sure that Tyge was going to ask for procurations.[237] The brothers should decide now whether or not they were going to give these services. But, said Bo, whether or not we give them, I am sure we are going to have trouble from Tyge. Without this consultation, in which the monks backed up Bo in his decision to refuse procurations, the abbot would not have met Tyge with so much self-confidence and stubborn determination. There is something fatalistic and despairing about the answer of Bo to his monks: we are lost whatever we do, so we might as well take the hard line:

> "Pro certo scio: sive dederimus, sive negaverimus maximum habebimus gravamen." unusquisque respondit se malle mori quam ei tam indebitas procurationes exibere.

---

235) SM II, 21o.
236) C.R. Cheney, *op. cit.*, pp. 43-44.
237) SM II, 211.

In the confrontation that came next, the abbot presented Tyge with two papal letters, one saying that certain prelates tried to escape justice by changing a voluntary favour into a duty and so claimed services to be owed because of ancient customs, thus burdening the monastery with their demands. The second letter asserted that no secular prelate could demand a Cistercian house to give procurations as a result of visitation, for such visitation was a purely Cistercian affair.[238] In a masterful exposition of this problem, Skyum-Nielsen has distinguished between the chance hospitality meant by the first letter, the visitation hospitality spoken of in the second letter, and the hospitality based on donations which Bishop Tyge was actually demanding, a third category not at all excluded by the papal letters.[239] These distinctions have shed much light on the controversy, but I cannot believe that at this point the Øm abbot was aware of such a nuance and was deliberately putting up some kind of legal smoke screen.

Tyge himself, in claiming procurations, at first only spoke of them as being owed to him because of custom.[240] Only when the papal bull seemed to exclude such a claim did he switch over to speaking of the prerogative as being based on the Djursland properties.[241] And even much later in the dispute, when the bishops of Viborg and Slesvig tried to settle it by referring to what the custom had been way back in the time of Bishop Peder Elavsen, they spoke only of the *custom* of visitation, and not whether or not it was based on the Djursland donations.[242] Even though Skyum-Nielsen is legally quite correct, I do not think the participants in the quarrel were themselves as aware of the issues involved as we can be today with our historical hindsight. We do know that by the end of the century the bishop of Ribe and the monks of Løgum could make the distinction between procurations based on the right of visitation and those based on donations to the monks by the bishop,[243] but this clear-

---

238) SM II, 211-212: Both issued by Alexander IV in 1255 and applying to all Cistercian houses. The fact that such privileges were issued at this time indicates that Cistercians in many European countries were having problems during this time in maintaining their independence from the secular church.
239) *Kirkekampen*, pp. 187-8: distinction between *visitatsgæsteri* and *donationsgæsteri*.
240) SM II, 211: "Sicut consuevistis," ait, "aliis episcopis servire, sic servite nobis."
241) SM II, 213: Si non vultis dare nobis ratione consuetudinis, oportet vos dare nobis ratione possessionum in Djursø, quod omnino denegare non potestis.
242) SM II, 239: "...procurationes, quas antecessores sui Arusienses episcopi in dicto monasterio *secundum approbatam consuetudinem* dinoscuntur habuisse."
243) DD II, 4, 339 (1298). The distinction is clear here, but it is interesting that the bishop's right of hospitality based on donation was summarily abolished in the same document because of the legal annoyances and complications the attempt to exercise it constantly entailed!

cut differentiation in a Danish source came almost thirty years after the start of the Øm controversy. So we cannot assume that the distinction was so obvious in the 1260's. The whole issue of procurations given to the diocesan bishop by an exempt Cistercian house was so full of doubt and uncertainty that the bishop of Viborg could as late as 1322 abandon any attempt to define the obligations involved for the monks because, as he wrote in a charter releasing them from further procurations, "the origin of such rights is lost in darkness."[244]

C. The Thirteenth Century Process of Definition

The problem of procurations is full of dead ends and false passages. The best solution is to look broadly at the general legal situation of the period. The thirteenth century brought definition and categorization, not only at the universities, but also in the legal obligations of everyday life. The great problem was that for a century or more many functions and duties had been performed without any careful theorizing about their legal basis. This seems to be the case with the Øm procurations. We know that the Øm monks at least as far back as Peder Elavsen housed and fed the Århus bishop and some of his men, but it is not until the time of Tyge that the monks and the bishop began to speculate about the basis or reason for that custom.

The monks tried to limit the practice to mere custom, which thus would have made it entirely voluntary, as stated in the papal decision. Tyge countered by pointing to the gift of the Djursland properties, which in his opinion obligated the monks to extend yearly procurations as a service in return. Bo answered by referring to the various privileges of "popes, kings, and archbishops", which confirmed the monks' holdings in Djursland.[245] Such a response implied that the monks owed nothing on these lands. This discussion could not proceed further, for Tyge, according to our writer, simply told the abbot to shut up and then went in to eat. In the monks' opinion, Tyge had been checkmated. Once again we may be getting a twisted account, but it is at least likely that Tyge did not have any immediate answer to Bo's contention.[246]

---

244) DD II, 8, 410 (1322) - "...sed quasi ab incerto auctore primitus emanasse, unde et minus solidam vel sufficientem iudicavimus ad intentionem nostram fundandam vel nostram conscientiam informandam."
245) SM II, 213.
246) Here I have a totally different perspective from that of Skyum-Nielsen, p. 187, where he writes that Tyge's non-answer did not show that he lacked better arguments." What does one do to defend a completely variant interpretation of the passage? The most reasonable answer, I think, must be based on one's perception of Tyge's personality. I find him a brilliant, complex individual who at times could be coolly rational and at

At a later, even more dramatic confrontation, Bo, instead of talking vaguely about the abbey's privileges in Djursland, referred to the "Testament of Sven".[247] Our writer says that a copy of this testament is found earlier in the volume.[248] He is thus pointing to the undated version of Sven's testament in the Exordium 1 which had this title, given in the original text, while the dated version lacks such a title.[249] It is this document that Bo is to have submitted to Tyge for his inspection. Their interpretation of the testament is clear: the gifts were given by Sven from his own patrimony and income and thus were personal and not in any way connected to his office as bishop of Århus. Therefore later bishops of Århus could not claim any favours from the Øm monks on the basis of their predecessor's gift.

Tyge, at least in the narration and in the documents included there, never really answered this contention. He merely charged that Øm had its writers, who could make any documents they pleased.[250] Buchwald pounced on this statement, as well as the earlier one telling the monks to shut up, as proof that the monks were forgers![251] It seems more likely to me that if the monks were busy falsifying documents, they would not have allowed such a charge into their narration.

The legal historian Erik Schalling has emphasized the importance of a falsified version of Bishop Sven's testament contained in Kristian Erslev's collection of testaments from the Danish Middle Ages and originally found in a copy book of Anne Krabbe.[252] Green-Pedersen has opposed Skyum-Nielsen's conclusion that the monks were using this falsified version against Tyge.

---

other times rash and furious. The second tendency I find in the Exordium 2, as in this incident. In accepting the Øm writer's report of such an incident as correct, I am taking a step Skyum-Nielsen would not allow. But if I come to doubt the basic veracity of a first hand account, then it is impossible to depend on *any* single statement in the Øm Book. This type of skepticism is for me too radical and does not lead to a fruitful understanding of the monks' situation.

247) SM II, 221.
248) *Ibid.*, "Istud privilegium longe superius transscriptum est in eodem volumine, et est rubrica, "Testamentum Suenonis"."
249) SM II, 179 - ch. 23 - Testamentum episcopi Suenonis (undated)
  18o - ch. 24 - Item aliud testamentum   (1183)
25o) SM II, 221: Dixit episcopus se nolle litteras aliquas recipere pro cibo suo. "Scimus", inquid, "quia habetis scriptores sufficientes; potestis litteras scribere, qualescunque vultis." Notice the contemptuous remark that precedes the accusation: dinner is more important to the bishop than documents. If our writer has correctly caught the tone, then the bishop is at this moment choked by his anger with the monks.
251) Buchwald, pp. 49-51.
252) Erik Schalling, "Kanonisk eller nationell rätt? Ett bidrag till diskussionen om 12oo-talets danska immunitetsstrider", *Kyrkohistorisk Årsskrift* 1937, 38 årgang. Uppsala, 122-29. Kristian Erslev, *Testamenter fra Danmarks Middelalder indtil 1450* (Cpn., 19o1), nr. 1.

This version is in fact much clearer than the genuine will in specifying the monks' freedom from any service to the bishop of Århus.[253] Green-Pedersen tries to prove in a complicated treatment of the subject that it is not at all certain that this falsification was composed at Øm until the fifteenth century, in a much later dispute with the Århus bishop.

Without taking sides and thus abandoning the Øm Book for the sake of a tedious polemic, a few remarks are in order. First, the testament of Sven as meant in the decisive passage is clearly referred to as the document already contained in the Exordium 1. There is thus no need to speculate about any utilization of the falsified testament in this particular case. Second, even if we discount the monks' bitterness, it is clear that Tyge acts in this situation in an explosive way and that the "charge" of falsification may well be nothing more than a shot in the dark, a sign of his own frustration and fury with the incorrigible monks. Third, when Schalling originally compared the texts of the falsified testament of Sven with that which if found in the Øm Book, he concentrated on the text of the dated testament, not the undated one. He did not notice that there is one decisive difference in the terms used between the two documents. In the undated one, Sven wrote: "what remains (after other claims have been settled) the brothers shall *libere* possess." In the dated testament *libere* is missing, and Sven only says he handed the property over to the brothers.[254]

Consider the difference between the two texts, the first so clear, the second so vague, and it is no wonder that the Øm writer refers to the section in the Exordium 1 entitled "Testamentum Suenonis", for it is only here that the monks' contentions find substantial backing. Schalling compared the text of some of the donations of Absalon to Esrum with the various documents of Sven to Øm and rightly concluded that in general Sven's language is more imprecise than Absalon's and leaves more room for an interpretation demanding some services to the bishop.[255] But again, the *libere* has not been taken into consideration, and even if it only contributes a little to the monks' legal case, it does show that they were not necessarily trying to bluff the bishop with a wildly distorted interpretation of the document. I think the monks acted in good faith, and even if Skyum-Nielsen could be right that the falsified document belongs to the controversy with Tyge, there was no need at this juncture for such a fake document to be produced. Possibly later, when the monks had become really desperate and thought they were witnessing the final destruc-

---

253) Skyum-Nielsen, pp. 187-8. Green-Pedersen, pp. 218-226.
254) SM II, 179: "...quod superest prefati fratres *libere* possideant"
        18o: "memoratis fratribus et loco assignavi."
255) Schalling, p. 13o.

tion of their monastery, they composed the falsification. But as far as I can see, the monks, no matter how stubborn and foolish in their blind insistence on their rights, were still being sincere in their answer to Tyge.

We are witnessing here, as I suggested before, a dispute that illustrates a basic difference between life and law in the twelfth and thirteenth centuries. In Bishop Sven's time, it had not been necessary to define precisely in his testament the exact services the monks would render the bishops in the future. But in an age that produced bishops like Tyge, it was essential to determine the nature and extent of the services. In order to do so, both bishop and abbot were forced to revert to the vague documents of the preceding century and to the customs that had grown up since then. The statement of the bishops who had been with Peder Elavsen in his day at Øm before 1246 shows that it was possible to state exactly what this custom entailed in terms of duties on the part of the monks.[256] But when either side tried to formulate or to go against a theoretical basis for such a custom, neither could come up with any sufficient answers. A later, more legally aware age was thus unable to legitimize itself by structuring the vague and unclear practices of an earlier period. Just as medieval theologians could say about the divine attributes that "noone gives what he does not have", so we must admit that despite the claims and counterclaims of the thirteenth century, the terms of the twelfth century testament of Bishop Sven were sufficiently open and vague to allow or exclude either interpretation.

From our comfortable distance, we can say that it would probably have been better for the monks if they had admitted both the complexity of the legal problems and the power of Bishop Tyge to make life difficult for them. Even if they did hold a papal privilege excluding procurations based on custom and good will, they should have seen that it was too late to go against such a well-established custom. The giving of procurations to the Århus bishop had probably in the past been a sign of good relations between him and the monks, and neither side had needed to define exactly what it was getting or giving. Only in the increasing rigidity of life and forms in the later thirteenth century did it become necessary to define exactly what the procurations consisted of and why they were given. The monks said they were voluntary, given out of the goodness of their hearts as a sign of friendship with their bishop. The bishop said they were compulsory, a contractual and inviolable agreement between bishop and monks. So the thirteenth century need for definition undermined the traditional and unquestioned alliance between bishop and monks. Peder Ugotsen had started the process and Tyge and Bo now finished it.

---

256) SM II, 24o.

On the European level we can see a parallel to this dispute in the condemnation of 219 "heretical" propositions at the University of Paris in 1277.[257] Until then the philosophers of the arts faculty had been able to speculate with a certain amount of freedom about Aristotelian propositions that contradicted Christian theology, such as the eternity of the world. But the open and flexible arts curriculum's content could no longer be tolerated. It was necessary now to draw a line between the orthodox and the heretical, just as at Øm it was essential to define the compulsory and distinguish it from the voluntary.[258] Life and thought are being concretized and compartmentalized: the fluidity of the twelfth century is turning into solid forms, more palpable, more easily identified. Whether at Paris or Århus, bishops can no longer accept vague propositions and open patterns of thought and behaviour. It is time to clamp down, to distinguish, and to reject.

This cultural interpretation which looks down from above at the chaotic surface of life, is not intended in any way to detract from the sordid but vital details of the confrontation. Tyge and Bo are not puppets in some deterministic historical frame of reference, but still should be related to their European background. In this way they become far more understandable and sympathetic than they might appear from their clashes in the Øm Book. With such a perspective we can look upon the narration as one of the greatest cultural legacies of the Danish Middle Ages, comparable to the abbey church at Sorø or the Jutlandic Law. In all three cases we find a manifestation of the way Danes were able to integrate European thought and creativity according to their own special needs and conditions.

D. The Dispute Intensifies

After the first confrontation, Tyge and Bo exchanged a number of letters and threats.[259] Finally Tyge came with armed men. As before, he summarized his demands on the monks by asking bluntly whether or not his dinner was ready. The abbot's answer, "I believe it has been prepared, but not here", must have been enough to enrage the volatile Tyge. He pointed to the bishop's house

---

257) Etienne Gilson, *History of Christian Philosophy in the Middle Ages*, (London, 1955), 387-41o. The condemned propositions have been grouped according to types by Pierre Mandonnet in his *Siger de Brabant*, (Louvain, 1911) II, 175-81.
258) J. Huizinga, *The Waning of the Middle Ages* (Penguin: Harmondsworth, 1965) deals with such categories and parallels between dissimilar areas of life. This approach can easily become too impressionistic, but it is also helpful in determining broad relationships between developments on a local and an international level.
259) SM II, 216.

and asked whether or not it was his. Bo, clearly provoking, said it was not.
What followed has been interpreted in various ways. Tyge is supposed to have
gone up the stair of the house and said, "We will take what we need." He
then went to the door of the chapel and pounded on it. When the monks heard
"that he would smash the door", they asked each other whether he was going
to use force against them.[260] Skyum-Nielsen has pointed out how this passage
was made more extreme in later accounts of the incident and has concluded that
Tyge only knocked on the door.[261] But the verb twice used, *frangere*, indicates
that Tyge used force to get the door open, probably in trying to see where the
brothers had hidden food. It is not clear whether or not the bishop smashed
in the door, but he certainly was pounding so hard that the monks were afraid
he was going to break it down.

Perhaps this is a small detail, but it illustrates the varying interpretations that have been placed on the Latin text. One can only return to the content of the words and then try to understand them in the context of the situation. Both the monks and the bishop were tense and upset after long having awaited this confrontation. Moreover Tyge was probably hungry. He felt wronged and maltreated. It is consistent with the explosive personality that we have seen up until now to conclude that he did act as our writer says. He was in such a state that he mistook the bell of the monks for the second meal as a signal to attack him.[262] All that we hear from this passage confirms our impression of him as a man who feels tricked, terrified, and very angry.

In the midst of this confusion the abbot, as during Tyge's first visit, consulted with the monks to find out what to do.[263] This time he only talked with the older members of the community, who suggested that the abbot give hospitality but not allow compulsory procurations. However much we can reflect on the inappropriateness of such a solution to the conflict, we must at least admit that from now on the Øm monks took a consistent position, until a few

---

260) *Ibid.*, Et accessit ad ianuam capelle (in the bishop's house), superius fregit eam. Cum hoc audirent monachi, quod *frangeret* ostium, mussitabant inter se: si vellet nobis vim inferre, quod vellent vim vi repellere.
261) Skyum-Nielsen, p. 188. Also p. 312, note 65.
262) Skyum-Nielsen has taken this mention of bell ringing for a second meal as proof that the monks broke the Cistercian Rule, which forbade them more than one meal a day, especially during Lent. This would contribute to his assertion of moral decline at Øm (p. 187). But as mentioned earlier, the monks' refectory was located in the old dormitory and so could have been much smaller than it needed to be to house all the monks and lay brothers at one sitting. So the words "prior refectio fratrum peracta erat, et secunda fieri instabat", would indicate that the first sitting of the daily meal was over, and the second was to begin. This interpretation makes better sense, for if the brothers did eat twice a day, they would hardly have taken the second meal immediately after the first.
263) SM II, 217.

years later they gave in to the compromise suggested by the bishops of Ribe and Slesvig.

The next day at Åbo Sysselsting, Tyge complained about what had happened and claimed that the monks had conspired against him. Moreover he accused the monks of harbouring an enemy of the king, the Cistercian monk Arnfast, who is one of the shady characters of this period. Our writer pauses here to give the story of Arnfast and to deny vigorously that the monks ever gave him shelter after he became *persona non grata* with the king. Here enters a new theme in the dispute: the question of the loyalty of the Øm monks to the king. Because of this question, the defeat of Øm would ultimately come, for all through the controversy both the young King Erik and his mother Queen Margrethe seem to have accepted Tyge's version of the events and became fully convinced that the monks were in league not only with the exiled archbishop Jakob Erlandsen (which was true), but also with the dreaded Duke of Southern Jutland (which was not necessarily true).

But Øm does not seem to have lacked a few influential friends, including the knight Jens Canne, who convinced Bo to go to the cathedral of Århus in order to try to arrange a settlement with Tyge.[264] Although the Øm Book almost always puts these laymen in the background, their presence helps us understand how serious the controversy had become. Such men must have felt pained embarrassment and maybe even real concern that two prominent churchmen were attacking and calumniating each other.[265]

The Århus meetings just brought more insults, until the nobles placed themselves between the two men and said they could not allow such a dispute between two churches.[266] Another meeting was arranged for the morrow at Dover church, one of the parish churches that the Øm monks held from the Århus bishop. Prepared for the worst the abbot brought with him all the sturdy young smiths, craftsmen, and labourers that he could summon from his estates, while the bishop appeared not only together with his diocesan officials but also with the local Benedictine abbots. The presence of these abbots in the episcopal

---

264) SM II, 218. Also a member of the bishop's own entourage had during the second confrontation at Øm advised the monks not to act in such a way and so encouraged Bo to consult with his elder monks (p. 217). The lay knights and property owners of the Århus area made frequent efforts to reconcile the bishop and the monks, an indication of how closely knit lay and ecclesiastical interests were at this time. The Cistercians, who were supposed to be both legally and spiritually immune and exempt from the affairs of the world, were right in the thick of them.
265) Might we here be seeing a medieval example of class solidarity? Upper class lay landowners are afraid of disagreement between upper class church landowners that would weaken the strength of this group in society against anonymous lower class land cultivators?
266) SM II, 219: Tunc nobiles, qui adfuerunt, interposuerunt partes suas; dixerunt; nulla ratione posse inter duas ecclesias tale certamen pati...

contingent indicates that Tyge wanted to use non-exempt Benedictines to oppose the exempt Cistercians' claims. In such an instance it seems as if Danish bishops like Tyge never really looked at Cistercians as any different in practice than the Benedictines, despite their claims. Tyge apparently was trying to play off the independence-seeking Cistercians against the loyal and submissive Benedictines.

The Dover meeting was a fiasco, just like previous encounters. The original issue of procurations was obscured by other charges. Tyge's gradual acceleration of claims and reprisals would mean ever greater miseries for the Øm monks. First of all as diocesan bishop, he deprived the monks of the parish churches they held and serviced.[267] Here he was within his rights, even though Bo protested by having the papal privilege for Veng church read aloud. Tyge's reply, "All your letters are not worth a bean", can only strengthen our impression of him as a passionate man whose anger swept him away and made him unable to listen to the other side.[268]

It could be countered that this is precisely what the Øm monks want us to think of Tyge. But the fact remains that in this confrontation, Tyge, being shown a papal letter that we are absolutely sure was legitimate could only answer that it was worth nothing.[269] There are only two ways for us to interpret such an answer. Either he was raging mad, or he was cynically saying that letters were worthless when what mattered was the use of force. For just after the Dover meeting Tyge began seriously to harass the Øm abbey peasants and labourers by summoning them to courts that were deliberately set at great distances from their homes.[270] To conclude with Buchwald that Tyge's remarks show he knew that the Øm monks were falsifiers of privileges – this would be to ignore the entire context of the situation and the undeniable evidence of the papal confirmation of Veng church.

Tyge's departure from reason and logic is also indicated by his attempt to depose Bo as abbot. He says that he has not chosen, confirmed, or placed Bo in office, and so he is not abbot. Obviously Tyge had no rights here, but Skyum-Nielsen gives him the benefit of the doubt by saying that the prejudiced monks apparently twisted the exchange.[271] What Tyge was really saying was that he had not given his blessing to Bo and so he could not function as abbot. This interpretation depends too heavily on the episcopal benediction of a Cistercian abbot as a necessary part of the abbot's installation. If we look

---

267) SM II, 219.
268) The Veng privilege of 1217 is in DD I, 5, nr. 1o5.
269) Green-Pedersen was the first to emphasize the importance of the Veng privilege as a counterweight to Tyge's loose assertions – pp. 221-2.
27o) SM II, 22o.
271) Skyum-Nielsen, p. 189 and p. 311, note 21.

at the general privilege for all Cistercian houses that was formulated in its full form by the start of the thirteenth century, we can see that even if the abbot was supposed to ask the bishop for his blessing, this is a mere formality.[272]

Even if Bo would have been guilty of breach of church discipline in refusing to seek Tyge's blessing, there is no indication that this could provide sufficient grounds for Tyge to depose him. Here, as in Tyge's attempt to perform a visitation at Øm, the bishop seems to be going as far as he possibly can and leaving it up to the monks to define the limits of his authority. But unlike with the question of visitation, he is not willing to retreat. In revoking the abbey's churches and trying to depose Bo, he seems to have sought the same control over Øm as he had over any of the diocese's Benedictine abbeys. Tyge had decided to use every means in his power to make Øm submit, first through its churches, and then through the harassment of its peasants. Aside from the passionate personality of Tyge, the monks themselves were responsible for this campaign, not only because they were too intransigent in the immediate issue of the procurations but also because they, like most other Danish Cistercians, had never before tried to define and delineate their independence from the local bishop. They had counted on his respect and benevolence, and when both were simultaneously withdrawn, they had no tradition of independence to butress themselves. Try as they might to assert what they legally were entitled to claim, it was far too late.

The treatment of the Øm labourers galvanized the abbot into further action. He complained to Niels, who was bishop of Viborg and royal chancellor, and to Jens Kalv, the king's marshall.[273] Their positive reaction in arranging yet another meeting at St. Clement's in Århus shows that they still had some sympathy with the abbot and some hope in a compromise.

On the day of the meeting, Tyge refused to let Bo read his privileges. He again demanded the procurations and based that claim on the Djursland hold-

---

272) M. Tangl, *Die Päpstlichen Kanzlei Ordnungen v. 1200-1500*, (Innsbruck, 1894), p. 23o, nr. 13. Si vero epsicopus, in cuius parochia domus vestra fundata est, cum humilitate ac devotione qua convenit requisitus substitutum abbatem benedicere et alia, que ad officium episcopale pertinent, vobis conferre renuerit, licitum sit eidem abbati si tamen sacerdos fuerit, proprios novitios benedicere et alia, que ad officium suum pertinent, exercere et vobis omnia ab alio episcopo percipere, quae a vestro fuerint indebite denegata.
This article makes it clear that the Cistercian abbot should get the episcopal blessing, but definitely does not imply that an unblessed abbot cannot hold office. Bo could point out his initial attempts at obtaining good relations with Tyge (pp. 2o9-21o) and, if the matter of benediction ever had come to the fore, could have gone to another bishop.
273) SM II, 22o-21.

ings. Bo countered by referring to the testament of Sven, and then Tyge uttered his famous remark about falsification of the documents.[274]

At this point in the Exordium 2 we hear finally of intervention by abbots of other Cistercian houses. From May, 1263, more than a year after the controversy had begun, we have a group of letters, appeals to the pope, and lists of Tyge's misdeeds.[275] It is not surprising that the heads of the other abbeys - and sooner or later all the Danish Cistercian abbots were involved - accepted the Øm abbot's version completely, for they were his colleagues. At this stage in the controversy, neither party seems to have been interested in going over the arguments once more. This is understandable, even if regrettable. But the real tragedy is the fact that the monks also appealed to the exile Jakob Erlandsen. The Øm author's commentary on this letter show clearly whose side the monks were on in the raging controversy between king and archbishop. Jakob is said to have been in Sweden "since he did not want to suffer the harm done the church in his province."[276] Skyum-Nielsen has already pointed out the "dangerous sympathy" that the Cistercians were showing and takes them to task for lacking legal and political sense.[277]

Such a way of looking at the Cistercians is perfectly fair, but we must add that in going to the archbishop the monks were only following normal procedure and appealing to the metropolitan against one of his suffragans. But these were not normal times, and the insistence of the Cistercians in acting as if they should proceed through customary channels reveals a certain naiveté that was hardly needed right now. Instead of carefully planning a suitable strategy, the Cistercians cried out for what they considered justice. One thinks of the unfortunate Esrum Cistercians depicted in Saxo. When the king threatened to kill a boy who had been brought up in the monastery, they wept bitterly. If Saxo's report is correct, the monks had no idea that it was all a trick.[278] Other instances of such unpolitic behaviour can be seen in the disappointing experience of Anselm as archbishop of Canterbury. He preferred to go into exile rather than be accused of acting for his own political advantage and thus against his spiritual well-being.[279] So often with medieval

---

274) SM II, 221.
275) SM II, 224-229.
276) SM II, 224.
277) Skyum-Nielsen, p. 19o: Det var en farlig sympati, der kun kunne skade ordenen og de enkelte klostre, sådan som situationen nu engang var, både hjemme og ude.
278) Saxo, pp. 436-7.
279) See R.W. Southern's *Saint Anselm and his Biographer:* A Study of Monastic Life and Thought 1o59-c. 113o (Cambridge, 1966), esp. pp. 122-6, "Principles of Conduct": "Anselm therefore was not only unpractised in the ways of the world; he disassociated himself from them on principle". It would be fascinating and rewarding to take the two archbishop-king quar-

church figures, we have to remove our cynical or pragmatic point of view and concede that what we look upon as lack of imagination or understanding may well actually have been a burning insistence on following divine law and its reflections in human rules.

But as the controversy became more bitter, the Øm monks dropped their concern for the rules of the game. Despite the bishop's prohibition, they held services in the parish churches. Our writer is clearly embarrassed to admit this fact and apologizes for it, but he does at least admit it. This concession on his part has to speak in favour of the general reliability of the account:

> Unde nullus sacerdos in ecclesiis nostris audebat alicui ecclesiastica sacramenta conferre. Unde necessitate compulsi, fecimus, quod potuimus, *licet inviti*.[280]

The writer also includes a letter from Tyge to Bo in which the bishop accused the monks of holding the liturgy in the parish churches and demanded they pay a fine which he levied on them as a result of their treatment of him when he was at the abbey. Our writer denies that the abbot had agreed to any such fine. Amid such charges and countercharges, we can see how hopeless the situation was becoming.

At this point Abbot Bo resigned his post. This was probably meant as a conciliatory gesture to Tyge. Bo's successor, Ture, had already been abbot at Esrum and, before then, at Vitskøl.[281] Now he was apparently living in retirement at Vitskøl. Buchwald thought he was chosen because he already was blessed by a bishop and so could immediately take up the Øm post without any trouble on this account,[282] but I think the main reason for his selection was his long experience as abbot. He could be expected to weigh the issues carefully and to make the right admissions to Tyge without compromising the Order.

rels of twelfth century England (Anselm-Henry I and Beckett-Henry II) and compare them with Danish parallels (Eskil-Valdemar I and Jakob Erlandsen - Erik Glipping). Such a juxtaposition would tell a great deal about the relative level of upper class culture and expression in two fringe European countries at different periods.

280) SM II, 225.
281) SM II, 229-230. In the manuscript there are unfilled spaces left for the number of years Ture had been abbot at Vitskøl and at Esrum. It is indicative of the haste with which this account was written and the suddenness with which it was abandoned that the numbers never were added.
282) Buchwald, p. 55.

9.

THE OUTCOME OF THE CONTROVERSY
1263 - 1268

A. The Aborted Compromise, 1264

On June 11, 1263, Ture became abbot at Øm. In the previous month Danish Cistercian abbots had issued appeals not only to the pope but also to the four main abbots of their order.[283] We know nothing about how the French abbots responded, except that the abbot of Clairvaux did write to the queen mother and ask her to look out for the interests of the Øm monks and defend them against Tyge.[284] But she seems to have been completely behind the bishop and at one point wrote a threatening letter to the abbot of Øm telling him to pay up the procurations or else risk her anger.[285] Just as letters to the Cistercian abbots did no good, so too the papal response was disappointing. Bo himself had gone to Rome to plead his cause, and at first the monks seemed to be getting somewhere. The letters issued after Ture's takeover at Øm more or less accept the monks' charges and accusations.[286] But Tyge seems to have had excellent connections at Rome, and all the orders contained in these letters were never enforced. Skyum-Nielsen thinks that they may for the most part be only drafts and never issued in final form, but it is just as likely that they were sent but had no effect after the change of papal policy.[287]

We might expect that the coming of a new abbot would at least temporarily have improved the situation. Our writer claims that Ture carefully investigated the causes of the controversy and tried to find a way to obtain the

---
283) SM II, 228-9.
284) SM II, 233.
285) SM II, 245-46. The abbot of Clairvaux wrote in the summer of 1264, while the queen mother's letter has been dated to 1266, May-August, and was sent to the Øm monks, so it cannot be looked upon as an answer to the Clairvaux abbot's letter. For dating, see Skyum-Nielsen, p. 32o, note 24.
286) Skyum-Nielsen, p. 313, note 92.
287) SM II, 233-36, especially the pope's letter to Bishop Tyge, p. 235. Here he orders Tyge to "desist from such exactions".

bishop's favour.[288] Unfortunately the account becomes sketchy here. Our writer says that he is not giving details of these negotiations, but they were a failure. His only explanation is that Tyge's heart was hardened and so he stepped up his maltreatment of the monks. It is frustrating for us that the writer gives the text of innumerable useless appeals to the pope, this time from the autumn of 1263, but does not tell us what happened over the summer. In any case Ture probably tried from May until the beginning of October to reach some compromise with Tyge, but his attempt failed. The likely reason is that he was not willing to make any concessions on the issue of procurations, while at the same time he encouraged his labourers to hold back their payment of the episcopal tithes. This was playing right into Tyge's hands, and enabled him to expand his campaign of harassment. A letter from 24 October by the Cistercian abbots to the pope says the bishop's summons to his courts and his fines and punishment were now being applied no only to lay labourers but also to the abbey's lay brothers.[289] On the seventh of October had come an attack on the monk Skjalm in the cemetery of the Djursland church of Rosmos.[290] Once again the distant possession provided easy prey for the bishops' men.

In the end of January, 1264, Brother Lars and the now retired abbot Bo were sent off to the Roman curia to acquire the papal letters that, as shown, did no good for the monks. In the same week after their departure came the most savage attack yet upon the monks. Bjørn, an Øm monk, and the two lay brothers Herman and Henrik were overnighting at Horsens on their way to Pomerania in order to buy grain.[291] The writer explains that there was famine in the whole of Denmark at this time, and perhaps this situation helps explain the repeated assertions of the abbot that he could not afford to feed Tyge and all his men. In any case, the Øm brothers never made their trip, for in the middle of the night, the bishops' men attacked them, led off the monk Bjørn as their captive, chaining his naked feet under a horse's stomach. One of the lay brothers, Henrik, tried to resist but was brutally kicked and died after a few days. The other, Herman, was robbed and left behind almost naked. As for Bjørn, he was kept in prison for nineteen weeks and treated so badly that after he returned home, he never became well again and could not fully use his limbs. Our narrator, who is so used to expressing anger, now pours forth his grief: when the brothers heard of this incident, they were overwhelmed with sorrow. On Bjørn's return to Øm, "there was not a single person, lay or monk, who if they had known him before, could keep themselves from weeping because of the

---

288) SM II, 23o.
289) SM II, 231.
29o) SM II, 231-2.
291) SM II, 238-9. "...ad emendum annonam in Sclaviam" means in the land of the Wends, which is likely to be Pomerania.

deformity of his body from lack of food and from the many other mistreatments he had received."[292]

The remarks in the next chapter about Bishop Tyge's acquisition of papal letters "under false pretences" have been exposed as incorrect and misleading.[293] But in view of the monks' sorrow and anger at the attack on Bjørn and the lay brothers, it is easy to see why they now saw lies and deception in everything Tyge did. A wild fear seems to have taken over life at Øm, and the brothers could no longer see events in realistic perspective. The monks, as individuals who need to explain their misfortune, could find some small comfort in thinking that Tyge was just as crooked in his behaviour at the papal curia as he was at home. Moreover they needed an explanation for the uselessness of their papal letters, and Tyge's activities provided an immediate excuse.

In a way it is pathetic to see this community looking desperately around for an explanation for its troubles and settling upon the cheapest answer, aside from the usual one of being punished for sins. But the monks have a deep need to find a person at the bottom of their misfortunes and not just a series of accidents. It may well be that some of the attacks on the Øm monks and their labourers were not instigated by Tyge but were carried out by people who knew they could take advantage of the generally chaotic situation and felt sure that Tyge would certainly not punish them. But the monks can only see the bishop's men lurking behind every tree, and at times the tone of their account approaches a mild hysteria.

But for a moment it seemed as if a solution was near, for on 26 November, 1264, bishops Esger of Ribe and Niels of Slesvig made their statement, already mentioned, concerning the practice of procurations in the time of Peder Elavsen.[294] Here it seemed as if there was a basis for future relations between Øm and Tyge, for they made known that Elavsen had never taken more than four

---

292) SM II, 239: "...non fuit aliquis, neque secularis neque claustralis, si eum ante noverat, qui se propter deformitatem ex inedia et aliis plurimis incommoditatibus sui corporis posset de fletu continere." It is important to notice how differently tears are used in an eleventh century source, like the letters of Saint Anselm, and in the thirteenth century section of the Øm Book. Anselm's tears came frequently and plentifully. They show sweetness, remorse for sin, affection for beloved monks. Øm's tears, which came rarely and only in extreme crisis situations, reveal bitterness and despair. I think the motivations given for tears and the way writers describe crying tell us a great deal about life in that society. Tears, even as literary conventions, are perhaps a direct entrance to a given society's general attitude towards emotion. At Øm tears are a vehicle not for love but for anger.
293) SM II, 239: "Non est oblivioni tradendum, quod procuratores episcopi Tukonis falsa suggestione litteras papales acquisierunt, ut idem episcopus duobus preesset episcopiis, scilicet Arusiensi et Roskildensi." Skyum-Nielsen, p. 191.
294) SM II, 239-24o.

clerks and five laymen with him to the monastery on Ash Wednesday and that he never stayed more than three weeks. Also Elavsen had been careful not to set any precedent in holding court in or near Øm but always left the vicinity of the abbey when the time came to hear cases. Tyge gave his oath to uphold these conditions, but by the time of next Lent, he had broken it. According to our writer, he met up at Øm with loo men, and at the same time continued with his attacks on the monastery's labourers.[295]

It has been suggested that Tyge came with so many men because he intended to collect not only the procurations for 1265, but also for the preceding years.[296] There were three vacant years after Peder Ugotsen and four years since Tyge had become bishop, so he was entitled, according to the most favourable possible reading of the agreement, at the very most to meet up with 7o men. The fact that he came with a hundred shows he had no intention of holding to the compromise but was resuming his policy of intimidating the monks. Even a great Cistercian abbey in the best of times would hardly have been able to house and feed a hundred men - or even seventy - for three weeks. Øm had been plagued by famine. Its lay labourers were dispersed, its granges under attack, its monks living in daily fear. And so come a hundred soldiers led by Bishop Tyge. No wonder the monks refused to give the procurations demanded, for there was absolutely no relationship between the agreement they had entered the preceding autumn and the demand being placed on them now.

B. The Coming of Guido

But even if the monks' reaction is understandable, they were still living in an unreal world. Soon after their denial of procurations to Tyge, the news reached them that the Cistercian cardinal legate Guido was on his way to Denmark to try to settle the dispute between king and archbishop. At this news, the monks "rejoiced, hoping to obtain from him justice for all the injuries inflicted on us by the bishop or by others".[297] The brothers failed to admit to themselves that sooner or later they would have to settle with Tyge. The wisest course would have been to follow the terms of the 1264 agreement and to appeal to Bishops Esger and Niels, who were supposed to act as arbitrators in any future disputes. So far as we know, the monks not only failed to do this; they also actually believed that Guido would have the time and power to crush Bishop Tyge. Once again we are confronted by a glaring example of Cis-

---

295) SM II, 241: Venit enim cum centum equitaturis et cursoribus plurimis, sed nec unum amovit a se, et sic ipse prior rupit fedus.
296) Skyum-Nielsen, p. 192.
297) SM II, 241: In gaudio exultavimus, sperantes ab eo et per ipsum iusticiam de omnibus iniuriis ab episcopo sive de aliis nobis illatis acquisituros.

tercian naiveté and deliberate ignorance of the ways of the world. But here the brothers were perhaps partly misguided by the naiveté of Guido himself, who already had sent a letter expressing support fot the Øm monks.[298]

The monks erred gravely here not in hoping for something from Guido, but in taking up all the old complaints against Tyge without considering or mentioning the 1264 settlement. Thus the Danish abbots' letter to Guido, sent in 1266 before 21 May, simply listed all Tyge's misdeeds and spoke of "procurations that are neither owed nor customary".[299] This was pure bravado to go back on an admission previously made. Even if the monks had felt all along that they did not owe procurations, they had bound themselves legally to their payment. By going back on their word, they were exposing themselves more than ever to Tyge's ruthlessness.

In the quarrel that followed, everyone got dirty. It is perhaps wrong for the historian to try to act as referee, judging who had more right on his side. By the end everyone was compromised and, as in most tragic human conflicts, no one won. But the jubilant reaction to Guido's expected arrival and the hope for a final victory confirms our picture of the monks as stubborn fighters, unwilling to admit the weaknesses of their cause. When they thought they had the advantage, they were even willing to hide part of the truth. When the Øm monks start stooping to such methods, it is possible to see them as falsifiers of documents. It may be sometime after this point that Sven's testament was doctored. But this is pure speculation.

Guido issued a letter to Bishop Tyge on 21 May, 1266, from Roskilde, in which he was careful enough to state at the beginning that the charges made in the letter were those made by the Cistercian abbots of Denmark.[300] Aside from this caution, however, he seems to have accepted the accusations fully, emphasizing most of all the attacks on the monks, their labourers, and their properties, and then going over to the individual charges. Guido's letter is long and eloquent. Not only does he tell Tyge that he is acting in a way unworthy of a bishop and thus causing scandal to the church, but also appeals to the inner workings of Tyge's conscience. The language mixes threats with exhortations, and even if it had no effect, we can see here one more manifestation of Cistercian solidarity, insisting that non-Cistercians give the monks their respect and even love.[301]

---

298) SM II, 237. The letter was from 6 June, 1264 and was sent to the two judges appointed by Pope Urban IV. Guido makes no bones about his affection for the Øm monks and practically warns the judges to treat the monks extra well.
299) SM II, 241-2.
300) SM II, 242-45, p. 242: "Aiunt enim, quod vos..."
301) In Guido's appeal to the inner heart (244-45) we can see the tradition of

During the summer of 1266, the monks' situation seems to have become even more precarious. The queen mother Margrethe wrote her letter warning the monks against opposing Tyge.[302] The monks went a second time to Guido because they had heard that Tyge continued to accuse them of "many crimes" before the king. Again Guido complied with the monks' wishes, and in a letter in August tried to communicate his interpretation of Tyge's demands for procuration. Tyge was in effect demanding a feudal payment and thus treating the monks as vassals: "quia tamen pretextu visitationis in feodis procurationes ab eis exigere."[303] We do not know if this was the formulation of the monks or of Guido himself, but in any case it once again skirted the inevitable fact that there was a long established custom at Øm for giving procurations, and no amount of theorizing would reduce this precedent to oblivion. Marc Bloch once skilfully pointed out how during the medieval period voluntary services, when done over a period of years, usually came to be looked upon as mandatory.[304] Customs had a tendency to solidify and justify themselves simply because that was the way things "always" had been. In trying to deny the force of precedent, first the monks and now Guido were flying in the face of everyday realities.

By August 1266, Guido was in Ribe, and by now it was becoming clear that his attempt to resolve the dispute between the king and archbishop of Lund was a failure.[305] Guido continued, as he moved south, to follow the desires of the Øm abbot and to summon Tyge to appear before him to account for his acts: first at Ribe, then Slesvig, and finally Lübeck.[306] As Guido moved further away from Zealand, his political importance diminished, but the Øm monks refused to give up. They probably already felt disappointed that he did not do anything decisive, like excommunicating Tyge when he had failed to show up, and our writer is forced to excuse Guido for his leniency:

> Bernard and of Cistercian self-righteous emotionalism. "Appendite itaque in libra rationis predicta quelibet, et vobiscummet ipsis disceptando de hiis, si vera sunt, vestra circumspectio colligat et discernat, et examinati iudicii rectitudo in pectore vestro dijudicet, utrum talia debeant de pontificibus predicari. Licet autem ad omnes nostre compassionis rivuli debeant derivari, eis inpendendo grate subventionis munimen, illis tamen precipue debent nostre insignia porrigi caritatis, quibus per religionis idemptitatem sumus et unionem coniuncti."
> There is a strange combination here of tenderness, threat, and authority that goes directly back to the personality and activity of Bernard.

302) SM II, 245-6.
303) SM II, 246.
304) Marc Bloch, *Feudal Society* (trans. by L.A. Manyon), vol. 1 - The Growth of Ties of Dependence (Chicago, 1965), p. 114, "...every act, especially if it was repeated three or four times, was likely to be transformed into a precedent." p. 113: "...the idea that what has been has *ipso facto* the right to be."
305) Skyum-Nielsen, 212-16.
306) SM II, 247.

> Quamvis episcopus propter contumaciam iudicandus esset, tamen legatus
> distulit propter nimiam sui cordis simplicitatem; erat enim erga omnes
> benignissimus, neminem volens iudicare, nisi nimis esset coactus.

Once again our monks have to find a rationalisation, a way out, to explain to themselves why they were unable to achieve what they sought. They never stop to wonder if their entire attitude is inappropriate. The fault must lie elsewhere. Moreover, they are unwilling to give up their belief in Guido, for he is their only "ally" left. But it could just as well be that Guido refused to go all the way with Tyge because he felt that it would be politically unwise to further complicate his relations with the monastery and its allies. If this is so, then it was the monks and not Guido who were being simple-minded.

C. The Lübeck Declaration and its Sorry Aftermath - November, 1266

Finally in a synod at Lübeck, and thus at a comfortable distance from Denmark, Guido did excommunicate Bishop Tyge. It was not for his treatment of the Øm monks, however, but for his position with the king against Jakob Erlandsen.[307] We are not given the full circumstances surrounding this act but instead are supplied with the entire text of a plea that Abbot Ture delivered before the meeting assembled there. Our writer says that Ture wanted to make Tyge's wrongs against Øm known "to the whole world", and what follows is a sad repetition of all the charges and complaints against Tyge with which we by now are so familiar.[308] There are some changes of approach, however, that are worth nothing. Ture gives much space to the problem of procurations and instead of claiming that they are not owed, goes through his version of the historical background for their payment. He admits that the monks gave such procurations in the past but were not obliged to them by any debt.[309]

Ture dreams of returning to the good old days before the death of Peder Elavsen in 1246 when debts and obligations were not so clearly defined or expected but when people more or less gave each other the benefit of the doubt

---

307) SM II, 247. The Øm writer does not try to hide the general reason for the decree and so cannot be accused of distortion here. But, as usual, he dismisses the entire archepiscopal-royal dispute with the remark that the king would not allow the archbishop to stay in Denmark. Just as in the Tyge dispute, the Øm monks show no interest in getting to the bottom of the matter but are content with a one-sided view. Also here the writer's growing fatigue with his account and the controversies involved becomes more apparent than ever. Concerning reasons why Guido excommunicated the king and bishop, he says, "Quare sic fecit, non fuit sine maxima causa, quod ad presens *propter nimiam prolixitatem* non est dicendum."
308) SM II, 248-52.
309) SM II, 248: "...quia nunquam fuerant antecessoribus suis in hoc vel in consimili servicio ex debito obligati."

when it came to mutual services. This picture of the past is idealized, for as we have seen from the Exordium 1, the monks did often have trouble with matters like their exemption from the tithe. But Ture's manipulation of the past for the sake of the present points to one of the most important results of the Øm controversy. With all the polemic on each side, the monks were forced to think about their past and about the kind of life they expected to lead in Danish society, to formulate their expectations, to rise out of daily life's routine. On a European scale, this need to formulate one's goals and the propaganda that resulted from it already had manifested itself for the first time in the Investiture controversy.[310] In both instances, the process of defining old ways inevitably changed them. And just as the investiture debate, despite its dark sides, had fruitful results in stimulating monastic reform and new expressions of religious feeling, so too the climate of debate and self-articulation at Øm seems to have been responsible for the writing down of Bishop Gunner's Life. This biography could provide an ideal vision of a past way of life that was superior to what the present could offer. And so the Life is much more than a hagiography: it is a model for the present situation at Øm.

Out of all the distortions and obsessions of the controversy with Bishop Tyge came the best biography of the Danish Middle Ages. We can look at Abbot Ture's bristling and fruitless accusations against Tyge at Lübeck as one side of the coin, and Gunner's Life as the other. They are a result of a deep yearning for *die schöne Vergangenheit,* when saints walked the earth and life was rich and good. But while Abbot Ture's polemic has lost contact with the political reality of the situation and is a pointless manoeuvre for an institution that has long since lost the battle, the biography of Gunner in contrast is a balanced, competent, and intensely personal description of a human being, light years away from any surface polemic. The fact that the same situation at Øm could give rise to two such different works only points out the unpredictability of human reactions to crisis situations. In one case the response is bitterness and hatred. In the other it is nostalgia and humour.

Even if there is a strained quality about Ture's polemic, sometimes bordering on the hysterical, he did succeed in making his abbey's plight into more than an isolated, exceptional phenomenon. After listing one by one the bishop's attacks on the monastery and its members, he says the "more intolerable" fact is that Tyge was trying to nullify and thus abolish the privileges of the Cistercian Order.[311] This recalls the charge already made by the Danish

---

310) See Brian Tierney, *The Crisis of Church and State*, 1o5o-13oo (Prentice-Hall, New Jersey, 1964), esp. section 4, "The War of Propaganda", pp. 74-84.
311) SM II, 251.

abbots in their letter to Guido, in which they said that because Tyge had no respect for the monks' immunities, other bishops might begin to abuse the privileges of Cistercian houses in their dioceses.[312]

Ture also claimed that Tyge had threatened to attack Øm after the legate had left Denmark.[313] This is exactly what did happen, and once again we can see the Øm monks' foolishness in heading towards destruction by handing over their fate to an outside authority and refusing to take the consequences of Tyge's powerful position. And yet such bravado is not entirely meaningless. Our monks were absolutely consistent in their stubbornness and, after the 1264 compromise's failure, refused to give an inch. Seldom in history do we find examples of a group of people who stick so recalcitrantly to a principle, come what may. But the abbot seems already to be aware of the final avalanche that such unmitigating pressure on Tyge would bring, for he ended his plea by saying that if Guido did not help the abbey, then there would be no one.

When Ture finally finished his long piece, our writer says that all who were there cursed such a bishop.[314] Nevertheless, Guido left Lübeck without doing anything more about the matter. Our writer makes no comment on this fact, but it indicates that the legate wanted no further involvement in the dispute. He had enough on his hands already in defending Jakob Erlandsen. But sometimes a defeated party cannot admit the inevitable, so Ture followed Guido to Bremen. There the abbot became ill and entrusted the whole matter to an ally. This was none other than the king's archenemy Jakob Erlandsen, and once again the monks showed a total lack of awareness of the delicacy of their situation. But in their perseverance and willingness to pursue people down into Germany, the monks acted similarly to the Sorø abbot earlier in the century who had sped to German towns and the deathbeds of various members of the relatives of Absalon in order to secure their rights and lands.

By now the people around Erik Glipping were probably convinced that the Øm Cistercians were in firm alliance not just with their Order but with Jakob's party also.[315] This open act probably did little to worsen an already hope-

---

312) SM II, 241: "...quod huius exemplo ceteris regni Dacie episcopis modo simili contra ceteras domus nostri ordinis debachandi materia generetur, quod utique iam ex quorundam illorum verbis...innotuit evidenter." This assertion, although it cannot be substantiated, provides a fascinating indication that the Øm-Tyge dispute may have provoked latent anti-Cistercian feeling in other parts of Denmark.
313) SM II, 251.
314) SM II, 252.
315) Concerning the development of the royal attitude, the first strike against the Øm monks came when Tyge claimed they had harboured the political fugitive and monk Arnfast (SM II, 217-8, February, 1263). The second, much more serious matter, was the appeal of Øm to the archbishop in May, 1263 (224). Not until after the failure of the November, 1264 compromise

less mess. At Magdeburg Jakob managed to get a letter from Guido which, instead of passing judgment on Bishop Tyge, handed the matter over to the investigation of the bishop-elect of Slesvig, Bonde. Guido seems to have been trying to edge out of the responsibility he once so eagerly had taken for Øm's fate. Still, he admitted the seriousness of the problem, for he wrote of the monastery as being "stricken by such and so many injuries that it seemed to be on the verge of final destruction, unless it be helped by a quick remedy."[316]

This letter is dated November 3o, 1266, and it was not until February 3, 1267, that Bonde wrote to the prior of the Århus Dominicans asking him to summon Tyge to appear at Flensburg on the twelfth of March to answer to the monks' charges.[317] By now the efforts to protect the Øm monks have taken on a farcical character. Tyge was certainly not about to go to Slesvig, unfriendly territory to the royal party. And the Dominican prior was not about to put on excessive pressure, for his order had during the dispute remained loyal to the king.[318] Our writer claims that Tyge went once more to the king and restated all his quarrels against the Øm monks. Because of Ture's activities at Lübeck and the efforts of Jakob Erlandsen, Tyge could say that the abbot had diminished the king's honour. Tyge was clever about linking his grievances to wrongs done to the king, and is supposed to have aroused the royal fury. This is the first time our writer speaks directly of the king's reaction. Until now the queen mother has been the most important personality, but by now the teen-age king seems to have been taking his own view of the Øm dispute. He threatened to ravage all the Øm possessions and to take the abbot captive if the monks did not give Tyge what he asked for.[319]

Perhaps a settlement could have been arranged between the king and the Cistercian abbots, but at this point the Duke of Southern Jutland issued a letter speaking of his love for the Øm monks and his desire to defend them.[32o]

---

do we have evidence of a royal reaction, and this only through the queen mother's warning to the Øm monks (May-August, 1266, pp. 245-6). At this point the writer accuses Tyge of lying to the king and charging the monks with many crimes (246).

316) SM II, 253. Et ipsum monasterium tot et tantis iniuriis laceratum finali destructioni proximum videatur, nisi ei celeri remedio succurratur.
317) SM II, 253-4.
318) Skyum-Nielsen, p. 227.
319) SM II, 254. Notice the way our writer has turned Tyge into nothing short of a demon, even if he could not possibly have been present when Tyge read the news that he was summoned to appear in court:
His perceptis, episcopus cepit furere et insanire, ac si prius non insanivisset; fremens ac dentibus stridens venit ad regem querelans, numquam aliquem episcopum talem aut tantam iniuriam perpessum fuisse, qualem ipse ab abbate et monachis de Øm sustinuisset. Item idem episcopus accusavit abbatem specialiter, dicens eum honori regio aput cardinalem legatum derogasse. Unde episcopus regem ad tantam illexit iracundiam..."
32o) SM II, 256.

The Cistercians had made one last attempt to sway the king away from his negative impression of Øm, but this new development nullified their attempt. Still, it is a fascinating letter, for it combines weeping with tough talking, including the threat that if the king did not hold Tyge back from further attacks against the monks, the abbot would continue to pursue their case in the ecclesiastical courts.[321]

But the Duke of Southern Jutland's declaration of concern was all that the king needed to back up Tyge with no questions asked. Tyge let loose with what looks like the worst series of attacks on Øm until now. Erik Abelsen's letter was composed on 22 February, 1267, and after this time Abbot Ture had to flee Øm and hide in the border country, sometimes in Ryd Abbey, sometimes at Løgum.

When the inquiry into Tyge's behaviour met in March, 1267 at Flensburg, the bishop had actually sent a man, but he was rejected as unfit because of accusations that he was a horsethief.[322] As said before, these last events at Øm approach the level of farce. But it is also tragic that our writer seems to have no concept of the ridiculousness of the abbey's position. Ture hides out in Southern Jutland together with Jakob Erlandsen, gives Tyge more ammunition for his propaganda barrages, while our writer speaks of Ture as an exile and the monks almost as martyrs. The summons of Tyge to Slesvig continued but remained unanswered. On 3 August, 1267, Bonde finally excommunicated Tyge. The documents contain the seals of the men most hateful to the royal party, Jakob Erlandsen and Peder, bishop of Roskilde. As Skyum-Nielsen has said, the monks had succeeded in making their dispute with Tyge into a national matter and had drawn themselves into the deadly rivalry between king and archbishop.[323]

Once again it would be wrong with our after-the-fact knowledge to take the monks to task for their stupidity. But I cannot help thinking that the Øm dispute would never have reached its intensity and bitterness if the Cistercians had simply resigned themselves to Tyge's demands for as long as he remained bishop. However sceptical we might be with the paranoid visions of the Øm account, it seems likely that Tyge was out to get the monks from the very beginning. But there were plenty of instances in which, if the monks had acted more diplomatically and had not drawn the issues into such sharp focus,

---

321) See especially the language of the conclusion: "Dignationem igitur vestram fusis lacrimis imploramus" (p. 255) as against "...nos coram iudice nostro ecclesiastico...prosequamur." These are crocodile tears with savage teeth underneath. It is strange that the abbots had not previously written the king, young as he was, but perhaps they had wanted to avoid royal intervention for fear of compromising their independence.
322) SM II, 257.
323) Skyum-Nielsen, p. 224.

they could have tempered the bishop's reaction. One can sympathize up to a certain point with the monks in their desire for independence, but they gradually lost a sense of what was most important to them: their survival as a religious community.

The final chapter of the Øm account provides a moving and terrifying picture of what life was like in the monastery after 1267.[324] Although some of the physical details about the monks' poverty may be exaggerated, the description is unique in the way it deals with monks' mental state. For once we penetrate right into the centre of their lives instead of seeing them through the eyes of outsiders or through the language of documents. To balance this psychological portrait of men in crisis, we would need a Danish Jocelin of Brakelond to tell us about a monastery in a time of calm and about its concerns of daily life. The closest we come to such a description is in the Life of Gunner.[325] But even here we are at a distance from the monks themselves. They provide a backdrop for Gunner when he visited Øm and tried to show the utmost respect for the abbot, or when he invited the monks by twos to the pleasures of his table.

During these days at the end of 1267, it looked as if Øm was going to disappear. The fact that it survived witnesses to the basic solidity of the foundation and the resilience of monastic life in Denmark, even at the end of the thirteenth century. Our writer says that barely half the monastic population remained at Øm during the worst times. "There were few who were not thinking about fleeing". The monks were prisoners in their own house - if they went outside, they were liable to be beaten up. Their labourers had long since left them, and even the lay brothers gave up their calling and often ran off with the monastery's possessions. This must have been all the easier to do with such scattered holdings, by now completely outside of the monks' control.

The king gave the monks until the 3oth of November to give Tyge his procurations. The monks tried to delay, and our writer mentions the abbey's friends, who surprisingly had not even now abandoned the monks. But the monastery was

---

324) SM II, 261-3.
325) The best attempt I have found by a modern writer to recreate the tenor of everyday life at Øm abbey is in H.N. Garner's *Søhøjlandet* (Cpn., 1965), pp. 6o-66, "Cara insula". Garner has a feel for the abbey's history and for the whole region that makes this book an inspiration to any historian who wants to go beyond the written sources and look at the landscape itself, as on p. 63: "Fra øst kom klostrets vogne gående, højt læssede med produkterne fra Djursland. Og peblinge kom fra hele Jylland for at lære latinen og læsningen, skrivningens svære kunst i klosterskolen. Fra værkstederne omkring klostret lød hammerslag og savenes hvin. Møllerne plaskede i klostrets kanaler, og ude fra klosterskovens kuplede tag steg røgen fra kulminer og højovne i vejret."

just living on borrowed time and hoping for a miracle. The last few lines of the Øm account are so graphic in their description of the state to which the monastery was reduced that they deserve to be cited:

> Alas, how often our privileges, our chalices, the ornaments of the church and other special possessions of the monastery we have buried in the ground, so that they not be taken away by force. And how often we have dug them up again, so that they would not be ruined by contact with the soil. It is not easy to account for all the times.
> In the end a final deadline was given to the abbot by the king, who commanded him that he personally appear in his presence. The king sent to him a letter that the abbot could come and go securely. But if he refused to come, the king would do what was his right.[326]

Perhaps the monks were tiresome. Perhaps they had no concept of law or of political facts. But here they are human beings in need and crisis, trapped in their own uncertainty, not knowing what to do. Ultimately the account of the dispute with Tyge becomes a tale not of problems of legal jurisdiction in thirteenth century Denmark but a story of what man does to man in the name of justice. After all the farce and self-deception of the preceding pages, there is something dignified and moving about the fact that the writer stops here and does not go on to tell us what we can almost be sure did happen. The abbot, forced to go to the king to save the house, capitulated to Bishop Tyge, gave him his promise of procurations, and went home a defeated man.

We know that in 1268 Jens of Dover, who already had been abbot in the beginning of the 1260's and then had been prior, became abbot again.[327] Ture apparently felt that his policy had failed, and so the leadership had to be given to someone else. But it was not a new man who took over, for there probably were no bright young men to try their hand. During the rest of the century, retired abbots were frequently recalled to the post, a sign that the monks failed to recruit new talent.[328] The abbot list peters out, and even if there may have been a much fuller description elsewhere, it is significant that the last continuators did not even bother to add dates or lengths of

---

326) SM II, 263. Proh dolor, quam sepe privilegia nostra, calices nostros, ornamenta ecclesie et alia precipua utensilia monasterii in terra occuluimus, ne vi auferrentur, quam sepe ea de terra levavimus, ne humo contecta putrescerent! Non est facile dicendum. Ad ultimum prefixus est abbati terminus finalis ex parte domini regis, mandans ei, ut personaliter se presentaret aspectui suo, mittens ei litteram, ut secure posset venire et redire; quod si venire contempneret, rex faceret, quod suum esset.
327) SM II, 2o3. Ture is said to have been abbot for five years, so he must have retired in 1268. Jens of Dover was "multum morosus atque religiosus".
328) Conrad of Ribe succeeded Jens of Dover. Then came Jens IV of Horsens, who is remembered for administering Øm so that it was "troubled or burdened by few controversies" (p. 2o3) - a sign of a reaction to the troubles in the 1260's and a desire to avoid embroilment in secular affairs. Conrad returned as abbot for seven months, then Jens of Dover for a third time, Jens of Horsens for a second, Oluf II for half a year, Peder Pave from

office. Apparently it no longer was so important to record the history of the abbey, for all the proud memories of the early days had now been blackened by the catastrophe. Continuity and contact with the past were no longer important, only the need to survive. History cannot be written by people who have ceased to believe in its magic and meaning, and so the abrupt ending of the Exordium 2 and the cryptic abbot list indicate not only a disillusionment with life in general but also a disappointment with the usefulness of writing history.

For us with our advantage of perspective, the Øm controversy provides one solid conclusion. There was one power in Denmark that ultimately decided the entire question not only of procurations but also of whether or not a bishop could treat a monastery in such a harsh way. And this was the cluster of people around the king, especially his mother. In 1264 Erik Glipping was about fifteen years old, and after this time he seems to have become directly involved in the controversy. All along, Bishop Tyge was aware of the decisive role the king could play in the matter and so made sure to cultivate royal sympathy. This was probably not difficult, for Tyge was a staunch supporter of the king's party. The monks helped matters along by their total lack of tact, in appealing first to Jakob Erlandsen and then to the international church, and their resulting implicit challenge to royal authority.

In the final analysis, the success or failure of monasticism in Denmark from the twelfth to the sixteenth centuries depended on the royal good will.[329] Local bishops could help or hinder. The international structure of the Cistercian Order could discipline houses and guard rights. And the pope could issue his flocks of bulls. But the Øm dispute shows us what we already have seen for the twelfth century's monastic expansion. When the king was favourable to a monastic house, gave it legal advantages, defended its interests, success was almost guaranteed. But when he turned against a monastery, then no other power in the world could compensate or successfully oppose this power. Power is a dangerous word for medieval historians to use, for power was seldom found in neat little defined packages. It was something that lay dispersed in the various classes and institutions of society and only becomes visible to us in

---

Vitskøl, Jens of Horsens for a third time. There are still many instances of exchanges among Esrum, Vitskøl, and Øm right up to 132o. But there is no instance of any exchange of abbot between Sorø and Øm. This could be because the abbacy of Sorø, by now the richest of the Danish Cistercian houses, was too big a prize for the abbot of humble and humbled Øm.

329) For the importance of the royal power for monasteries in the 15th century, see Niels Skyum-Nielsen, "Ærkekonge og Ærkebiskop - Nye træk i dansk kirkehistorie, 1376-1536", *Scandia*, XXIII (1955-56), H. 1, 1-1ol. Skyum-Nielsen shows in this article how the archbishop of Lund worked together with the king to limit drastically the last vestiges of monastic independence.

the rare moments when behind the facade of documents and declarations we can see a final outcome to a conflict. At Øm we can be almost certain that the result of years of controversy was a defeat for the monks, and this defeat came because royal power backed Bishop Tyge of Århus. The monks themselves perhaps recognized and admitted this reality to themselves, for after Ture went to the king, they wrote no more about their dispute, and thus seem to have given up their fight.

10.

THE AFTERMATH OF THE DISPUTE

A. Øm and its Sisters

The history of the Danish Cistercians in the 1260's will always be dominated by the Øm dispute, but this fact should not keep us from realizing that life went on more or less as usual in the other abbeys. Despite the large number of letters to pope, legates, and king, which expressed solidarity with Øm, the other abbots do not seem to have given up all their other interests in order to concentrate exclusively on saving Øm. Esrum, despite its defeat in the jurisdictional dispute of the 1250's, continued its attempt to gain and maintain influence in the lands south and east of Denmark. In June, 1264, we find Abbot Esbern of Esrum at Greifswald witnessing a document by which Duke Barnum I gave the town the law of Lübeck.[330] The following summer, Barnum followed the advice and assent of the Esrum abbot in taking Greifswald as a fief of the Cistercian abbey at Eldena.[331] It also seems that Esrum did what it could to keep up good relations with the Danish king. In 1265 Erik Glipping took Esrum under his protection.[332] This act itself in other times would tell us little about the royal-monastic relationship, but at the height of the Øm controversy it means that one or both parties were eager to express their devotion to the other. Significantly enough, this declaration of protection was renewed in April, 1268, just after the probable culmination of the Øm controversy.[333]

We do not know of any royal privileges to other Cistercian abbeys during the years of the controversy, but already in 1269 both Vitskøl, Øm's mother, and the borderland abbey Løgum must have declared their loyalty to Erik, for both received from him immunity from all war tax (*leding*), and all other payments to the king.[334] The royal privilege to Vitskøl points out that the mon-

---
330) DD II, 1, 429 - 1264 26 June.
331) DD II, 1, 464 - 1265 26 May.
332) DD II, 1, 488 - 1265 15 July.
333) DD II, 2, 100 - 1268 5 April.
334) DD II, 2, 136 - 1269 2 February (Vitskøl); DD II, 2, 147 - 1269 30 June (Løgum).

astery was founded by Erik's predecessors. In mentioning this fact, the king emphasizes the age and benevolence of his royal line.

These royal privileges indicate that all parties were eager to return to normal times, and even Øm in June 127o received a royal charter confirming its properties in Purup, Vor herred, warning against anyone challenging the monks' holdings.[335] There may have been other royal privileges issued to Øm which have been lost, but this single notation assures us that Øm had managed to return to the royal favour. Or, perhaps more accurately, the royal favour had been imposed on Øm.

By 1267-68 Øm could no longer continue to demand the full attention of the other neighbouring abbeys. A serious problem had arisen at the nearby abbey of Tvis that caught the attention of the Cistercian General Chapter in 1268.[336] According to the report from eight Danish abbots, the monks and lay brothers had revolted against their abbot and had bodily injured him. The Chapter ordered the abbots of Herrisvad and Ryd to go to Tvis, discover what had happened, and if they found that the charges contained in the letter of the Danish abbots were true, to restore the abbot to office and punish severely the conspirators according to the Order's penalties for such behaviour. Already in 1254 the abbots of Sorø and Ås had been charged with trying to depose the abbot of Herrisvad, but this is the first time we hear of a revolt in a Danish Cistercian abbey of monks against their own abbot. In the 124o's a similar event in the Norwegian Cistercian abbey of Hovedö in Oslo fjord had been so violent that the monks had put their abbot on a desert island and left him there to die.[337] Just as we can see from the Exordium 2, life in the thirteenth century could be extraordinarily violent and savage, even in the places where ideals of community and brotherly love were supposed to dominate.

We do not know if there is any relation between the Tvis revolt and the probable settlement of the Øm controversy, but we can at least conclude that at the end of the 126o's the Danish Cistercians were caught up with other matters, while Øm apparently tried to return to a normal existence. One abbey's single overwhelming attempt to establish once and for all its independence from episcopal power had failed miserably. At least until the fifteenth century, we know of no other abbey that got into a similar dispute with its bishop.

---

335) DD II, 2, 154 - 127o 7 June. Originally in the fragment of Øm Kloster Inventarium of 1554 printed in *Suhms Nye Samlinger*, III, 328.
336) Canivez, 1268 nr. 37.
337) Canivez 1243, nr. 43.

B. The Life of Bishop Gunner

Sometime in 1264, or soon after, an Øm monk began to write the Life of Bishop Gunner.[338] I have already mentioned this biography in so many other contexts that there is no reason to give a full review of its contents here. But as pointed out before, the biography tells us a great deal about the attitudes and dreams of the Øm monks in the 1260's, probably after it had become clear to them that they could not win in the dispute with Tyge. It is a natural human reaction in defeat and depression to try to posit some other, better way of life. The author of the Life looked back on what he remembered of Gunner and what others told him and found comfort and nostalgic joy. The Life of Gunner is not any implicit attack against Tyge in order to make clear to him that a good bishop acted quite differently than he did to the Øm community. Nevertheless I still think the biography belongs to the 1260's and not to the 1250's, not only because its mention of the bishop of Børglum would put it after 1264, but also because the tone of sweet memory belongs to the struggles of an institution trying to find inner sources of strength through its traditions.[339]

In the introduction the author says that the purpose of the Life is to provide an example for the monks and those who read it so that they can be brought to "salvation and advancement and honour in life."[340] This is the purpose of any hagiographical work, but as Ellen Jørgensen noticed long ago, the Life of Gunner is more a biography than a hagiography.[341] It has none of the miracles and cures that usually characterize writing about saints. The element of the supernatural is completely missing. Gunner appears as a warm, loving human being, always eager to turn problems into humorous incidents, playing with language, with learning, and with people.

One of our writer's main concerns is to show how attentive Gunner was to the niceties of liturgical observance, even after he became bishop and really did not have time for the tedious monastic hours.[342] Despite inconveniences, he lived more or less in the same way he had as a monk, and our writer care-

---

338) SM II, 265-273.
339) The best piece of evidence for dating in 1264 or after is that Jens is mentioned as bishop of Børglum (269). He was appointed by the pope on 23 July 1264 (DD II, 1, 438). Before that he had been royal chaplain. The papal letter says that the bishopric of Børglum had been vacant for a long time.
340) SM II, 265.
341) *Historieforskningen og Historieskrivningen i Danmark indtil år 1800*, (Cpn., Photographic Reprint, 1960), p. 24.
342) SM II, 267-8.

fully notes the few exceptions Gunner made to this practice. The use of very technical details here shows what we might expect from a Cistercian: a vital interest in the liturgy and an assumption that the readers of the Life will also be fascinated by exactly what observances Gunner kept as bishop. In these descriptions we are able for once to capture the feeling of Danish Cistercians for the practices of their daily lives. We can see how such habits had become an end in themselves, not to be questioned, but to be carried out no matter what. Certainly there is here something of the quibbling with minutiae of which Bernard once had accused the Cluniacs. In this respect as elsewhere in the realm of episcopal jurisdiction, I cannot find the Cistercian way of life as practiced in thirteenth century Denmark to include any special qualities that can distinguish the monks from their Benedictine colleagues.

The illustrations of Gunner's learning, just as those of his concern for the liturgy, provide one of our rare insights into an almost completely obscure side of monastic life in Denmark. [343] Our writer says that Gunner was well educated and clever both in arts and theology and that when smart clerics came back to Denmark after their studies in Paris, he would usually stump them with one of his "horned syllogisms". [344] Our author is very impressed with Gunner's small tricks and perhaps here betrays a monk's jealousy of men privileged by a Paris education and a *Schadenfreude* in their discomfort at not being able to solve Gunner's riddle.

The example given does not speak for the claimed high level of learning in Gunner. Instead it indicates an interest on his part for dilettantish word games. If we remember that Gunner is being seen through someone else's eyes, then we have to qualify the preceding statement and say that Gunner may well have been a learned man but that in this biography our author's own limitations have failed to show him as such. Our author thus does not indicate a very high level of learning at Øm in the 1260's But he is only one of the monks and cannot represent them all.

As another example of Gunner's attitude to studies, our author tells us that Gunner loved to propose questions for disputation and then afterwards would laugh at the opponents and say, "You should have answered in such and such a way. That is the question's solution." If Gunner did respond in this manner, he was much more taken by the sport of the competition than the quest for understanding.

The portrait of Gunner's learning thus lacks depth and could indicate that our author and perhaps Gunner himself were not very interested in the philo-

---

343) SM II, 268-69.
344) See Hans Olrik's explanation of this term in his translation of the Gunner biography, col. 1o, nr. 3.

sophical and theological problems of the day. But even if here we are far from the intellectual concerns of Paris, there is another area of life in which our writer tells us far more than thirteenth century scholastics ever could: in the descriptions of the incidents and humour of everyday life. We see Gunner on festive occasions, trying to make both lay and religious happy and satisfied.[345] There is an atmosphere of almost carefree joy in some of these passages that tells much about Cistercian attitudes. For even if the rule was strict and unyielding, our author treasures the memory of Gunner because he knew how to relax that rule, to consider the feelings of the members of his household, and to make all who came into contact with him feel appreciated and even loved. When he visited the nuns of Asmild or other foundations of noble ladies, he often had trouble in getting away from them.[346] The ladies probably flirted for his attention and hung on every word of his conversation. For Gunner knew how to laugh.

Even when he punished people, he did it with a certain style and charm. We are shown Gunner on a tour of inspection in his diocese, trying to make sure that the linen used in the liturgy was kept clean, and discovering that an unlettered priest named Knud had been using an altar that did not contain a relic stone.[347] Knud offered the bishop a fat ox as compensation for his offence, and Gunner accepted the offer, but also gave the priest a penance. He stuck to the rules and did not allow himself to be bribed, but he still did not seem to mind the gift of a fine ox.

There are so many superbly drawn details in this short biography that one emerges from reading it with a feeling of relief. Here at last is something substantial about life in Denmark in the thirteenth century. For once all the information is on the surface and not deeply submerged and requiring careful excavation by historians. We can see Gunner's talent for smoothing over what could easily become an unpleasant incident when Archbishop Uffe in visiting him at Viborg insisted that the bishop take precedence to him in passing through a doorway.[348] Gunner refused, but then Uffe gave him a long list of reasons for doing so. Finally Gunner, who apparently loved nothing better than such erudite teasing, agreed to do what Uffe wanted. The word used to describe Gunner's attitude in this situation, *hilariter*, ways a great deal about him. Life was to be lived with humour and joy.

But also with justice. If peasants came with their requests, Gunner could joke with his people, "Oh no, here comes trouble", but then he would treat

---

345) SM II, 27o-72.
346) SM II, 273.
347) SM II, 271.
348) SM II, 274.

them well.[349] Gunner represents the confidence, flexibility, and hilarity of an age and a group of men that firmly believed in themselves and their place in society. In reflecting back upon these times and these men, our author reminded himself and his fellow monks that the ideal life could also be a happy one.

During the thirteenth century the writing of biographies was not nearly as popular as it had been in the twelfth. The *Magna Vita* of Bishop Hugh of Lincoln was the last major contribution to this genre of which I know, and we really have only one other contemporary biography with which to compare the Life of Gunner: The Little Flowers of Saint Francis.[350] This is a work whose composition is full of disputes and is a much more politically oriented work than Gunner's Life. Even so, we can at least see from a brief comparison of the two works that the Øm monks are interested in portraying an earthy, practical, affectionate man, while the Franciscans set out to capture the ethereal, soft gentleness and nature mysticism of a genius. Gunner as shown in his biography is much more easily believable to us today than Francis, and thus the latter is much more exciting.

But the very lack of ambition and relatively relaxed tone of the narrative about Gunner enables us to use the account as a help in studying attitudes and conditions at Øm. Our monks looked back with some longing at a better, more generous age, when they could feel protected and appreciated. There is thus a definite relationship between Gunner as seen in his Life and Sven as seen in the Exordium 1. In both cases the monks, by telling us about someone outside their monastery who was decisively important to them, reveal their deepest hopes and dreams. It is no accident that the making and the unmaking of Øm came through the interaction of strong bishops with the monks.

Gunner's Life would probably not have been written if he had remained abbot of Øm. If this had been the case, his personality would have been known to us only through a few lines in the abbot list about his trials and efforts for the sake of the monks. In becoming bishop, he enabled an Øm writer to externalize the monks' interior life by writing about him. So we see men in whose lives tiny details like the form of prayers had immense symbolic importance, but who also valued a witty remark or a kind act so much that it was remembered and recorded years later.

349) SM II, 275: "Bella mihi, video". The remark is a fragment of Ovid's "Bella mihi, video, bella parantur". (Remedia amoris, v. 2) In such a case of classical citation, there is something distinctly twelfth century humanistic about Gunner, and such a man typifies what I consider the archaic quality of thirteenth century culture in Denmark, still caught up in the styles and pursuits that Central Europe had left behind years before.
350) Trans. and introduced by Serge Hughes (Mentor-Omega, New York, 1964).

C. The Tradition of Biography at Øm

It might be worthwhile to look more closely upon the models for biography that our Øm author could have drawn on. As the Life of Gunner itself shows us, Øm and the Danish Cistercians by no means lived in an intellectual vacuum but were influenced in various ways by outside currents of thought. Naturally the most common form of biography that could have given an impulse is hagiography, a genre that was well developed in Denmark by the mid-thirteenth century. Øm's "grandmother" abbey, Esrum, had a near neighbour, Æbelholt, which could lay claim to the greatest saint of the period, the Abbot William, who was already canonized within a few decades of his death in 12o3.[351] William was a reformer on a grand scale, and the Life tells us how he got into trouble with his fellow canons at St. Victor in Paris when he insisted on a strict way of life. He is thus the kind of man who could have appealed to the Danish Cistercians, with their ascetic legacy from Bernard. And yet this Life belongs more to the European tradition of hagiography than to the anecdotal style of biography with a human face that we have discovered in Gunner's Life. Danish historians have long expressed their displeasure that there is so little in William's Life that can tell us anything definite about him as a person or about Æbelholt Abbey.[352] The emphasis is on miracles, signs, prophecies, and we have such an abundance of them that William already before his death is collecting teeth removed from his mouth and telling one of the Æbelholt brothers, "Keep these teeth with you and be careful not to lose them!"[353] It may well be that William was convinced of his own holiness and considered himself already a living reliquary, but it is much more likely that the Æbelholt monks are remembering William in such a way because it was necessary for them to integrate his life with the common, stylized life of every saint of the Church.

Hagiography thus means stylization and generalization, while in the biography we look for near-realism and local colour, the process of individualization that is so closely linked with the cultural developments of the twelfth century.[354] If we look at ways of describing holy men in the Cistercian Order

---

351) Sancti Willelmi Abbatis Vita et Miracula, *Vitae Sanctorum Danorum*, M.Cl. Gertz (Cpn., 19o8-12), pp. 3oo-369.
352) *Danske Helgeners Levned*, trans. by H. Olrik. Selskabet til historiske kilders oversættelse (Cpn., 1968 reprint) II, 171. See also remarks in Tue Gad, *Legenden i dansk middelalder* (Cpn., 1961), pp. 173-77.
353) *Vitae Sanctorum Danorum*, p. 344: "Habe custodiam horum dentium penes te et noli illos amittere."
354) Colin Morris's *The Discovery of the Individual 1050-1200* (Harper Torch, New York, 1973) provides the best survey of currents of thought and life that led to this change.

itself, we can find in many instances a continuation of the hagiographical traditions. The Life of the Blessed David, monk of Himmerod in Eifel near Trier provides a typical example.[355] Himmerod was founded in 1134 by the Bishop of Trier and soon became one of Clairvaux's most prominent daugters. Its location made it a potential stopping place for Danish Cistercians on their way to the General Chapter. David's Life starts out with a prologue lifted word for word from another, earlier hagiography.[356] We learn little or nothing about his personal habits: he is holy in a purely conventional sense. His nights were spent in ceaseless prayer; his days in constant labour. But so were every other saints' from Martin of Tours onwards.[357] The pattern was set, and the only valuable individual details concern David's initial noviciate at Clairvaux and the founding of Himmerod. We are told that David suffered from his youth from some disease that almost prevented him from becoming a monk until St. Bernard was won over to him. As far as his life at Himmerod is concerned, the only personal anecdote is that when he came to table he would not realize he was supposed to eat but would begin praying. Another brother would have to remind him of his duty to eat. But again, this could easily be an anecdote lifted out of an earlier Life. From chapters five to thirty-one we are told only of his miracles, starting with his casting out of devils and finishing with visions and a miracle performed after his death. As a man David is totally passive, an instrument of divine power and invisible to us as a person. As a saint David is a superman, lifted beyond and above the human level and capable of almost anything.

David died in 1179, and this Life was probably composed soon after, or at the latest around 1204 when his bones were translated form the chapter room to the church in Himmerod.[358] The author of the Life was not a Cistercian but a monk from the Benedictine house of St. Eucharius at Trier. This house had a close relationship with Himmerod from its very beginning, and it is perhaps a sign of the times that there could be such cooperation between the rival orders and also that the Cistercians would have the writing of a hagiography handed over to the Benedictines. Because of the well-developed tradition behind him, the Benedictine author could merely borrow from earlier models and add a few essential Cistercian details.

---
355) "Vita B. David Monachi Hemmenrodensis", *Analecta Sacri Ordinis Cisterciensis*, XI, 1955, 27-48, commented by Ambrosius Schneider. See also C. Wilkes, *Die Zistercienserabtei Himmerode im 12. u. 13. Jahrhundert. Beiträge zur Geschichte des altens Mönchtums und des Benediktinerordens*. Heft 12 (Münster i. W., 1924).
356) *Vita David*, p. 32.
357) See the Life of Martin of Tours by Sulpicius Severus, ch. 36 - trans. by F.R. Hoare in *The Western Fathers* (Harper Torch, New York, 1965).
358) *Vita David*, p. 31.

The Life of Gunner can thus be traced neither to a typical hagiography of a Danish saint, nor to a twelfth century German Cistercian-Benedictine example. If we turn to England, which supplies early abbots at Sorø and Esrum, we have a lively tradition for biography in English Cistercian abbeys. The Life of Ailred of Rievaulx by Walter Daniel is the first work that comes to mind, but its basic purpose of defending the memory of Ailred against criticism from the Order immediately distinguishes it from the calm, almost placid Life of Gunner.[359] There is an undercurrent of polemic in Walter Daniel that reminds us more of Bernard's own writings than of anything we can find in Gunner's Life.

Another, lesser known possibility is the short Life of Gervase of Louth Park.[360] Here, as with Walter Daniel and our Øm writer, we have a monk who remembers his abbot with love and devotion. But any careful description of Gervase's personality traits is absent. We know only that the monk who wrote the short biography was tremendously devoted to him. The author is not interested in listing a string of miracles. Nor is he concerned with giving us individualized anecdotes. His sketch, which is called a "lamentatio", is meant basically to console the other brothers on the loss of their beloved abbot.[361]

Here we stumble on a dimension in Cistercian writing that belongs to the twelfth century and is disappearing in the thirteenth: an emphasis on open and almost unrestrained emotion. Our writer makes little attempt to contain his sorrow on the death of Gervase. He is so caught up by the abbot's death that he feels the whole community is in danger of dissolution now that the abbot is gone. Sometimes the author addresses Gervase himself, sometimes the other monks, and sometimes "sweet Jesus". Our parents left us, he tells Gervase, but you took us on.

> I lost someone like you, and when will I find someone similar? Now a fear which I have felt has come over me, and what I feared has come about. Why do I pretend? Why remain silent? Let the tears burst forth, let the sighs come out from the innermost heart....[362]

---

359) *The Life of Ailred of Rievaulx* by Walter Daniel, trans. by F.M. Powicke, Nelson Medieval Classics (Edinburgh 1950), LXV-LXVI. "Ailred found enemies in monastic circles as he had found them at King David's court, and Walter Daniel's Life was written in part as a passionate refutation of the suggestions that he was ambitious, a wirepuller, fond of luxurious living, a successful prig who in his time had been no better than he should have been."
360) C.H. Talbot, "The Testament of Gervase of Louth Park", *Analecta sacri Ordinis Cisterciensis* 7, 1951, pp. 32-45.
361) The text ends with the words, "Explicit cuiusdam condolentis amici lamentatio de morte Gervasii abbatis de Parcho Lude" (p. 44), while it opens with the words, "De Vita et virtutibus eiusdem et de morte ipsius" (39).
362) *Ibid.*, p. 44: Te talem ac tantum perdidi et quando tibi similem recupe-

The language borders at time on hysteria. Immediately we catch the difference between the way a twelfth century English brother could regret the death of an abbot and the way a thirteenth century Danish brother could do so. The biography of Gunner celebrates him more than it laments him. He had been dead for many years when it was written, and even if his biographer probably had known him personally there is always a distance between subject and writer. The fact that Gunner was known and described as a bishop, not as an abbot, helps to create that distance, but at the same time the entire drive for intimacy so emphasized in our English source is missing here. The author of the Lamentation pointed out that he had been specially chosen to be the friend of Gervase among all the monks, and instead of creating problems of jealousy from other monks, this relationship seems only to have given the monk the necessary qualification to represent the community in writing about Gervase. Assumed here is the twelfth century idea of friendship in all its facets, something that there is no room for in our thirteenth century Life.

Another theme that is prominent in Gervase's Life and lacking in Gunner's is the Bernardine separation of the material from the spiritual in the attempt to rid one's life of all that is not concerned with community life, prayer, and meditation. Gervase himself complains in a statement contained in the same manuscript as the biography that he had been weighed down by secular cares.[363] They had distracted him, and now he regrets all the time he had to spend eating with guests in the hospice while the brothers were fasting in the refectory. For a moment we capture a sense of a pure Cistercian spirituality, yearning for the eternal and being constantly frustrated by everything else.

This consciousness of a split world is something that our biographer of Abbot Gunner has no room for. Gunner is capable of everything, whether it is the maintenance of the Cistercian rule in his everyday life, entertaining friends, or visiting his parish priests. The Øm monk's account gives the impression of a harmony and balance in his existence. For a moment we can see how well the Danish Cistercians could adjust to prevailing political and social conditions instead of harping on the clear contradiction between daily duties and the original reform and other-worldly impulse of the Order. As

    rabo? Ecce timor quem timebam evenit michi, et quod verebar accidit. Quid dissimulo? Cur sileo? Erumpite lacrime, procedant ex intimis cordis suspiria...

363) The Testament, p. 28: Recordare miser homo, recordare et noli oblivioni tradere quantas occupationes habuisti, quanta tedia sustinuisti multociens de secularibus....
    p. 39: Memorare nunc, debilis et pusillanimis homuncio, quam tociens conscientia tua pavebat, cum tu pluribus escis inhiabas in hospitio et monachi fratres inediam paciebantur in refectorio?

we have seen in the abbot list, the original twelfth century emphasis on spiritual abbots is replaced in the thirteenth century by applause for leaders who could cope with the business of the world. But this does not mean that such men were only worldly creatures. To borrow from the language of the nineteenth century American medievalist, Henry Adams, Gunner's biography provides us with a case of thirteenth century unity when for a moment the oppositions between ends and means, material and spiritual, unity and diversity - all of these cease to exist.

The open and nearly violent emotions of the twelfth century English monks thus make a fine contrast with the calm and almost jocular musings of our thirteenth century Danish writer. But we are as distant as ever from seeing the Life of Gunner in the context of a European tradition of biography. A final possibility can be quickly eliminated, tempting as it might be: the secular tradition. If we take Einhard's Life of Charlemagne, for example, we can see the continuation of Suetonius's personality portraits using physical descriptions, political accounts, and intimate details of private life. There is no reason why the Danish Cistercians would have been ignorant of such a popular work. But if we look at the training the most promising monks received at Paris in the thirteenth century, with its heavy emphasis on theology or law,[364] then it is hard to find any openness to such a type of writing. The library of the Øm monks at the Reformation was hardly overstocked with such secular books,[365] and even if we find some historical writers who at times dealt with personalities, there is nothing that points to any interest in classical biographies.

In order to determine the type of model that might have influenced our Øm writer, we can get some help from the first part of the Older Zealand Chronicle.[366] It has long been thought that the section dealing with events down to 1251 had a Cistercian author, and in 1922 M. Cl. Gertz wrote in his introduction to this chronicle that its composer had used the *Exordium Magnum* of the Cistercians, the *Vita Prima* of St. Bernard, the miracles of Thomas of

---

364) The study of canon law was theoretically forbidden to Cistercians in the thirteenth century, but there were probably many exceptions, as Abbot Gunner himself. "Les Cisterciens et l'Etude du Droit", P. Colomban Bock, *Analecta Sacri Ordinis Cisterciensis* 7, 1951, 14-2o.
365) Suhm, *Nye Samlinger til den Danske Historie* III (1794), pp. 317-24 lists the books in the monks' library according to a 1554 inventory. The historical books at Øm are almost exclusively ecclesiastical: Peter Comestor's *Scholastica historia*, Adam of Bremen's *Gesta Pontificum Bremensium*, *Historia Josephi*, and Josephus *De bell. Judeorum*. As for saints' lives, the monks were much better equipped, with the lives of Bernard, Clement, Mary Magdalen, Martha, Lazarus, Lives of the Fathers, of martyrs, and the Golden Legend of Jacob of Voragine.
366) SM II, 2o-72.

Canterbury by Benedict of Peterborough, the Acts of Thomas the apostle, the Life of Martin of Tours by Sulpicius Severus, together with Jordanus's Life of St. Dominic and Thomas of Celano's Life of Francis.[367] This chronicle was written by a Cistercian living on Zealand, and most probably by one from Sorø, for there is much information about the descendants of Skjalm Hvide, who were so important in the endowment of this monastery. Sorø and Øm can hardly be said to have had an intimate relationship, for they were different from each other and had different mother abbeys. Even so, they were both descendants of Clairvaux in the Esrum line, and it would have been natural for the Øm abbot to stop at Sorø on the way to Esrum. The first abbot of Øm, Brienne, had died at Sorø after giving up office.[368] Thus there were contacts, and so it is likely that the books being read and used in the first half of the thirteenth century that went into the making of the Sorø part of the Older Zealand Chronicle were also known to the Øm monks.

This is especially the case with the passages from the Exordium Magnum that tell of the early days of the Cistercians in Scandinavia and the life of Archbishop Eskil.[369] As already pointed out, Eskil made a deep impression on a number of Clairvaux monks, and the Exordium Magnum contains the story of a dream he had as a little boy in which the Virgin appeared to him and made him promise to serve her. The compiler of the Older Zealand Chronicle was content to lift this story almost word for word from the Exordium Magnum, for the account responds to a Danish Cistercian interest in linking the Order's early days with the personality of Eskil. It is thus here, in twelfth century Cistercian literature from Clairvaux, that we have the best chance of uncovering the tradition that could have influenced our Øm writer.

The Exordium Magnum account of Eskil is based itself on two main sources, the *Liber Miraculorum* by Herbert of Clairvaux,[370] and the third book of the Vita Prima of Saint Bernard, by Godfred.[371] Both these monks had direct contacts with Eskil. We have a copy of a letter that Godfred sent to him after Bernard's death.[372] Herbert tells us twice in the course of the *Liber Miracu-*

---

367) SM II, 7.
368) Øm Abbot List, SM II, 192, 195.
369) SM II, 48-52.
370) A shorter version of the *Liber Miraculorum* is contained in *Patrologia Latina* (PL) 185, 1274 ff., but it does not include the section on Eskil. Fortunately Lauritz Weibull printed the text of another manuscript that does include this narration: "En samtida berättelse från Clairvaux om ärkebiskop Eskil av Lund", *Scandia* IV, 1931, 27o-29o. Weibull dates the writing of the *Liber* to between 1178 and 118o - just at the time when Eskil was a monk at Clairvaux.
371) For the difficult problem of the composition of the *Vita Prima*, "Etudes sur la Vita Prima de Saint Bernard", Adriaan Hendrik Bredero, *Analecta Cisterciensia* 17, 1961 and 18, 1962.
372) DD I, 2, 114 - written soon after Bernard's death on 2o August, 1153.

lorum that he has written down stories as he heard them from Eskil himself.[373] Herbert is interested in actions, not in personality. He emphasizes the sensational and the unusual. We have first of all the famous vision Eskil had as a boy in Saxony that foresaw his work for the Cistercians. Then he is archbishop of Lund building his monasteries. He is celebrated for his conversion of the pagans. The power of his excommunications is illustrated by two stories about how recalcitrant sinners were found dead, strangled by devils. There follows the story of how Eskil in celebrating mass at Ribe discovered that the host had divided up into five sections, a sign of the schism that was to come in which Bishop Elias of Ribe would side with King Valdemar and the Emperor Frederick against Eskil and the legitimate pope Alexander. This leads Herbert into a description of Elias's terrible death, before which he cursed his sons as "evil sons of whores" for wanting his money. His body was found cast up on a beam, and it was clear to everyone that a demon had suffocated him and then lodged him up there. Finally we have a milder story of how Eskil had a brother who had offended him and died without confession. One time this brother appeared to him at Clairvaux while Eskil was praying in the oratory. Eskil could see only the upper part of his body, for the rest was consumed by fire. On the next day in coming into the monks' chapter, he begged their prayers and masses for the dead man.

This string of stories is consistent with the usual fare in the *Liber Miraculorum*. Herbert was interested in the marvellous and so was glad to add Eskil's accounts to his work. The result is neither biography nor hagiography, for there is no interest in depicting the person behind the stories. If we turn to the Exordium Magnum, however, we can quickly see how these lurid stories had been integrated into a new context, the story of the best-known brothers of the Cistercian Order until about 1180. The Exordium Magnum cuts away one of the two accounts of deaths after Eskil's excommunication and uses the remaining one only in order to emphasize Eskil as the just and righteous man.[374] Similarly the vision of the dead brother is taken up only after a long introduction about how Eskil came to Clairvaux at the end of his life and spent his days in constant prayer.[375] The individual incident is given less prominence than the point that Eskil was a devout man. The only section of Herbert's *Liber* that is incorporated word for word into the Exordium is the account of Eskil's boyhood vision.[376] This is done apparently because the story appeals to the Cistercian passion for showing how the spread of the Order was ordained

---

373) Weibull, "En samtida berättelse...", pp. 283, 289.
374) PL 185, 1087.
375) PL 185, 1088.
376) PL 185, 1085-1086.

by God with men such as Eskil as his instruments. Likewise, the Exordium points to Eskil's conversion of pagans to Christendom, but instead of making the *Liber*'s extravagant claims about Eskil bringing Saxony, Sweden, Norway, Denmark, and the Slavic lands to Christendom, the Exordium Magnum limits itself to claiming for Eskil the foundation of two Cistercian houses in Denmark, one of the Citeaux line, the other from Clairvaux.[377]

This careful and sober attention to detail is also something to be found in the Life of Gunner. The one great difference is that the Exordium Magnum integrates some of the miracle accounts from earlier sources, while the thirteenth century Life is devoid of miracles. Thus the Exordium Magnum uses the Vita Prima's story that when Eskil was to return to Denmark soon before Bernard's death in 1153, the saint blessed some bread for him that remained fresh three years later.[378] This miracle is integrated almost word for word into the Exordium Magnum, but this time not so much to illustrate Bernard's powers but to show the link between Eskil and Bernard and thus delineate the spread of the Order.

If we look at the Vita Prima of Bernard, the Liber Miraculorum, and the Exordium Magnum individually, we have to admit that none of them could have been a direct prototype for the Life of Gunner. Bernard's Life is one more instance of hagiography (even though in different forms because of different authors), with a liberal dose of miracles and the same frustrating problem as noted with the Life of William of Æbelholt for us to break through the tales and extract some historical reality. The Liber Miraculorum, besides being a source whose presence we cannot determine among the Danish Cistercians, is nothing more than a naive collection of fantastic and often gruesome tales in which any interest in personality is totally submerged to the search for the sensational. The Exordium Magnum is more a history of the early years of the Order and an apology for its purposes than a series of biographical sketches. In the back of the mind of Conrad of Eberbach, the probable writer, looms the threat of the Benedictines, the Cistercian claims to spirituality, and the scandal surrounding the origins of the Order in its split from a Benedictine house.[379] Despite the immense activity of Bernard, the Cistercian Order still had to defend itself, and in the context of such a polemic, influential men like Eskil, who so totally adopted the Cistercian piety in ending their lives as simple monks, were much in demand.

Any description of a person is bound to manipulate him, but the important

---

377) Weibull, p. 279; PL 185, 1086-87.
378) Exordium Magnum, PL 185, 1087. Vita Prima, PL 185, 335. The episode of the bread also enables us to date the Vita Prima to 1156.
379) SM II, 428.

point with these twelfth century Clairvaux writings is that they were not primarily concerned with biography. Nevertheless, there are elements present that easily could have influenced our Øm writer. Because the Cistercians were interested in describing living people and seeing their historical contribution to the legitimization of their Order, it was not good enough to continue along the same hagiographical lines as the Benedictines had followed and to write merely for edification. The adaptation of the Eskil stories from Herbert's pen to Conrad's points to a need for an integrated, rationalized sketch of a person in which the sensational is sacrificed for the historical. Conrad was willing to prune away some of the episodes with the devil so that he would not distract from the portrait of Eskil the founder and Eskil the monk. Miracles were no longer sufficient. It was necessary to establish a certain tradition, to point out exactly which abbeys Eskil founded and find out what kind of monk he had been at Clairvaux. The result is a concentration on time, place, and circumstance that far from eliminating all the lively details of the Liber Miraculorum instead gives them a coherence contributing to a finished protrait of one person important to the Cistercian Order.

It is this type of writing at Clairvaux that may have provided an inspiration for our Øm writer, for it could assure him that it was acceptable to give concrete and lively anecdotes in describing men who had been important for the Order. Local colour and individualized details become not only legitimate but also necessary in establishing monastic history. Our Øm author may well have been influenced by traditional hagiographies, just as the composer of the first part of the Older Zealand Chronicle had been. But the Life of Gunner's freshness of approach and concentration on everyday details belong to the Clairvaux tradition.

Nevertheless the Exordium Magnum can only go part of the way in explaining the appearance of this unique account in thirteenth century Denmark. Almost all twelfth century Cistercian literature lacks the humour and delight in human weakness that we find so unforgettably expressed in the Øm story of how the abbot spoiled Bishop Gunner's system for keeping track of the amount he drank. To explain the appearance of such an episode, we are given some help by the Exordium 1 from Øm itself, for its sketch of Bishop Sven of Århus does manifest something of this same pleasure in small and funny details.

Perhaps the most memorable anecdote is the one about the bishop's men trying to cheer him up by telling him they thought they could see a Cistercian monk approaching. The author of the Exordium 1 obviously included this story because it illustrated Sven's devotion to the monks and the joy they gave him. But at the same time there is a note of wistfulness here, just the suggestion

of a smile in the picture created of the naive and hopeful Sven.[380] Although
the description of Sven is much briefer and more stylized than that of Gunner,
the former shows the same use of minor anecdotes as proof of concern for the
monks that we find in the Life of Gunner. The humour in the Exordium 1 may
only be embryonic, but the sense of delight in the great protector and donor
is certainly well developed. Our Øm monks at least had a precedent in their
own writings for describing the character of a man who was important for their
survival and prosperity.

In the final analysis, textual comparisons are inadequate as complete explanations for the genesis of the Life of Gunner. Its author is no genius
in his knowledge of men; nor is he a historian who would live up to many of
today's demands. He is merely a monk who is writing down what is remembered
of Gunner in his monastery. But perhaps precisely because his approach is
so unsophisticated, so unconscious of models and precedents, so uninvolved
with proving anything through the intervention of the supernatural, the Life
of Gunner can be ranked among the best medieval biographies we have.

As indicated before, the immediate historical background for the 1260's
at Øm probably provides the best explanation for the appearance of such a
biography. In the aftermath of the dispute with the bishops of Århus, polemic
or self-justification is no longer useful. They had been tried and found
wanting. The monks are interested only in reminiscing about a better time and
a better bishop. The Life of Gunner can be seen as the result of a combination
of factors: Gunner's attractive and mild personality; the monks' aversion to
further disputes; their yearning for a more harmonious past; and the presence
of a monk at Øm who had a talent for writing. From the twelfth century Clairvaux tradition he could draw on a passion for anecdotes with local colour to
illustrate spiritual or personal facts. But our Øm monk did not need to include the supernatural side of these accounts. He may have left out this
dimension because he preferred to present Gunner through his everyday life.
But the very fact that our author emphasized the banal at the expense of the
marvellous points to an acceptance of the conditions and possibilities of
the material universe.

This process is generally called secularization, but this empty word has
to be qualified in a non-twentieth century sense. At Øm abbey in the thirteenth
century secularization means the hallowing of the material so that it replaces
the need for the supernatural. In other words, the bishop's treatment of the
Asmild nuns or his diocesan visitations are sufficient for our author to illustrate his goodness and saintliness as a man. It is now in the context of daily

---

380) SM II, 187.

life - instead of miracles - that the Cistercian ethic can be found. The heroic age of the Order, with its bishops like Eskil and Sven, is over. Spirituality has become so integrated in the routine of life that it can be almost unself-conscious. I cannot help comparing this naive consciousness with the mentality reflected in high gothic sculpture, with its near-realistic qualities that still on closer inspection betray stylized forms. There is a delicate balance in such art between the attempt to imitate life and the attempt to elevate individual things to generalized spiritual forms. At its best, such art convinces the viewer and manages to combine a faithful realism with genuine spiritual qualities. I think for example of the statues on the north portal of Chartres cathedral from c. 122o: here are saints that could easily come to life but still would be saints and not ordinary men.

The trouble with such balance and completeness is that it depends on ideal conditions in society: economic backing, devout churchmen, and popular support. At Øm the primary danger was that later bishops would lack the easy acquaintance with and acceptance of the Cistercian background that their predecessors had taken for granted. Peder Ugotsen and Tyge came to challenge the fundamental economic and legal assumptions that made this harmony possible. And so at the very time when one Øm monk was celebrating a bishop who had integrated all levels of existence for the monastery, the abbey was emerging from the earthquake of another bishop who had obliterated all hope for any continuation of such a complete way of life.

It must have been a genuine consolation for the monks to be able to read about Gunner and the good old days, for the scraps of evidence we have about Øm after 1268 point to a community that was standing still. From 127o to 13oo we have records of only two property transactions, and one of them is merely a confirmation of a 1264 deed.[381] The other, in 1287, could be a donation, but it stands alone as the only known property gain for the monks in these years. Otherwise we are limited to the information that in 1284 Bishop Tyge's successor, ironically also called Tyge, remitted forty days of punishment from all those who helped in the building of a stone church.[382] This privilege was issued at Øm and shows that the Århus bishop was once more residing some of the time at the monastery.

---

381) *De ældste danske Archivregistraturer* I (ÆA) A2o - 1293; T47 - 1287.
382) DD II, 3, 122.

11.

THE FOURTEENTH CENTURY:
ECONOMICAL REVIVAL AND DECLINE

After 13oo Øm begins to get back on its feet, at least in terms of property holdings. The Skanderborg Register and the fragment of the Øm catalogue that survived both contain a number of entries from these years. Especially from 131o to 1346 the monks seem to have been adding to their holdings according to a definite pattern. First they tried to expand their properties around Skæring, and also immediately to the northwest of this area, in Trige, apparently so they could solidify and broaden their halfway holdings on the road to Djursland.[383] The disputes with Tyge had probably taught them better than ever that they needed to have well defined areas of their own at regular intervals between Øm and Djursland if there was ever going to be a chance to hold onto the distant estates. In 1317 and after, we also find the monks trying to enlarge their holdings in the area immediately to the northeast of the abbey, in Dover and Illerup parishes.[384] The monks had never gained an overwhelming share of the land here in earlier years, and there were probably many possibilities for expansion.

During these same years the abbot of Øm pops up occasionally in various documents, indicating that he had begun again to involve himself in affairs other than the immediate ones of the house. In 1311 the Øm abbot, Oluf a canon in Århus, and the prior of Ring abbey, together with the citizens of Horsens witnessed a letter issued in 13o2 by Junker Kristoffer and others, concerning the title of a farm in Horsens.[385] We know from the account of the dispute with Tyge that Øm had properties near Horsens,[386] and can thus see here a continuing involvement with the area. A papal letter from 1312 calling upon Bishop Kristian of Ribe and the abbots of Løgum and Øm to be guardians and judges for Archbishop Esger of Lund, in order to protect his properties, may or may not indicate that Øm again had become strong enough for its abbot to take on such a duty.[387] Added to our other shreds of evidence, the papal

---

383) DD II, 5, 224 - Trige, 13o2; DD II, 6, 322 - Skæring, 131o.
384) DD II, 7, 529 - 1317; DD II, 8, 79 and DD II, 8, 8o - 1318.
385) DD II, 6, 337.
386) SM II, 196.
387) DD II, 6, 415.

letter points to the same increase in confidence that we can see when the monks begin in the 1330's to acquire lands outside the Dover or Skæring area, as in 1333 when they took on Skovsrod in Tulstrup parish north of Dover.[388] In 1341 the monks got a property in Flensted in Låsby parish, the next one to the north after Tylstrup.[389] If we looked at these acquisitions on a map and drew arrows from Øm out to the new holdings, then by the 1340's the arrows would be getting longer and longer. One of the last additions during this period of expansion came in 1346 when the monks obtained a mortgage on a farm in Snede parish, Nørvang herred, which is halfway between Horsens and Vejle.[390] This is the furthest yet we have come from the Skanderborg area, and the almost reckless self-confidence in getting distant possessions that we noticed in the twelfth century seems to be returning.

But it did not last. The Black Death, the invasion of the Holsteiners, and the resulting social chaos apparently put the brakes on expansion. From 1348 to 1356 I can find no additions to Øm's holdings at all, and even if there is some revival in the 1360's, there no longer seems to be any definite plan for deliberate expansion into selected areas. The monks got what they could, whether it was in Vor herred south of Mossø, in Veng parish to the northeast, or in the Skæring area. The rest of the century brought a modest number of new acquisitions, as can be seen from Poul Rasmussen's figures and graph.[391] But the clear growth pattern of 1310 to 1346 did not recur.

One of the factors that kept the monks from really recovering from the catastrophes of the preceding century may have been the attitude of the Århus bishops. We have no direct evidence of how they treated Øm, and it may be accidental that it is not until 1376, more than a hundred years after the ending of the Tyge dispute, before we hear of an Århus bishop making any gesture indicating cooperation with Øm. In that year Bishop Olav made known in a charter recorded in the Skanderborg Register that Niels Godsen and his wife had deeded to Abbot Hans in Øm all their property rights in Hårby mark, Veng parish.[392] Øm's apparent isolation from the Århus bishops - or what looks like isolation to us with our lack of sources for these decades - could easily have been compensated for by royal interest in the foundation. But unlike Vitskøl or the Zealand abbeys, Øm had no royal roots, and the only medieval royal charters listed in the Skanderborg Book are exlusively from the very last period of the monastery's existence. What a contrast with Esrum, whose *Codex* contains royal privileges from every period of Denmark's medieval era.

---

388) DD II, 11, 99.
389) DD III, 1. 167.
390) DD III, 2, 309.
391) Poul Rasmussen, pp. 146-49.
392) Sk. Reg. L16 - ÆA I, 232.

We do fortunately have one document from the end of the fourteenth century that may tell us something definite about Øm's condition. In 1395 the pope appointed the bishops in Ribe, Odense, and Viborg as guardians of Øm for five years.[393] The text here is of a standardized kind and so does not tell us anything about Øm individually, but the implication is that in some way or other Øm has been under attack and needed special protection. A few days later the same type of bull was issued in appointing the abbot in Essenbæk, the provost in Lübeck and the dean in Roskilde as guardians for Ring Benedictine convent on Skanderborg Lake.[394] It may be only a coincidence that the two houses, so geographically close to each other, both were given guardians at the same time, but it could also indicate that the monastic foundations in the Skanderborg area were either under attack or in decline.

As we leave Øm at the end of the century, we find at least one hopeful sign: a renewed involvement with properties in Djursland and dealings with the townspeople in Grenå.[395] At the same time as Sorø began on a much larger scale to buy and sell properties in the towns of Zealand, and even as far away as Malmø in Skåne,[396] the Øm monks began to come to terms with the existence of a town in Djursland. We know so little through the brief notations in Skanderborg Register that it is dangerous to draw conclusions, but it is still possible to observe a marked flexibility in the way monasteries adapted themselves to changing social conditions. The archetypally rural Cistercian monasteries were beginning to accept not only the fact of towns but also the necessity of having good relations with them.

---

393) Alfr. Krarup and Johs. Lindbæk, *Acta Pontificum Danica* II (Cpn., 19o7), nr. 856.
394) *Acta Pontificum Danica*, II nr. 858.
395) ÆA I, 223 - Sk. Reg. H8o, H81. ÆA I, 225 - Sk. Reg. H91 (1397); I, 226 - H 98.
396) The last section of the Sorø Donation Book is entirely given over to transactions with town properties, SRD IV 522-3o.

12.

THE REFORMATION BOOK LIST AT ØM: CULTURAL REVIVAL

To get an absolutely complete picture of Øm's history, using all the sources we have, it would be necessary to deal with the notations of the Skanderborg Register for the fifteenth and sixteenth centuries. Poul Rasmussen has already given us a general idea of what they contain: a decided increase in acquisitions around 14oo, followed by a sharp decline, and then a modest increase after 145o, and finally a falling off up to the time of the dissolution.[397] The history of Øm's possessions thus follows more or less the pattern of other Danish Cistercian abbeys: a heady period of expansion in the twelfth century, followed by thirteenth century consolidation at a slower pace, crises and revivals in the thirteenth and fourteenth centuries, and a decline during the years around the coming of the Danish Reformation.

If we turn from the property records to the one other substantial source for the later history of Øm, the 1554 inventory, we find a book list for the abbey library.[398] No list has come down to us for any other Danish monastery, and so before we summarize our findings on Øm, it would be worth looking at its contents, especially because it has not previously been analyzed.[399]
The list is divided into three parts, the first containing the books which belonged to the abbot, the second naming Øm manuscripts which the monastery as a whole owned but which the abbot was keeping for the time being, and the third section naming the titles in the monks' library. These latter are for the most part printed books, for titles that are in manuscript form are speci-

---
397) Poul Rasmussen, pp. 149-5o.
398) Suhm, Nye Samlinger III, pp. 312-324.
399) Some remarks in Ellen Jørgensen, "Studier over danske middelalderlige Bogsamlinger", *Historisk Tidsskrift* 8. Række, 4. Bind (1912-13), pp. 49-5o. Already J.B. Daugård in *Om de danske klostre i middelalderen* (Cpn., 183o) noticed the list (p. 1o9) and remarked appropriately that the presence of so many theological works in the collection did not necessarily mean that the monks studied them. Anne Riising, *Danmarks Middelalderligs Prædiken* (Cpn., 1969), p. 47, used the list to conclude that "man i Danmark ligesom i udlandet lagde størst vægt på de forholdsvis overkommelige mindre håndbøger, og at netop postiller og prædikensamlinger optrådte i størst antal." The best introduction to the subject of medieval monastic libraries is in David Knowles, *The Religious Orders in England*, Vol. 2, pp. 331-353.

fically named.[400] This fact means that the 1554 list does not tell us very much about the exact contents of the library a few centuries before, when printed volumes did not exist. Still, we can assume that the monastic library's choice of subjects and authors did not change radically from the thirteenth to the sixteenth centuries. The interests of the Øm monks, as a conservative group in society, are likely to have remained just as static as those of parish priest were in their sermons. Anne Riising has pointed out in her thesis on preaching in Denmark in the Middle Ages that the content of sermons varied very little from 13oo to 15oo.[401] She finds the communication of priests with laymen to have been one of the least changing factors in society. I think a similar analysis of libraries, if it were possible, would reveal a corresponding lack of development.

Another problem we have with the Øm list is the placement of the manuscripts that the abbot had borrowed from the monks' library. Did he take them merely to see that they were better cared for or was he actually interested in reading and using them? The notation in the list says only that the manuscripts were kept (*asservati*) by the abbot and were still in his care, *adhuc in custodia illius existentes*.[402] In the uncertain situation of the abbey in its last years before dissolution, it is likely that Abbot Peder did want to give special care to these valuable manuscripts, but he still could also have been concerned in using them, especially when we consider the quality and interests of his own library. His collection contained many of the works of the Fathers, and the one of them who is not richly represented among his own books, Gregory, has six titles among the manuscripts Peder borrowed from the monks.

What kind of books did the monks have to their credit? Out of 174 titles, plus 4o antiphonaries, I have found 19 having to do with the Bible or being Biblical commentaries, 24 of Patristic theology, 31 of medieval theology, 9 law, 6 history, 63 devotional, liturgical and anonymous sermons, 8 saints' lives and biographies, 1o handbooks, and 4 that I cannot identify. It is a collection geared to devotional life and not to hard study. The large number of books of edification is by no means balanced by a representative cross-section of medieval theologians. Certainly two of the great thirteenth century masters are there: Aquinas and Albert the Great. But they are alone. For the twelfth century the only writer who is well stocked is, as we would expect, Bernard, with seven entries. All the early theologians of Paris, such as Hugh of St. Victor, Abelard, etc., are missing. The Sentences of Peter Lombard

---

4oo) As p. 32o (*Nye Saml.* III), "Expositio orationis dominicae in papiro manu scripta"; p. 322, "Liber sermonum manu scriptus".
4o1) Riising, p. 454.
4o2) *Nye Samlinger* III, p. 316.

are there, as well as work of Richard of St. Victor, and at the other end of the great period there is a volume of Ockham. But even here in the theology section the emphasis is not so much on the heavy tomes of the masters (except with Thomas and Albert), but on sermons, such as those of Peter of Paris (Peter Auriol), a great Franciscan master who died in 1322, and John of Abbeville, another Paris master who died a century earlier. Likewise the subtle and difficult but centrally important nominalist theologian of the fifteenth century, Gabriel Biel, is only represented by his sermons, including his Sunday sermons for the liturgical year. At the end of the medieval period, any monk of Øm who was vitally interested in the development of scholastic theology would not have been able to get very far in his abbey's library. There was too much light, popularized reading matter and very little of the theological Summae. He could get a start, nevertheless, with the works of the Fathers: Jerome, Augustine, Bede, Ambrose, Cyprian, Origen, and Gregory are all included, but if he even wanted to read such a basic work of Augustine's as the Confessions, he would have been out of luck.

Only if our prospective reader was mainly interested in literature in order to be edified and encouraged in being a good monk would he have been able to be completely happy with his library. Here he could find innumerable popular collections of sermons, such as the *sermones dormi secure, Pomerium sermonum de sanctis*, and *sermones thesauri novi*. He could broaden his devotion to Mary by reading books dedicated to her, or he could find much material for meditations on the scriptures.

We know that the Benedictine Rule prescribed that each monk during Lent was to read a book from the library,[403] and we can assume that the Cistercians followed this provision. In the Øm list we can see the outcome of the practice that we might have expected: the brothers, not being intellectuals or scholars, preferred to read books for self-improvement, thus keeping to the Rule and leaving the secrets of theology to others. Another practical use of the library books would have been in the preparation of sermons. Here the brothers had again a great selection to choose from. As we move through the thirteenth century, we find many cases in Denmark of Cistercian monks taking over parish functions, and thus the obligation to preach. We can thus look upon the library at Øm as a collection of books with a primarily pragmatic function: either to fulfill the Rule or to provide inspiration - or complete texts - for sermons.

But not all the books can be limited to these purposes, for there is some variety. Monks who were interested in history could dabble with Peter Comes-

---

403) *La Règle de Saint Benoît* II, Adalbert de Vogüé *Sources Chrétiennes* (Paris, 1972), ch. 48.

tor's *Historia Scholastica* or with their own Cistercian Exordium Magnum. Or they could read the *Gesta pontificum Bremensium*, the work of Adam of Bremen. If they had legal problems, they had a fairly adequate collection of canon and civil law, while if they needed some general information, they could try Vincent of Beauvais and his thirteenth century encyclopedic Specula. Finally, if they were interested in reading some edifying saints' lives, they had a fairly broad choice, from the Fathers to St. Bernard, and including Jacob of Voragine's extremely popular Golden Legend, which contains saints' stories and short treatises on church festivals.

The brothers could lay claim to a library that was perfectly respectable, even if intellectually uninspiring. A 1514 catalogue from the Cistercian abbey of Lehnin in Brandenburg lists 6oo titles,[404] and if we add the abbot's 113 titles to the monks' 174, then Øm could come up to half this number. And just as at Øm, the Lehnin monks were strong on patristics, theology, law, and devotional books. They also had some textbooks on Latin grammar, a volume of Aristotle, a Seneca, Macrobius on the Dream of Scipio, and Boethius on the Consolation of Philosophy, plus Euclid's Geometry. Thus even though the nineteenth century German historian of Lehnin sighed that the monastery was weak in the classics, the monks there at least had something, while the Øm monks had nothing at all.

It was to be expected that Cistercian libraries would not contain so many of the classics as the Benedictines had, for their collections were so much older. But after the first hundred years or so, many Cistercian abbeys began to acquire classical literature. Already in the thirteenth century a catalogue for Rievaulx abbey in Yorkshire shows a work of Seneca, and a 14oo catalogue from a much smaller English Cistercian abbey has many more such entries.[405] Øm does not seem to have had any interest at all in the pagan writers, unless we suppose that earlier manuscripts were lost by the time the 1554 inventory was taken.

In terms of numbers of books, however, the monks had nothing to complain about. If we assume (and this is a large assumption) that there were twenty monks, then they had plenty to choose from for their reading,[406] especially if they read only because of duty and not because of interest and curiosity. What is so surprising in the Inventarium is not the monks' library. It is the abbot's. Peder must have been a phenomenal man. Through the substantial per-

---

4o4) M.W. Heffter, *Die Geschichte des Kloster Lehnin* (Brandenburg, 1851), p.79.
4o5) M.R. James, *A Descriptive Catalogue of the Manuscripts in the Library of Jesus College*, Cambridge (London, 1895), pp. 44-52. Knowles, *Religious Orders* II, 346.
4o6) I have used this number because the only Scandinavian source that gives us a number, the foundation account for Vitskøl, says that 22 monks came to Vitskøl from Varnhem (SM II, 141).

sonal library he built up, we can see how he followed the theology of the Reformation. The list of his books contains the works of just about every single prominent German and Swiss Reformation theologian.[407] We find 15 works by Martin Luther, 14 of Brentius, including many of his famous Biblical commentaries. Other names are Musculus, a former Benedictine who ended up as Protestant professor at Berne; Martin Bucer, a former Dominican who after his conversion to Luther tried to mediate between him and Zwingli. After Zwingli's death, he became leader of the reformed churches in Switzerland and Southern Germany and in 1549 went to England to become Regius Professor of Divinity at Cambridge. We even have the works of a Cistercian turned reformer, Corvinus, abbot in Lower Saxony. Abbot Peder's books also include the Augsburg Confession of 153o, which was made studiously moderate in order to leave open the possibility of reunion with the Catholics, and the acts of the conference of Ratisbon in 1541, when Catholic and Protestant theologians under the Emperor Charles V tried to reach agreements and actually succeeded on many points.

Abbot Peder was well stocked not only with Reformation theology. Also his collection of Bibles and Biblical commentaries and works of the Fathers is far superior to that of the monks. He had, for example ten volumes of Augustine "with index", and all the works of Jerome in ten tomes, also "with index", plus works of Tertullian, Origen, John Chrysostom, Cyprian, Rabanus, and Leo the Great. His library was almost devoid of devotional books, except for a psalter or two, and his works on medieval theology included only Bernard, Peter Lombard's Sentences, and Juan of Torquemada (d. 1468) on the Psalms, plus Rupert of Deutz on the minor prophets of the Old Testament. There are no Summae or commentaries on the Sentences. In this library we meet the impact of the Reformation on monastic Denmark. Here we find an abbot who not only took seriously his pledge to be loyal to the new religion but also apparently went about studying it with great care and devotion.

The immediate cause of Abbot Peder's devotion may well lie in a Copenhagen University Ordinance of 1o June 1539, according to which all monasteries outside towns were obliged to provide schools for the education of priests.[408] They were to have a theologian as master of studies and others to teach grammar, dialectic, and rhetoric. These teachers could either be the monastery's own brothers or could come from the outside. The students were to live in obedience and chastity, to sing daily in the choir, and to wear the monastic

---

4o7) The biographical notes that follow about Reformation figures are based on the following reference books: *Oxford Dictionary of the Christian Church*, F.L. Cross. 1957. *Lexikon für Theologie und Kirche*. *Dictionnaire de Theologie*.

4o8) Holger Fr. Rørdam, *Kjøbenhavns Universitets Historie* I, 52 (Cpn., 1868-9). See also *Academia Sorana*: Kloster, Akademi, Skole (Cpn., 1962): Kai Hørby, "Skolen og Adademiet gennem 4oo år", p. 14.

habit. In other words they were to form a monastic community so long as they remained in the monastery.

This decision sheds a great deal of light on Abbot Peder's library, which was ideally suited to the education of priests in the Protestant faith. The abbot himself apparently had control of the books to be read. It may well have been he who was the first master of studies. We can also understand why it was that he had certain books from the monks' library. He needed the texts of the Fathers like Ambrose and Gregory the Great in order to supplement his own collection of Augustine, Jerome, Tertullian, Origen, John Chrysostom, and Cyprian.

Although the likelihood of a school for training priests at Øm during these years detracts somewhat from our initial enthusiasm for the intellectual interests of Abbot Peder, a second look at our book list should be sufficient to make us realize that, school or no school, we are dealing with a very unusual man. Any young candidates for the priesthood would have been engaging in intellectual overkill if they ever began plowing through the imposing tomes that Peder could offer them. In the final analysis the great number and variety of volumes have to be ascribed to Peder's own special interests. He may have had plans to convert the abbey into an influential educational centre and thus give it a new role so that it could continue as a viable institution under the new regime. Or he may simply have been heartened by the prospect of devoting himself to the study of the new theology. Whatever his motives, the result is clear: a library that more than fulfilled the University requirements and provided the basis for a deep knowledge not just of the latest developments in Reformation theology but of the tradition of theological thinking from the Greek fathers, Ambrose, and Augustine right through the Middle Ages.

The evangelical direction of the reformed church is clearly reflected in Abbot Peder's selection. Many of the works of Luther and Brentius cited in the list are their commentaries on various books of the Bible:

    Summarium Lutheri in psalmos
    Lutherus in Ecclesiasticum
    Brentius in Exodum, Leviticum
    Idem in Job et Amos; in Esiam
    Brentius in totam evang. Lucae et Johannis

Together with this category we find catechisms or short outlines of the content of faith. These must have been especially useful in the training of priests, and they could easily be collated with the decisions of various church councils that I already have mentioned: "Cronica Martini (Lutheri) et acta conventus Ratisbonensis in uno volumine". Strangely enough, but again a sign of Abbot Peder's intellectual vitality, he had a number of books by Erasmus, such as his annotations on the New Testament. Erasmus's works are far outnumbered by

THE ØM INVENTORY OF 1554: COMPARISON BETWEEN ABBOT'S AND MONKS' BOOKS
(clear columns indicate abbot; striped columns indicate monks)

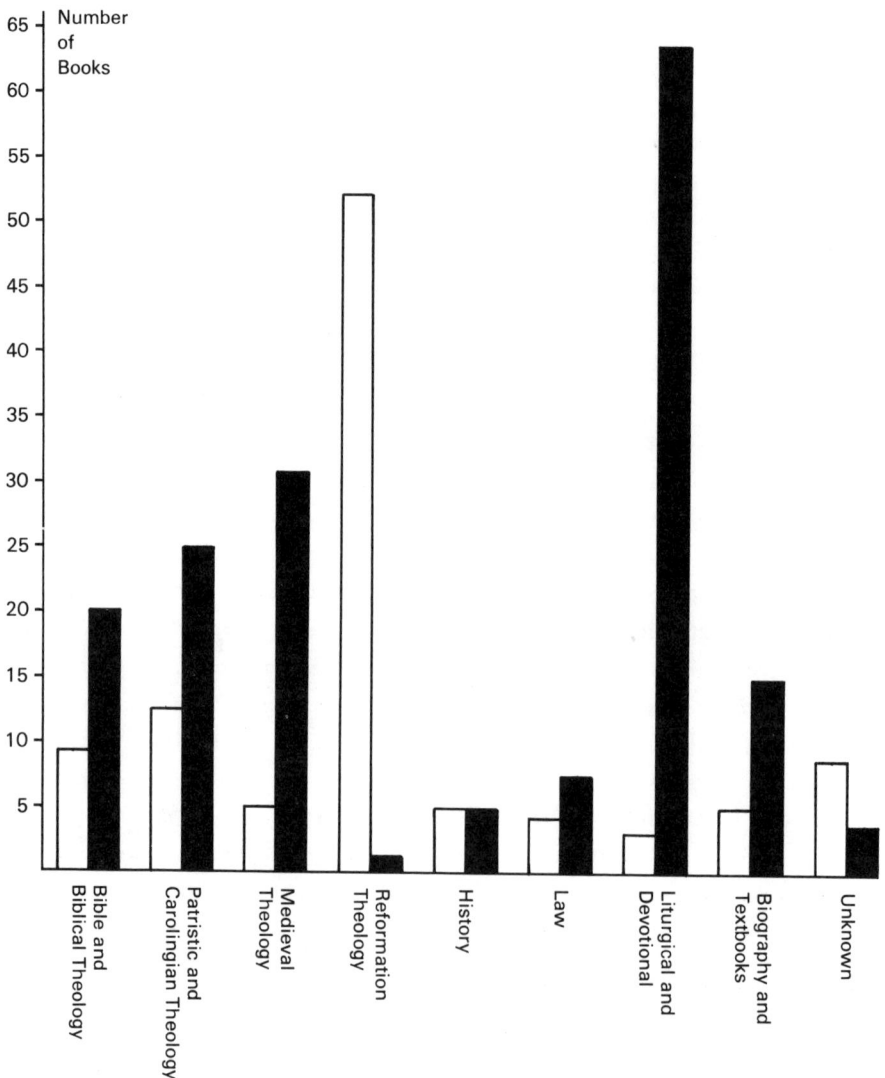

113 books are listed as belonging to Abbot Peder.
174 books are listed as belonging to the monks, plus 40 antiphonaries.
Not included are the 19 books held by the abbot but belonging to the monks' library: 8 Patristic theology, 5 Medieval theology, 6 unknown.

those of Luther (15 vs. 4), but the very fact that Peder included Erasmus shows that for him the break with Rome was not yet so final that it excluded all acquaintance with the reformers who had stayed within the Catholic Church. Another reformer who remained Catholic after an early flirtation with Protestantism is Johann Faber, who ended by becoming a zealous defender of orthodoxy. Abbot Peder nevertheless had a commentary of his on the gospels.

Abbot Peder was clearly interested in building up a library that gave a thorough introduction to the thoughts and doctrines that belonged to the Protestant north. He even seems to have been interested in seeing how other Protestants, who once had been Cistercians, had absorbed the new faith. His library contained the *Postilla Corvini*, by Antonius Corvinus from the important abbey of Loccum on Lower Saxony. He had left the monastery in 1523 and had helped to spread the new faith in his region.

It is a typical commentary on the difference between the Danish and German Reformations that Corvinus had to leave his Cistercian home in order to preach and live his new faith, while Peder could continue as abbot of his monastery after he had adopted Protestantism. Once again we can see the marvellous adaptability of the Danish Cistercians to changing conditions. Some historians might use this instance of continuity as an indication of lack of religious fervour and conviction. But to us in our age of passionate intensity, there is something refreshing about this renewal and adjustment.

The Øm library can be looked at statistically, according to subject matter. What immediately strikes us in our graph is the way the monks' and abbot's books roughly equal each other, except in the categories of medieval theology, reformation theology, and devotional literature. Here is the essential difference between pre- and post-Reformation libraries: the former full of exemplary literature, the latter stocked with Biblical commentaries.

Abbot Peder is our surprise and source of light at the end of the medieval period.[409] He warns us not to speak flippantly about unmitigated decadence of Danish monasticism up to the Reformation.[410] He stands not only for the amazing tolerance shown in many aspects of the Danish reformation, at least outside towns, but also for the vitality and interest of the monks in adapting themselves to the new system. Peder's intentions and plans with his books will

---

409) For the practical details of his life as abbot, see Holger Fr. Rørdam, "Efterretninger om de to sidste abbeder i Øm Kloster", *Kirkehistoriske Samlinger* 3. Række, 3. Bind (1881-2), 94-111, esp. 94-1oo. For an appreciation of Øm's survival at the Reformation, H.N. Garner's *Søhøjlandet* is again an excellent account, in such lines as: Alle privilegier i behold. Klosterlivet gik sin vante gang, medens man gik til billedstorm inde i byerne, og medens man andetsteds i Europa drev munkene ud, slog den ihjel, der mukkede....(p. 64)

41o) Such a facile view provides an easy way out for the historian who wants to summarize an area of life without really penetrating it. See for example, Erik Arup, *Danmarks Historie* II A (1961), p. 277.

never be completely clear to us, but the list itself shows us that he was trying to reconcile himself to and to understand the Reformation. His books containing decisions form councils where Protestants and Catholics tried to get together may even indicate that Peder was trying to establish in his own mind the basic unity of the Christian religion. But whatever his purpose, Peder reveals to us an intellectual curiosity and a desire to educate priests that speak highly for the state of Øm Abbey on the very eve of its dissolution.

As we look back over this immense stretch of four hundred years to the fragile beginnings of Øm and the unhappy wanderings, the tragedies of the dispute with Tyge, and the silences of the next centuries, with this hint of great riches at the end, there is one theme that seems to give unity and meaning not only to Øm's history but to that of the Danish Cistercians in general: resilience. Every time we from our perspective might think that the monks were decisively defeated, as in 1268 or at the Reformation itself in the 152o's, they surprise us a few years later with stubborn signs of life. The monks could profit from a society in which changes were not as radical or hasty as in our time, but even so it is still amazing how they could persist.

Institutions can often perpetuate themselves because they already exist and are too cumbersome to dispose of. It would be easy to say that Øm survived until the Reformation simply because it was such an institution. But something must have been there in the fourteenth and fifteenth centuries that we cannot trace because of inadequate sources: a desire to continue, a feeling that the monastic way of life was a valid and worthwhile one. We are still burdened by the Reformation's preference to look upon the Middle Ages as a time of regression or at least passivity, and yet it must have required a constant effort to maintain a monastery like Øm. The manifestations of this work are forever lost to us except in modest ruins and cryptic sources. But is it just by chance that when the Reformation came, it was Øm that continued to exist, while the remaining monks from the abandoned Vor monastery across the lake were given refuge at Øm? Or is it by chance that the monastery that survived the nextlongest in Denmark, right into the 158o's, was Cistercian Sorø? Only Benedictine Ringsted outlived it by a few years. Even at the end, when monasticism no longer has a social or religious role to play in Denmark, the Cistercians show a remarkable stamina. Such persistence points to more than the dead weight of one more institution cluttering up the medieval landscape.

Future historians will see the Øm monks in new lights. My judgments about them seem perhaps already in the mid-197o's to be inadequate or trite. But no matter what historical interpretation does to the Øm Book, we are left with one undeniable fact about the monks, something we no longer can say about ourselves: they knew how to survive.

BIBLIOGRAPHY

A. Manuscript Sources

COPENHAGEN Royal Library MS. E don. variorum 135, 4° - The Øm Book
MS. Ny Kgl. Samling 2o43,2° - Edvard Ortved's papers concerning the Cistercians in Denmark and Norway

B. Printed Sources (unless otherwise given, place of publication is Copenhagen)

Becker, T. A., De ældste Danske Archivregistraturer I (1854),IV (1885).

Bruun, Chr., Broder Russes Historie 1555 (1868).

Canivez, J. M., Statuta Capitulorum Generalium Ordinis Cisterciensis (Bibliothèque de la Revue d'Histoire Ecclésiastique 9-14B, Louvain, 1933-41)

Christensen,C.A., Corpus Codicum Danicorum Medii Aevi 2 (196o) (includes facsimile of the Øm Book).

Christiansen,C.P.O., Bernard af Clairvaux. Hans Liv fortalt af Samtidige og et Udvalg af hans Værker og Breve (Selskabet for historiske Kilders Oversættelse, 1926).

Dänische Bibliothec oder Sammlung von Alten und Neuen Gelehrten Sachen aus Dännemarch VI (documents for Vitskøl Abbey) (Copenhagen and Leipzig, 1745).

Danske Magazin 1-6 (1745-52) and Nye Danske Magazin 1 (1794).

Diplomatarium Danicum (Det danske Sprog- og Litteraturselskab, 1938-   ).

Erslev, Kristian, Testamenter fra Danmarks Middelalder indtil 145o (19o1).

Gertz, M.Cl., Scriptores Minores Historiae Danicae Medii Aevi I-II (Selskabet for Udgivelse af Kilder til dansk Historie, 1917-1922. Photographic reprint, 197o).

Gertz, M.Cl., Vitae Sanctorum Danorum (Selskabet for Udgivelse af Kilder til dansk Historie, 19o8-1912).

Hoare, F.R., The Western Fathers (Harper Torch Book, New York, 1965).

James, M.R., A Descriptive Catalogue of the Manuscripts in the Library of Jesus College, Cambridge (London, 1895).

Julian, R.P.D., Nomasticon Cisterciense (Solesmes,1892).

Jørgensen, Ellen, Annales Danici Medii Aevi (Selskabet for Udgivelse af Kilder til dansk Historie, 192o).

Jørgensen, Ellen, Catalogus Codicum Latinorum Medii Aevi Bibliothecae Regiae Hafniensis (192o).

Jørgensen, Ellen, "Ribe bispekrønike", Kirkehistoriske Samlinger 6R, I (1933), 23-33.

Krarup, Alfred, Bullarium Danicum. Pavelige Aktstykker vedrørende Danmark 1198-1316 (1931-32).

Krarup, Alfred and Johs. Lindbæk, Acta Pontificum Danica II (19o7).

Langebek, Jakob and Suhm, P.F., Scriptores Rerum Danicarum Medii Aevi I-IX (1772-1878).

BIBLIOGRAPHY

Migne, J.P., Patrologiae Latinae cursus completus, Vol.185 - the Vita Prima og Bernard of Clairvaux (Paris, 1853).

Moltesen, L., Bullarium Danicum. Pavelige Aktstykker vedrørende Danmark 1316-1536 (19o4).

Nielsen, O., Codex Esromensis. Esrom Klosters Brevbog (Selskabet for Udgivelse af Kilder til dansk Historie, 188o-81. Photographic reprint, 1973).

Olrik, Hans, Danske Helgeners Levned (Selskabet for historiske Kildeskrifters Oversættelse, 1893-94. Photographic reprint, 1968).

Powicke, Maurice, The Life of Ailred of Rievaulx by Walter Daniel (Nelson Medieval Classics, Edinburgh, 195o).

Saxo, Saxonis Gesta Danorum I, ed. J. Olrik and H. Ræder (1931), II: Indicem Verborum, ed. Franz Blatt (1957).

Schneider, Ambrosius, "Vita B. David Monachi Hemmenrodensis", Analecta Sacri Ordinis Cisterciensis 11 (Rome 1955), 27-48.

Southern, R.W., The Life of Saint Anselm by Eadmer (Oxford Medieval Texts, 1972).

Suhm, P.F., Samlinger til den danske Historie I-II (1779-81).
Nye Samlinger til den danske Historie (1792-95).

Talbot, C.H., "The Testament of Gervase of Louth Park", Analecta Sacri Ordinis Cisterciensis 7 (Rome, 1951), 32-45.

Thorkelin, G., Diplomatarium Arna-Magnæanum I (1786).

de Vogue, Adalbert, La Règle de Saint Benoît (Sources Chrétiennes, Paris, 1972).

Weibull, Lauritz, "En samtida berättelse från Clairvaux om ärkebiskop Eskil av Lund", Scandia 4 (1931), 27o-29o.

C. Secondary Literature.

Andersen, Niels Knud, "Striden mellem Øm Kloster og Aarhusbisperne. Et Forsøg på en ny Forstaaelse", Danske Teologisk Tidsskrift (1939), 129-46.

Arup, Erik, Danmarks Historie I (1925, photographic reprint, 1961).
II (1932, photographic reprint, 1961).

Asschenfeldt Birkebæk, C., "Mossø klostrenes omstridte fiskegårde ved Vosgård", Århus Stifts Årbøger 56 (1963), 41-58.

Baker, L.G.D., "The Genesis of English Cistercian Chronicles", Analecta Cisterciensia 25 (Rome, 1969), 14-41.

Bartholdy, Olga, Munkeliv i Løgum Kloster (Løgumkloster, 1973).

Bloch, Marc, Feudal Society 1-2, trans. L.A. Manyon (Chicago, 1965).

Bock, P.Colomban, "Les Cisterciens et l'Etude du Droit", Analecta Sacri Ordinis Cisterciensis 7 (1951), 14-2o.

Boserup, I.(ed.),Saxostudier. Saxo-kollokvierne ved Københavns Universitet (Museum Tusculanum, Opuscula Græcolatina, 2, 1975).

Buchwald, G.v., "Die Gründungsgeschichte von Øm und die dänischen Cistercienser", Zeitschrift der Gesellschaft für Schleswig-Holstein-Lauenburgische Geschichte 8 (1878), 1-121.

Cheney, C.R. Episcopal Visitation of Monasteries in the Thirteenth Century (Manchester, 1931).

Dansk Biografisk Leksikon, red. af Poul Engelstoft under medv. af Svend Dahl, Bd. 1-26 (1933-44).

..._gaard, J.B., Om de Danske Klostre i Middelalderen (1830).

Garner, H.N.,   Søhøjlandet (1965).

Garner, H.N.,   Atlas over danske klostre (1968).

Garner, H.N.,   De Venders (Højbjerg, 1972).

Garner, H.N.,   Øm Kloster Museum. Vejledning for besøgende. The Abbey of Øm. English Guide (Historisk Samfund for Århus Stift, 1973).

Gilson, Etienne, History of Christian Philosophy in the Middle Ages (London, 1955)

Green-Pedersen, Sv.E., "Øm klosters grundlæggelse og dets forhold til bisp Sven af Århus", Århus Stifts Årbøger (Historisk Samfund for Århus Stift, 1964), 174-246.

Green-Pedersen, Sv.E., "Studier over de danske cistercienserklostres forhold til ordenens internationale styrelse og til den danske kirke og det danske samfund ca. 1340" (unpublished thesis, 1969).

Haugsted, Ejler, "Benediktinernes Kirke i Venge", Århus Stifts Årbøger 30 (1937) 165-195).

Heer, Friedrich, Mittelalter (1961). English translation: The Medieval World (Mentor, New York, 1963).

Heffter, M.W.,   Die Geschichte des Klosters Lehnin (Brandenburg, 1851).

Huizinga, J.,   The Waning of the Middle Ages (Penguin, Harmondsworth, 1965).

Høirup, Henning, "Gunner af Viborg", Fra Viborg Amt (Historisk Samfund for Viborg Amt, 1961), 32-59.

Hørby, Kai,   Academia Sorana: Kloster, Akademi, Skole (1962).

Isager, Jacob,   "Syvogtyve abbeder i Øm", Århus Stifts Årbøger 57 (1964) 133-40.

Isager, Kr.,   "Skeletfundene i Øm Kloster", Århus Stifts Årbøger 35 (1942) 46-66.

Isager, Kr. and Sjöval, Einar, Skeletfundene ved Øm Kloster (1936)

Isager, Kr. and Sjöval, Einar, Krankenfürsorge des dänischen Zisterzienserkloster Øm (Copenhagen and Leipzig, 1941).

Jørgensen, A.D., "Striden mellem Biskop Tyge og Øm Kloster", Aarbøger for Nordisk Oldkyndighed og Historie (1879), 111-153.

Jørgensen, Ellen, "Djævelen i Vitskøl Kloster", Danske Studier (1912), 15-17.

Jørgensen, Ellen, Historieforskning og Historieskrivning i Danmark indtil Aar 1800 (Third edition, 1964).

Jørgensen, Ellen, "Studier over danske middelalderlige Bogsamlinger", Historisk Tidsskrift 8. Række, 4. Bind (1912-12), 1-67.

Jørgensen, Poul Johs., Dansk Retshistorie (1947).

Kjærsgaard, Erik, Borgerkrig og Kalmarunion 1241-1448 (Politikens Danmarks Historie: Second edition, 1970).

Knowles, David, The Monastic Order in England 940-1216 (Cambridge, 1966).

Knowles, David, The Religious Orders in England I, 1216-1340 (1962).

Koch, Hal,   "De ældste danske Klostres Stilling i Kirke og Samfund indtil 1221", Historisk Tidsskrift 10. Række, 3. Bind (1936), 511-582. Reprinted in: Danmarks Kirke i den begyndende Højmiddelalder (Det historiske Institut ved Københavns Universitet. Historiske Afhandlinger. Bind 8. 1972).

Koch, Hal,   Den Danske Kirkes Historie 1: Den ældre Middelalder indtil
                 1241 (195o).

Koch, Hal,   Kongemagt og Kirke (Politikens Danmarks Historie 3: Second
                 edition, 1969).

Kristensen, Anne K.G., Danmarks ældste Annalistik. Studier over lundensisk
                 Annalskrivning i 12. og 13. Århundrede (Skrifter udgivet af
                 det historiske Institut ved Københavns Universitet. Bind III,
                 1969).

Lange, Christian, De Norske Klostres Historie i Middelalderen (Christiania,
                 1856).

Lind, J.,   "Klosterhaven i Øm", Århus Stifts Årbøger 24 (1931), 13o-42.

Lorenzen, Vilhelm, De danske cistercienserklostres Bygningshistorie (1941).
                 Vol. XI of: De danske klostres Bygningshistorie (1912-41).

Mahn, Jean-Berthold, L'Ordre Cistercien et Son Gouvernement des Origines au
                 Milieu du XIIIe Siècle (lo98-1264) (Bibliothèque des Ecoles
                 Francaises d'Athènes et de Rome, 161: Paris, 1945).

McGuire, Brian Patrick, "Patrons, privileges, property - Sorø Abbey's first
                 half century", Kirkehistoriske Samlinger (1974), 5-39.

McGuire, Brian Patrick, "Property and Politics at Esrum Abbey: 1151-1251,
                 Mediaeval Scandinavia 6 (Odense, 1973), 122-15o.

McGuire, Brian Patrick, "Love, friendship, and sex in the eleventh century:
                 The experience of Anselm", Studia Theologica 28 (Oslo, 1974),
                 111-152.

Meer, Frédéric van der, Atlas de l'Ordre Cistercien (Paris-Bruxelles, 1965).

Morris, Colin,   The Discovery of the Individual lo5o-12oo (Harper Torch, New
                 York, 1973).

Nielsen, Holger Garner, "Om tamt og vildt ved Øm, Århus Stifts Årbøger 55
                 (1962), 24-34.

Nielsen, Holger Garner, "Øm Kloster. Cara Insula gennem fire århundreder."
                 Århus Stifts Årbøger 62 (1969), 9-65.

Nyberg, Tore,   "Klostren i abbot Wilhelms brev", Kirkehistoriske Samlinger
                 (1971), 44-57.

Nyberg, Tore,   "Lists of monasteries in some thirteenth century wills. Mona-
                 stic history and historical method: a contribution", Mediaeval
                 Scandinavia 5 (Odense, 1972), 49-74.

Nørlund, Poul,   "Klostret og dets Gods", Sorø: Klostret, Skolen, Akademiet
                 gennem Tiderne I (1923), 53-131.

Nørlund, Poul,   "Jorddrotter paa Valdemarstiden", Festskrift til Kristian
                 Erslev (1926), 141-17o.

Nørlund, Poul,   "De ældste Vidnesbyrd om Skyldtaxationen", Historisk Tidsskrift
                 9. Række, 6. Bind (1928-29), 54-95.

Nørlund, Poul, and Johannes Brøndsted, Seks Tværsnit af Danmarks Historie
                 (1941. Reprinted 1966).

Olrik, Hans,   Viborgbispen Gunners Levned (Selskabet til historiske Kilde-
                 skrifters Oversættelse, 1892 - Reprinted: Historisk Samfund
                 for Århus Stift, 1968).

Olrik, Jørgen,   Øm Klosters Krønike (Historisk Samfund for Århus Stift, 1954).

Ortved, Edvard, Cistercieordenen og dens Klostre i Norden I - Cistercieordenen Overhovedet (1927).
II - Sveriges Klostre (1933).

Petersen, K.N.Henry, "Øm klosters feide med bispen af Aarhus i midten af det 13. århundrede", Historisk Archiv I (187o).

Rasmussen, Poul, Den Katolske Kirkes Jordegods i Århus Stift. Herreklostrenes jordegods i det 16. århundrede og dets historie (Østjydsk Hjemstavn, Skanderborg, 1957).

Rashdall, Hastings, The Universities of Europe in the Middle Ages I-III (1895) (revised edition by M.Powicke and E.B. Emden, 1936).

Riising, Anne, Danmarks Middelalderlige Prædiken (1969).

Rosenthal, Joel T., The Purchase of Paradise. Gift Giving and the Aristocracy, 13o7-1485 (Studies in Social History: London, 1972).

Rørdam, H.F., Kjøbenhavns Universitets Historie I (1896-9).

Rørdam, H.F., "Efterretninger om de to sidste abbeder i Øm kloster", Kirkehistoriske Samlinger 3. Række, 3. Bind (1881-2), 94-111.

Schalling, Erik, "Kanonisk eller nationell rätt? Ett bidrag till diskussionen om 12oo-talets danska immunitetsstrider, Kyrkohistorisk Årsskrift 38 (Uppsala, 1937).

Skyum-Nielsen, Niels, "De ældste privilegier for klosteret i Væ. Et nyfund", Scandia 21 (1951-52), 1-27.

Skyum-Nielsen, Niels, "Ærkekonge og ærkebiskop. Nye træk i dansk kirkehistorie", Scandia 23 (1955-57), 1-1o1.

Skyum-Nielsen, Niels, Kirkekampen i Danmark 1241-129o. Jakob Erlandsen, samtid og eftertid (1963. Reprinted 1971).

Skyum-Nielsen, Niels, Kvinde og Slave. Danmarks historie uden retouche 3 (1971).

Smidt, C.M., Øm Kloster. Cara Insula (Historisk Samfund for Århus Stift, 1924. Third edition, 1962).

Smidt, C.M., Cistercienserkirken i Løgum (1931).

Smith, Gina Gertrud, "De danske nonneklostre indtil ca. 125o", Kirkehistoriske Samlinger (1973), 1-45.

Southern, R.W., Western Society and the Church in the Middle Ages (The Pelican History of the Church, 2: Harmondsworth, 197o).

Southern, R.W., Saint Anselm and his biographer (Cambridge, 1966).

Tangl, M., Die Päpstlichen Kanzlei Ordnungen v. 12oo-15oo (Innsbruch 1894).

Tierney, Brian, The Crisis of Church and State 1o5o-13oo (Prentice Hall, New Jersey, 1964).

Wilkes, Carl, Die Zisterzienserabtei Himmerode im 12. und 13. Jahrhundert (Beiträge zur Geschichte des alten Mönchtums und des Benediktinerordens 12, Münster in Westf. 1924).

Wissing, Jürgen A., Das Kloster Lögum im Rückblick. Errinerungen, Betrachtungen und Vermutungen (Heimatkundlichen Arbeitsgemeinschaft für Nordschleswig. Heft 26. Apenrade, 1972).

INDEX

Note: Medieval and reformation personal names are usually given according to Christian names. In accordance with the Danish alphabet, the letters æ, ø, and å are placed at the end of the alphabet, in the order given.

Abel (duke of Southern Jutland, mid-1200's), 63-65; payments extorted from Øm, 67.
Abelard, 129.
Absalon, 10; role in Cistercian foundations, 11, 16, 17, 28-9; situation after his death, 23; and Eskil, 35; iiin Saxo, 49-51; other mentions, 36, 53, 101.
Adam of Bremen, 118n, 131.
Adams, Henry, 118.
Ailred of Rievaulx, 21, 48n, 116.
Albert the Great, 129, 130.
Alexander III (pope 1159-81),on Eskil and Veng, 31; 120.
Alexander IV (pope 1254-61), 81n.
Alvastra (Swedish Cistercian abbey), 13-14.
Ambrose, 130, 133.
Amilius (Øm abbot, c. 1173-80), 43, 55.
Andersen, Niels Knud, 21n.
Annals (various Danish), 9-10, 15-16, 18, 67.
Anne Krabbe copy book, 83.
Anselm (archbishop of Canterbury,d.1109), 91.
Apé (peasant near Øm), 29, 42, 46.
architecture of Øm, 70; compared with other Danish abbeys, 71.
Aristotle, 131.
Arkona (fortress on island of Rügen), 50.
Arnfast (Cistercian monk of Ryd, 1200's), 88, 101n.
Arup, Erik, 115n.
Asgot (Øm abbot, 1255-60), 69, 70, 78.
Asschenfeldt Birkbæk, C., 40n.
Asser Rig (Absalon's father), 52.
attitudes:
    Bishop Sven and Øm, 47-48; expectations of Øm monks at start of 1260's, 73; defensiveness of monks, 80; their narrowness, 85, 95; Tyge as a demon, 102n; Øm in defeat, 104-105; attitudes reflected in Gunner's biography, 111; as reflected in French Cistercian literature, 119-121.
Augsburg Confession (1530), 132.
Augustine, 130, 132, 133.
Baker, L. G. D., 24n.
Barnum I (duke of Pomerania), 108.

Bec (Benedictine abbey in Normandy),57.
Bede, 130.
behaviour:
    patterns (monks-bishop) that reinforce each other, 79; naiveté that leads to catastrophe, 91; lack of will to compromise and paranoia at Øm, 103-4; Øm in defeat, 104-5.
Benedict of Petersborough, 119.
Benedictines:
    competition with Cistercians in Denmark, 29, 53; possible decline by 1150, 55; abbots backing Bishop Tyge, 88-9; tradition of hagiography, 115; as threat to Cistercians, 121; rule, 130; libraries, 131.
Bergen (Cistercian convent on Rügen), 17.
Bergen (Norway), 14.
Bernard of Clairvaux, 10, 34, 58, 111, 115, 116, 118, 119, 121.
biography:
    of Bishop Sven of Århus, 46-8; of Bishop Gunner of Århus, 110-113; at Øm and elsewhere, 114-124; Cistercian practices in England, 116-7; secular tradition, 118; Cistercian in France, 119-122; Cistercian in Denmark, 122-3.
Bjørn (Øm monk, mid-1200's), 94.
Bloch, Marc, 98.
Bo (Øm abbot 1262-3), 46, 73, 82-3; provoking Tyge at Øm, 86-7; meeting with Tyge, 88-9; Tyge tries to depose, 89-90; second meeting at Århus, 90-91; resignation, 92.
Bock, P. Colomban, 118n.
Boethius, 131.
Bonde (Bishop of Slesvig in 1260's),102.
Boserup, Ivan, 49n.
Brandan (Øm abbot 1193-97), 55-6.
Bredero, Adriaan Hendrik, 119n.
Brentius, 133.
Brienne (first Øm abbot), at Veng and to Rome, 31, 36-7, 42, 54-5, 119.
Broder Russe, 14n.
Bruun, Christian, 14n.
Buchwald, G. v., dispute over Øm Book, 20-1; 28n, 29n; *Sueno vita*, 43-4;

claims monks are forgers, 83.
Buris Henriksen, 14n.
Cambridge, 132.
Cara Insula, 14-15 (see also "Øm").
Cecilie (daughter of Skjalm Hvide), 52.
Charlemagne, 118.
Chartres, 124.
Cheney, C. R., 68n, 69n, 80.
Christensen, C. A., 54n, 76.
Christina (Swedish queen), 12-3.
Cistercians:
   early Danish foundations, 9-13; statutes of General Chapters, 14n; Danish convents, 16; contrast between twelfth and fourteenth centuries, 18; use of narratives, 22-3; partisan mentality, 27-8; 119-20; competition with Benedictines, 29, 53; problems and changes c. 1200, 53, 56; intellectual expansion, Paris and Denmark, 58; conflict in the 1260's, 75n; limitations of episcopal influence, 89-90; naiveté, 96-7; impotence of the Order against kings, 106; Danish abbeys continue life as usual despite Øm, 108-9; tradition of biography, 119-122; emotional content of Cistercian writing, 116-7; change in Cistercian spirituality from 1100's to 1200's, 124; flexibility in changing social conditions, 127; libraries, 131.
Citeaux, 9, 25; visitation, 61.
Clairvaux, 10, 15, 23, 55, 74; involvement in Øm dispute, 93; 115; its literature as source for Danish writing, 119-20; Eskil there, 120-22.
Cluniacs, 111.
Codex Esromensis, 24n.
Colbaz, 16 (see also "Annals").
College de Chardonnet, Paris, 58n.
Conrad of Eberbach (Clairvaux writer, late 1100's), 9n, 121-2.
Conrad of Ribe (Øm abbot in 1270's),105n.
convents (Cistercian in Denmark), 16-7.
Copenhagen University, 132.
Corvinus, 132, 135.
Cyprian, 130, 132, 133.
Dargun (Cistercian abbey in North Germany), foundation, 16; claimed by Esrum, 75.
Daugaard, J. B., 128n.
David (monk of Himmerod), 115.
definition:
   as phenomenon of thirteenth century culture, 82-6; at Øm, 100.
demon at Vitskøl, 13.
Denmark:
   favourable conditions for monasticism, 16; transition from foreign monks to

Danish, 55; social stability until 1241, 59; troubles in 1240's, 64:, comparison of its culture with England's, 92; archaic quality of thirteenth century culture, 113n; royal power and monasteries, 106; catastrophes of mid-1300's, 126; difference between Danish and German reformations, 135.
Djursland, 41; testament of Bishop Sven, 44; limitations of properties, 45, 52; disadvantages, 64; new properties on way to it, 72; as basis for procurations in 1260's, 81-2, 125, 127.
Doberan (Cistercian abbey in N. Germany), rival of Esrum in 1250's, 74.
Dominicans, 102.
Douie, D. L., 48n.
Dover (church near Øm), 41; meeting between Århus bishop and Øm abbot, 88-9, 125, 126.
dream of Apé, 26, 42.
Duby, Georges, 64n.
Eadmer (monk of Canterbury c. 1100), 57.
Ebbe (bishop of Århus, early 1200's), 60.
Einhard, 118.
Eldena (Cistercian abbey in N. Germany), 108.
Elias (bishop of Ribe in 1100's), 120.
Emer (chaplain of Knud 6), 33.
England, 55; comparison of culture with Denmark, 91-2; tradition og Cistercian biography in, 116-7.
episcopal blessing (of new abbots), 88-90.
Erasmus, 131, 135.
Eric (count, helped found Øm), 36.
Erik Abelsen (duke of Southern Jutland in 1260's), 73; intervention in Øm dispute, 102-3.
Erik Glipping (Danish king 1259-86), 25, 101; anger with Øm, 102; Cistercian abbots attempt to pacify him, 103; the king as probable decisive factor, 104-6; his relations with Cistercian abbeys in late 1260's, 108-9.
Erik Plowpenny (Danish king 1241-50), 63-5, 67.
Erslew, Kr., 83n.
Esbern (Esrum abbot in 1260's), 108.
Esger (bishop of Ribe in 1260's),67,95.
Esger (archbishop of Lund, early 1300's), 125.
Eskil (archbishop of Lund, 1137-77), Cistercian foundations 9-11, 13, 55;

memory of, 14n, 35; 15, 17; his use of Cistercians, 31, 35; 53, 62; as seen in Exordium Magnum and Liber Miraculorum, 119-22.
Eskil (bishop af Århus in 1100's), 27, 30; schismatic, 38.
Eskilsø, 39.
Esrum, 9, 10; foundation date, 11, 41; daughter foundations, 16-7, 55; problems after 1200, 24; 29; technical skill of monks, 40; abbots from Sorø, 56; church, 70; dispute over Dargun, 74; exchanges of abbot with Øm, 106n; continuing power bid at home and abroad, 108; royal privileges, 126.
Essenbæk, 40, 127.
Euclid, 131.
excavations (at Øm), 63n, 70.
Exordium Magnum, 9-10, 23, 119-20, 131.
Exordium Parvum, 22, 28n, 34.
expansion in 1100's, limits, 38.
Farmer, H., 48n.
Firgårde (Dover parish), 72n.
Flensborg Fjord, 17.
Flensburg, 102, 103.
Flensted (Låsby parish), 126.
Fountains (Cistercian abbey, Yorkshire), 14; foundation narrative, 24.
Francis of Assisi, 113.
Franciscans, 113.
Frederick I (emperor, 1152-90), 120.
Fünen (Fyn), 15.
Gabriel Biel, 130.
Gad, Tue, 114n.
Garner, H. N., 17n, 39n, 63n, 104n, 135n.
General Chapter (at Citeaux), 14, 22, 25, 57-8, 59, 61; and morality of Danish abbeys, 61; decision on Dargun paternity, 74; 75; Tvis scandal, 109.
Gerald of Wales, 23n.
Germans in 1240's, 63.
Gertz, M. Cl., 9n, 20n, 51n; 54, 77, 114n, 118.
Gervase (abbot of Louth Park in Lincolnshire), 116-7.
Gilson, E., 86n.
Glücksborg (Slesvig), 17.
Godfred (Clairvaux writer in 1100's), 119.
grange system, 64n; decline after 1250, 74.
Greenland, 13.
Green-Pedersen, Sv. E., 10n, 23n, 25n, 28, 30n; 36, 39, 43, 45n, 50n, 51n; authorship of Exordium 2, 76-7; 83-4.
Gregory the Great (pope 590-604), 48, 130.
Greifswald, 108.
Grenå (Djursland), 127.
Guden Lake (Gudensø near Øm), 14, 40.
Gudenå (stream near Øm), 27.

Guido (papal legate in Denmark in 1260's), 25; his coming, 96-7; misled by monks, 98; fails to satisfy them, 99, 101-2.
Guldholm (Slesvig), 17, 53.
Gunner (Øm abbot, 1216-21; Viborg bishop 122-51), 21, 22, 41, 56, 58; achievement, 60-2, 100; his biography, 110-13; its author, 110; dating, 110n; possible reasons for its emergence, 123-4.
hagiography, 110; for William of Æbelholt, 114.
Halland (Danish province now in Sweden) 17.
Hans (Øm abbot in 1300's), 126.
Harlev, 36.
Haugsted, Ejler, 64n.
Heer, Friedrich, 39n.
Heffter, M. W., 131n.
Henrik (abbot of Varnhem, then Vitskøl in 1100's), 13, 35; role at Øm, 27-8.
Henrik (Øm lay brother in 1260's), 94.
Herbert of Clairvaux, 10n, 119-20.
Herman (Øm lay brother in 1260's), 94.
Herrisvad, 9, 10, 15, 29, 57, 59, 61, 69, 74, 109.
Het-Münster (convent in Germany, 58n.
Himmerod (Cistercian abbey in S. Germany), 45n, 115.
Holme, 15, 61, 69.
Holstebro, 15.
Honorius III (pope 1216-27), 60.
Horndrup (Tåning parish), 66, 72n.
Horsens, 41, 64, 67, 117, 126.
hospitality, see "procurations".
Hovedø (or Hovedøya, Cistercian abbey near Oslo), 14, 39; revolt in 1240's, 109.
Hugh (bishop of Lincoln, end of 1100's) 47-8, 113.
Hugh of Saint Victor, 129.
Huizinga, J., 86n.
humour:
 in Gunner's biography, 112; in Cistercian literature, 122; in the Øm Exordium 1, 123.
Høirup, Henning, 21n.
Hørby, Kai, 132n.
Hårby (veng parish), 72n, 126.
Iceland, 13.
Illerup, 41, 125.
Innocent III (pope 1198-1216), 60.
Isager, Jacob, 69n.
Isager, Kr., 64n.
Jacob of Voragine, 118n, 131.
Jakob Erlandsen (archbishop of Lund

1254-74), 74, 91, 101-2, 103, 106.
James, M. R., 131n.
Jens I (Øm abbot 1222-29), 56.
Jens II (Øm abbot 1246-9), 63-66.
Jens III of Dover (Øm abbot 1260-62; again in 1268 and in 1270's), 71, 73, 105.
Jens IV of Horsens (thrice Øm abbot in 1270's and later), 105n.
Jens (Benedictine abbot at Veng), 27,29.
Jens (bishop of Børglum after 1264),110n.
Jens (prefect of Viborg chapter), 60.
Jens Canne (knight and friend af Øm in 1200's), 88.
Jens Judesen, 66.
Jens Kalv (royal marshall), 90.
Jensgård (Glud parish, Bjerge herred), 63.
Jerome, 130, 132, 133.
Job, 48.
Jocelin of Brakelond (monk of Bury St. Edmunds c. 1200), 104.
Johann Faber, 135.
John Chrysostom, 132-3.
Jordanus, 119.
Josephus, 118n.
Juan of Torquemada, 132.
Jutta (Erik Plowpenny's queen), 64-5.
Jørgensen, A. D., 20.
Jørgensen, Ellen, 13n, 14, 21, 110, 128n.
Kalvø, 14, 15, 29; move from Veng, 36; move to Øm, 39; 42, 55.
Kirkstead (Cistercian abbey in Lincolnshire), 14.
Knowles, David, 18, 23n, 55n, 128n.
Knud 6 (Danish king 1182-1202), 33.
Knud (priest mentioned in Gunner biography), 152.
Koch, Hal, 10n, 18, 23, 30n.
Kollens, 37.
Krarup, Alfr., 127n.
Kristian (bishop of Ribe, early 1300's), 125.
Kristoffer (junker), 125.
"Lamentatio" of Gervase of Louth Park, 116-7.
Lange, Christian, 39n.
Langebek, J., 28n.
Lars (Øm monk in 1260's), 94.
Lateran Council (Fourth, 1215), 30.
lay brothers:
   wealth, 71; attacked by Tyge's men, 94; abandonment of Øm, 104.
learning:
   at Øm and Paris, 58, 118; as seen in Gunner's biography, 111-2; study of law 118n; as seen in Øm library at Reformation, 129-135; at other Cistercian abbeys, 131.

Lehnin (Cistercian abbey in Brandenburg), 131.
Leo the Great, 132.
"Liber Miraculorum" of Herbert of Clairvaux, 119-121.
libraries:
   at Øm, 118; book list in 1554 inventory, 128-9; Cistercian vs. Benedictines, 131; possible explanation for Øm library, 132-3; Abbot Peder's intentions, 135.
life:
   at Øm (attempt at recreation of), 104n; violence of in 1200's, 109; as seen in Gunner's biography,111-2.
Lind, J., 64n.
Lindbæk, Johs., 127.
Loccum (German Cistercian abbey), 135.
Louth Park (Cistercian abbey in Lincolnshire), 116.
Ludrö, 13, 15.
Lübeck, 25, 98; plea of Abbot Ture at, 99-101; 127.
Lugnås, 13, 15.
Luplau Janssen, C., 24.
Lyse (Norwegian Cistercian abbey near Bergen), 14.
Læsø, 60.
Løgum: foundation, 15-6; 1238 dispute settlement, 61; church, 71; decision on procurations, 81; refuge for Ture of Øm, 103; 125.
Macrobius, 131.
Magdeburg, 102.
Magnus of Viborg (Øm abbot, 1233-5), 56-7, 73.
Malmø, 127.
Mandonnet, Pierre, 86n.
Margrethe (local noblewoman in mid-Jutland), dispute with Cistercians, 35-8; 80.
Margrethe (sister of Oluf of Øm), 67.
Margrethe Sprænghest (Danish queen, mother of Erik Glipping), 25; early demands on Øm, 73; letter to Øm 1266, 98; probable decisive role, 106.
Martin (monk at Øm in 1170's), 40.
Martin Bucer, 132.
Martin Luther, 132, 133, 135.
Martin of Tours, 115n, 119.
Mesing (Hjelmslev herred), 37.
Michael (Øm abbot 1235-46), 57, 61, 64n, 70.
monasticism:
   various historical approaches, 18-9, 47n; attitudes of self-protection at Øm, 34.
morale vs. morals, 63, 87n.
Morimund (one of the four first daugh-

ters of Citeaux), 74
Morris, Colin, 114n.
Moss Lake (Mossø), 14, 40, 41, 65, 126.
motives for monastic history, 23-6.
Musculus, 132.
Narratiuncula (for Vitskøl), 12n.
Niels (Øm abbot, 1197-9), 24, 56, 73.
Niels II (Øm abbot, 1229-33), 56.
Niels (bishop of Slesvig in 1260's), 67n.
Niels (bishop of Viborg in 1260's), 74, 90, 95.
Nielsen, Holger G., 64n.
Nielsen, O., 24n.
Norway, 13, 55, 121.
numbers of monks, 55.
Nyberg, Tore, 16n.
Nødebo, 24n.
Nørlund, Poul, 24n, 42n, 64n.
Odense, 127.
Olav (Århus bishop in 1300's), 126.
Olav Quiter (supervisor of Tåning grange), 64, 71.
Olrik, Hans, 21n, 111n, 114n.
Olrik, J., 49n, 63n, 73n.
Oluf (Øm abbot 1249-55), 67, 69.
Oluf II (Øm abbot in late 1200's), 105n.
Oluf (Århus canon, 1311), 125.
Origen, 130, 132-3.
Ortved, Edvard, 9n, 11n, 13n, 16.
papal privileges for Øm, 81.
Paris University, 86, 111.
peasants:
    treatment of Øm's by Bishop Tyge, 89-90; abandonment of Øm, 104; in Gunner's biography, 112-113.
Peder (bishop of Roskilde in 1260's),103.
Peder Elavsen (bishop of Århus, d. 1246), 64n, 65-6, 67, 82.
Peder Pave (Øm abbot, late 1200's), 105n, 106n.
Peder Sørensen (Øm abbot in 1500's), 129; interets and personality, 131-6.
Peder Torstensen (enemy of Sorø in 1100's), 52.
Peder Ugotsen (bishop of Århus, 1249-59), 65-6; Lenten procurations, 67, 78; 72, 124.
Peder Vognsen (bishop of Århus, 1191-1204), 52.
Pedersborg, 52.
Peter Comestor, 118n, 130-1.
Peter Lombard, 129, 132.
Peter of Paris, 130.
Petersen, Henry, 21.
Petrus Olai, 15.
pittances, 52, 71n.
Pomerania, 55, 94.
poverty as ideal at Øm, 49.

power: royal power triumphant at Øm, 106-7.
Powicke, Maurice, 21n, 116n.
Premonstratensians, 12.
procurations, 78, 81-2; position discussed by Øm monks, 87-8; king's demand for Tyge, 104-5.
Purup (Østbirk parish), 72n, 109.
Radulf (bishop of Ribe in 1100's), 15.
Randers, 40.
Rashdall, Hastings, 59n.
Rasmussen, Poul, 29, 36n, 40n, 41n, 45n, 72, 126, 128.
Ratisbon, Conference of (1541), 132.
recruitment: Danish vs. French, 55.
reformation, 132-6.
resistance to Cistercian foundations, 12.
Ribe, 15, 59, 98, 127.
Richard of Saint Victor, 130.
Rievaulx (Cistercian abbey, Yorkshire), 131.
Riising, Anne, 16n, 68n, 128n, 129.
Ring (convent near Skanderborg), 41, 125, 127.
Ringsted (Benedictine abbey near Sorø), 17n, 136.
Roskilde, 13; Cistercian convent of, 16; 127.
Rosmos (Øm farm, Djursland), 78.
Rügen, 16, 50.
Rupert of Deutz, 132.
Ryd: foundation, 17; refuge for Ture of Øm, 103; investigation of Tvis, 109.
Ræder, H., 49n.
Rørdam, Holger Fr., 132n, 135n.
Sabro, 33.
St. Clement's cathedral, Århus, 46.
St. Eucharius (Benedictine monastery, Trier), 115.
St. Michael (Benedictine monastery, Slesvig), 17.
St. Victor (Augustinian house, Paris), 114.
Saxe Torbernsen, 24n.
Saxo, 10; uses of Absalon and Sven of Århus, 49-51; and Esrum monks, 91.
Saxony, 120, 121.
scandal (at Øm), 68-9.
Schalling, Erik, 21n, 83-4.
sculpture, 124.
secularization, process of, 123-4.
Seem, 15.
Seneca, 131.
Sens, 32.
sermon literature at Øm, 130.
Silkeborg, 14, 55.
Skanderborg, 41, 126.

INDEX

Skanderborg Lake, 14, 39n, 127.
Skanderborg Register, 72, 125-6, 128.
Skjalm Hvide (founder of West Zealand magnate family), 52, 119.
Skjalm Vognsen (bishop of Århus, early 1200's), 52.
Skyum-Nielsen, Niels, 10n, 21n,, 26, 28n, 38n, 42n, 49n, 54, 58, 60, 63, 68, 72, 78, 79n, 81, 82n, 83n, 87, 89, 91, 93, 95n, 96n, 103, 106n.
Skæring (near Århus), 72, 125-6.
Skåne, 9, 12.
Slangerup (Cistercian convent, Zealand), 16.
Slesvig, 17, 53, 61, 98, 102.
Smidt, C. M., 63, 64n, 70-1.
Sminge, 14, 27; transfer to and from, 29-31; 37, 39.
Smith, Gina Gertrud, 10n, 16n.
Snede (parish between Horsens and Vejle), 126.
solidarity: of Danish Cistercian abbeys with each other, 61, 91, 93, 97; first attempt to save Øm, 103; abbeys continue life as usual, 108; of upper class to solve controversy, 88n.
Sorø:
  foundation and wealth, 11-2, 15, 41, 55; daughter at Ås, 17; problems after 1200, 24, 101n; foundation account, 27-8; 29; self-defence, 30; need for running water, 39; canals, 40n; abbots to Esrum, 56; deposition of abbot, 69n, 74, 109; church. 70; pittances, 71n; fire, 74; no more abbots from Øm, 106n; authorship of Older Zealand Chronicle, 118-9; contact with Øm, 119; acquisition of towns, 127; survival in 1500's, 136.
Southern, R. W., 12, 48n, 55n, 57n.
Stefan (Herrisvad abbot, then bishop of Ribe in 1100's), 40.
Stephen (skilled Esrum monk, 1100's), 40.
Stephen (archbishop of Uppsala), 52.
Suhm, P. F., 28n, 118n.
Sulpicius Severus, 115n.
supernatural:
  in Exordium 1, 29; in abbot list, 57; in French Cistercian literature, 121-2; in Gunner's biography, 123-4.
Sven (bishop of Århus), 22; foundation of Øm, 27-30; 33, 35, 36, 39; donations on Djursland, 41; initial resistance to monks, 43-4; testaments, 43-4; character as seen by Øm, 46-8, 122; as seen by Saxo, 49-51; books given monks, 68; testaments as used in 1260's controversy, 83-4.
Sven Pave (son of abbot Oluf of Øm), 67.

Sweden, 121.
Sødring (island, Randers fjord), 66.
Talbot, C. H., 116n.
Tangl, M., 90n.
Tautra (Norwegian Cistercian abbey), 39n.
tears: as cultural expressions, 95n.
Tertullian, 132-3.
testaments of Sven, 43-4, 83-4.
Thomas (apostle), 119.
Thomas Aquinas, 129-30.
Thomas Becket, 118-9.
Thomas of Celano, 119.
Thorkelin, G., 46.
Thorkil (Øm abbot, 1199-1216), 24, 56.
tithes, problem of, 23, 30, 46; Vitskøl solution, 74; withheld from Tyge, 94.
Tommerup, 12.
tower at Øm, 65.
towns and the Cistercians, 127.
Trier, 115.
troll, 14.
Tuel Lake, 39.
Ture (Esrum abbot, from 1263 Øm abbot), 25, 76, 92; first clashes with Tyge, 92-3; appeal at Lübeck, 99-101; help from Jakob Erlandsen, 101; flight from Øm, 103; probable 1268 retirement, 105n.
Tvis, 15, 16, 59; and Løgum, 61; 69; crisis in 1260's, 109.
Tyge (bishop of Århus in 1260's), 22, 26, 65, 72, 73, 76; insists on procurations, 78, 81-2; first visit to Øm, 79; personality, 78-80, 82n, 83n, 84; attempt at visitation at Øm, 80; rage, 86-7; decisions at Dover, 89; second Århus meeting, 90-1; rejection of 1264 compromise, 96; alliance with king, 102, 106-7; excommunication, 103; his challenge to Øm, 124.
Tåning (Øm grange), 41, 64.
Ubby Tordsen, 61.
Uffe (archbishop of Lund, early 1200's), 112.
Urban IV (pope 1261-4), 97n.
Valdemar I (Danish king 1157-82), foundation of Vitskøl, 12; 27; Veng, 32, 35-7; his importance to monks, 38-9; as seen in Saxo, 50-1.
Valdemar II (Danish king, 1202-41), 59, 61.
Valdemar (bishop of Slesvig in 1100's), 17, 18.
Varnhem (Swedish Cistercian abbey), 12, 13, 15, 55, 131n.
Vättern (Swedish lake), 13.

INDEX

Venern (Swedish lake), 13.
Veng, 14, 15, 27, 29; Cistercian residence, 31-2; outcome of troubles, 35-6, 39; holdings of Benedictines, 40; 42, 55, 60; papal privileges for Øm, 89; 126.
Viborg, 21, 56; and Bishop Gunner, 58-60, 112; 127.
Vincent of Beauvais, 131.
visitation, practice of: at Herrisvad, 61; at Citeaux, 61; by bishop, 68n, 69n, 81.
Vissing (Benedictine convent near Øm), 40; destruction in 1240's, 65.
Vita Prima of Bernard of Clairvaux, 119.
Vitskøl: foundation, 12-3, 131n; 25, 41; advantages, 42; 55, 56; and Viborg, 60; and Løgum, 61; church, 71; episcopal tithes, 74; 92; exchanges of abbot with Øm, 106n; relationship with Erik Glipping, 108-9; advantages of royal roots, 126.
Vole, 37.
Volgast, 49.
Vor (Benedictine monastery near Øm), 40, 136.
Vor (herred south of Mossø), 126.
Væ (Premonstratensian abbey, Skåne), 17n.
Walbert (Esrum abbot, 1100's), 16-7.
Walter Daniel, 21, 116.
Weibull, Curt, 49.
Weibull, Lauritz, 10n, 119n.
Wilkes, Carl, 45n, 115n.
William (abbot of Æbelholt), 39, 40, 53.
William (abbot of Øm, 1180-93), 55.
William of Ockham, 130.
Wissing, Jürgen A., 15.
Ynes, 63.
Zealand Chronicle, Older, 118-9.
Zwingli, 132.
Æbelholt, 39, 114.
Øm Abbey:
  foundation, 14-5, 27; library, 22, 131-6; preface to Exordium 1, 23; early problems with Bishop Sven, 28-30; troubled alliance with ruling class in 1100's, 38; choice of site, 40; fishing dispute, 40n; lands and limitations, 41-2, 52; twelfth century optimism, 45; period of happiness, 51; weaknesses after 1200, 52-3; early abbots, 54-6; practical abbots, 56-7; scandal at pub, 58; failure to obey General Chapter, 59; reason for success to 1240's, 61-2; decline in morale, 63; panic reaction of monks in 1240's, 65-6; trouble with Peder Ugotsen, 67-8; library and unknown scandal, 68-9; consecration of church 1257, 70-1; new property acquisitions, 72; beginnings of troubles in 1260's, 73-81; second visit of Tyge, 86-7; helped by other abbots, 91; resistance to Tyge's decrees, 92; monks and lay brothers attackes, 94; 1264 compromise fails, 95-6; seeks help from Guido, 97-9; manipulation of the past, 100; defeat, 102-5; royal privilege of 1270, 109; contact with Sorø, 119; dependence on bishops, 124; late 1200's records, 124; situation after 1300, 125-7; treatment by Århus bishops, 126; development in 1400's and 1500's, 128; book list, 128-9; library and Reformation, 131-6; survival, 136.
Øm Book (containing: Exordium 1, abbot list, Exordium 2, Bishop Gunner biography): introductory, 20-1; sections 22; composition of Exordium 1, 24, 30, 53; composition of Exordium 2, 24-6, 56-7; purpose of writing, 33; chronological chaos, 34; veracity, 37, 43, (by archaeology) 64, 78n,82n, 83n; description of Bishop Sven, 46-8; style and polish, 48; books and writing, 49, 60, 77; early abbot list, 54-6; Gunner's biography, 58-9, 100; lost chronicle, 67; lost full account of abbots, 69; distinction between Exordium 1 and 2, 77; criterion for accuracy in Exordium 2, 79; its incompleteness, 92; writer's growing fatigue, 99n; seeing Tyge as a demon, 102n; diminution of abbot list after 1260's, 105-6; loss of interest in history writing, 106; comparison between Bishop Sven's and Gunner's biographies, 113; Exordium 1 as influence on Gunner's biography, 122.
Øm Kloster Inventarium (1554), 109n, 128, 131.
Åbo Sysselsting, 88.
Århus, 46; contrast with Viborg, 59; attitude of bishops in 1240's, 65-6, 70; 86; cathedral meeting, 88.
Ås, 17; and Løgum, 61; 69, 104.
Åsgård (Øm canal), 65.

□ □ □ □ □ □ □ □ □ □ □

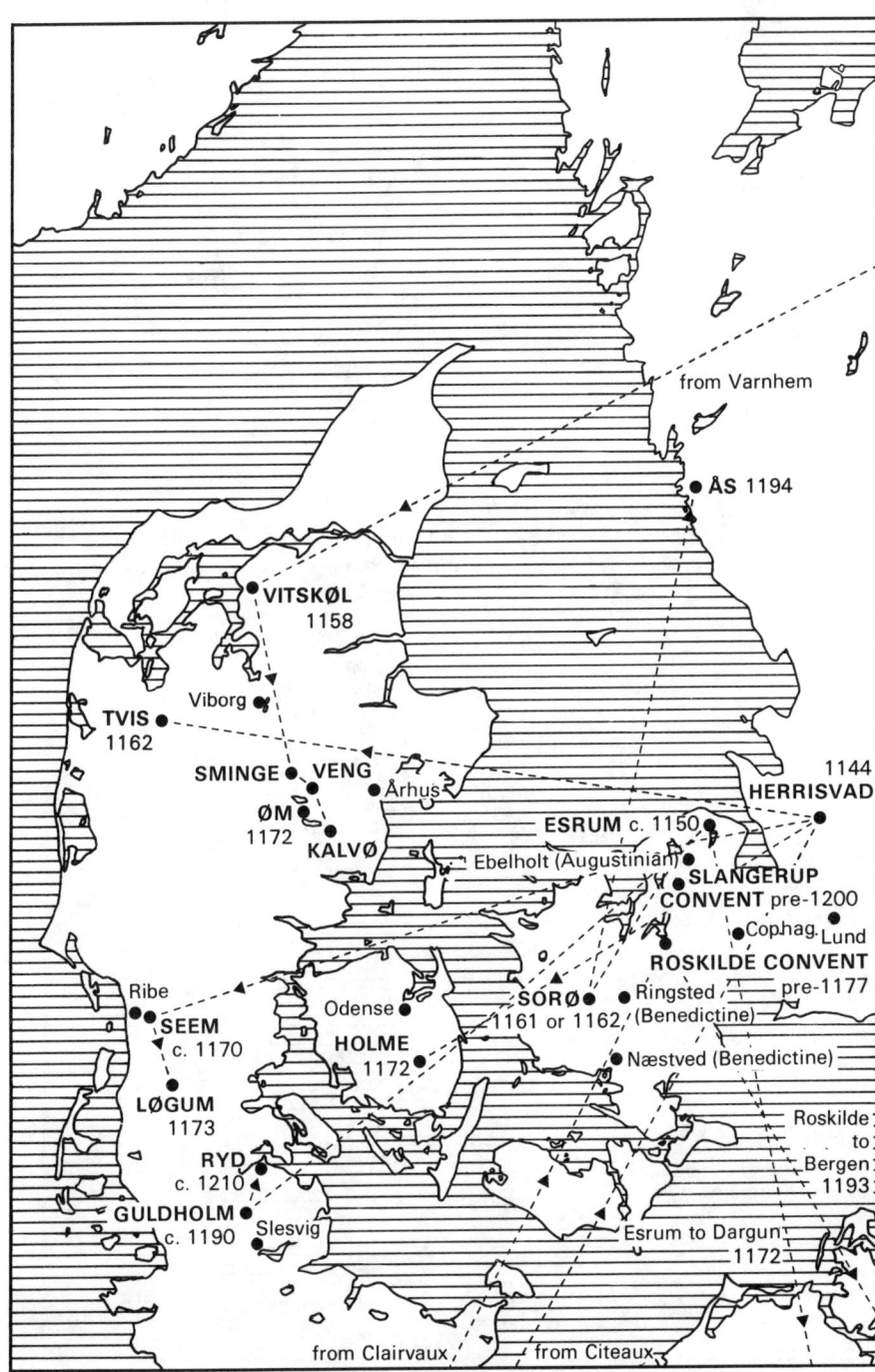

EARLY CISTERCIAN DENMARK

Note that in 1193 Roskilde Cistercian Convent founded a daughter convent in Bergen on the island of Rügen.

Also Esrum monks in 1172 founded Dargun in Mecklenburg, which in turn founded Kolbaz, near Stettin in 1174/5.

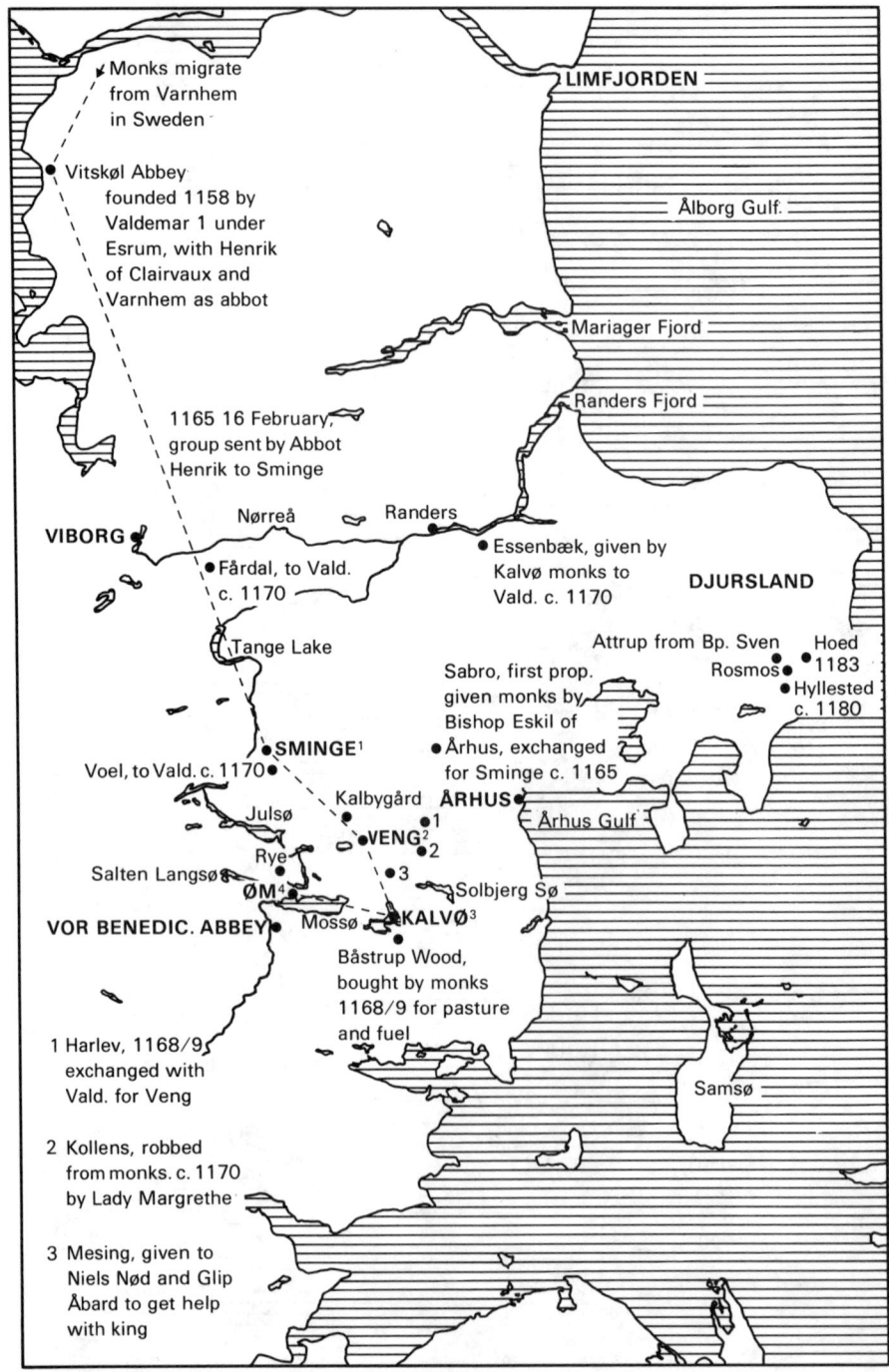

ØM ABBEYS'S EARLY HISTORY (1165-1185)

1. SMINGE - the monks gave it up to Bishop Sven, perhaps already in 1165, but he eventually returned the property to them. Then c. 117o they gave it to King Valdemar I, who at his death willed it to his concubine!
2. VENG - the monks were here 1165-1168, then exchanged it with Valdemar but regained it c. 117o.
3. KALVØ - 1168/9-1172.
4. ØM - arrival at sprin, 1172.

Note: Kalbygård (Lårby parish, Gern herred) belonged to Veng, given by monks to Bishop Sven of Århus but returned to them 1183.

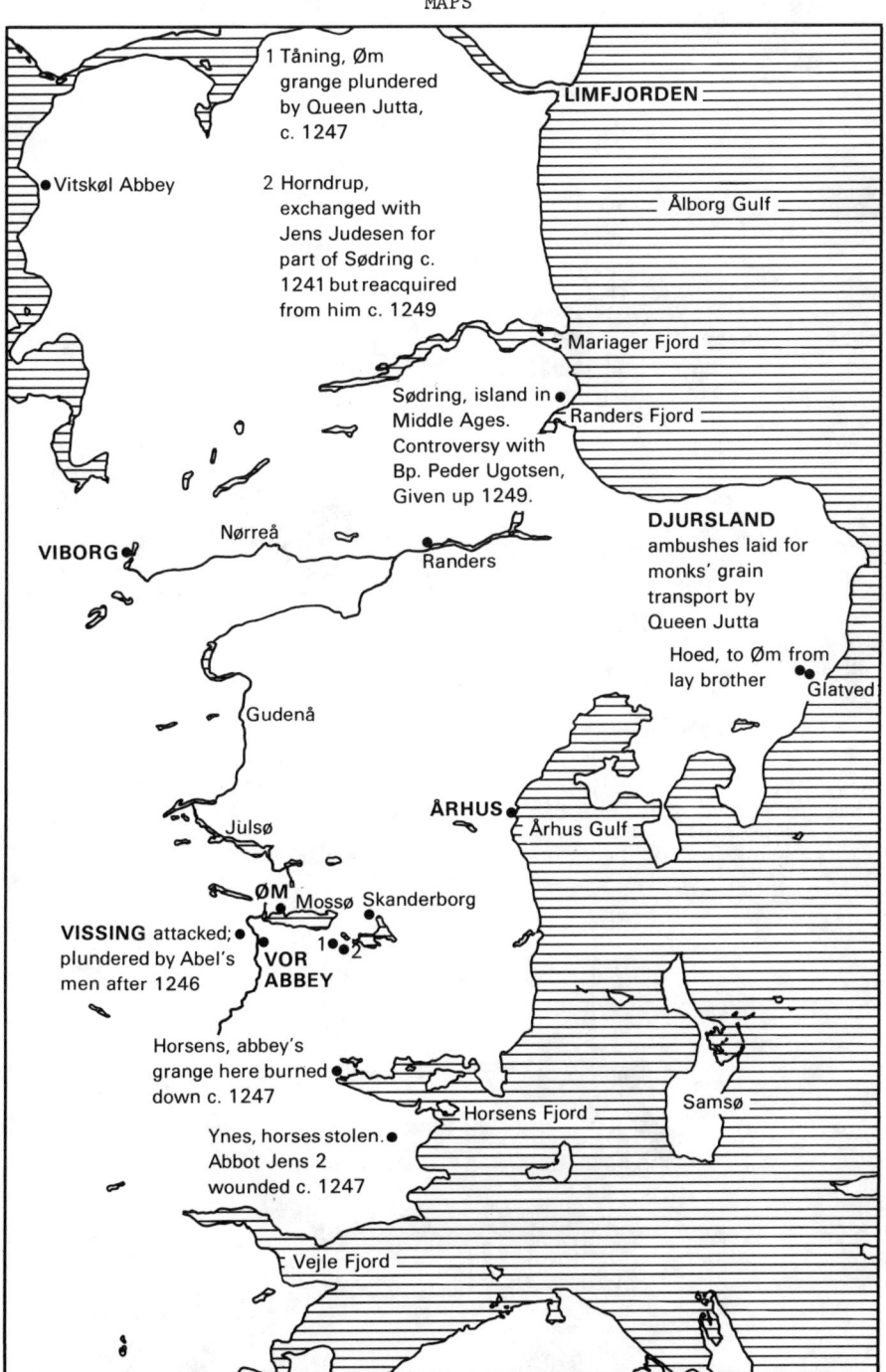

CHANGES AND CATASTROPHES IN THE 1240's FOR ØM

PLAN OF ØM ABBEY

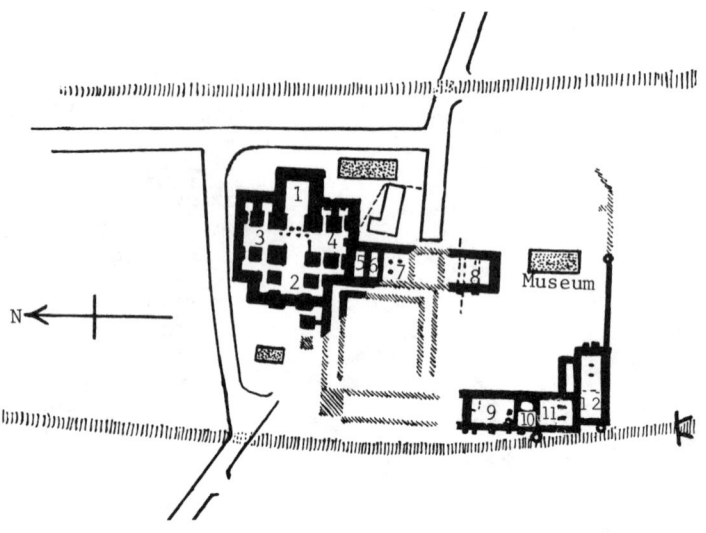

ØM ABBEY RUIN before summer, 1975 (drawing based on work of C.M. Smidt).
(Øm Kloster Museum)

1-4	The abbey church	7	The chapter house
1	The choir	8	Not certain
2	The nave	9	Identified as laundry (with canal behind)
3-4	North and south transepts		
5	Identified as the vestry	10	Bakery 11 Kitchen
6	Identified as the library	12	Refectory

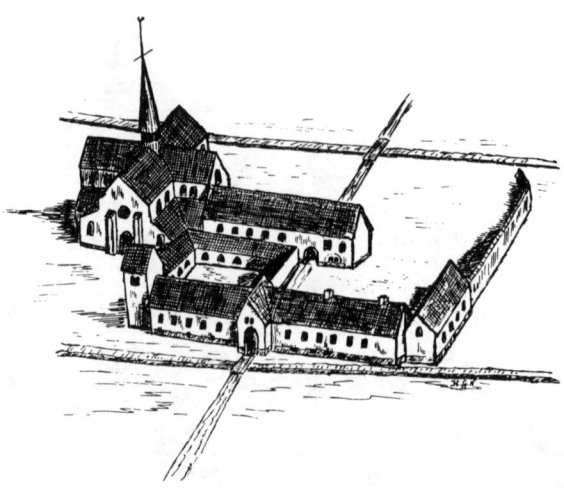

Attempt at reconstruction of Øm abbey complex as it might have appeared after 1257, with canals (Note that certain details will have to be revised because of the excavations that started in 1975).
(Øm Kloster Museum)

Plate 1. Aerial photograph of the abbey ruin in 1965 (since then, the road has been altered and new areas have been excavated). (Nationalmuseet)

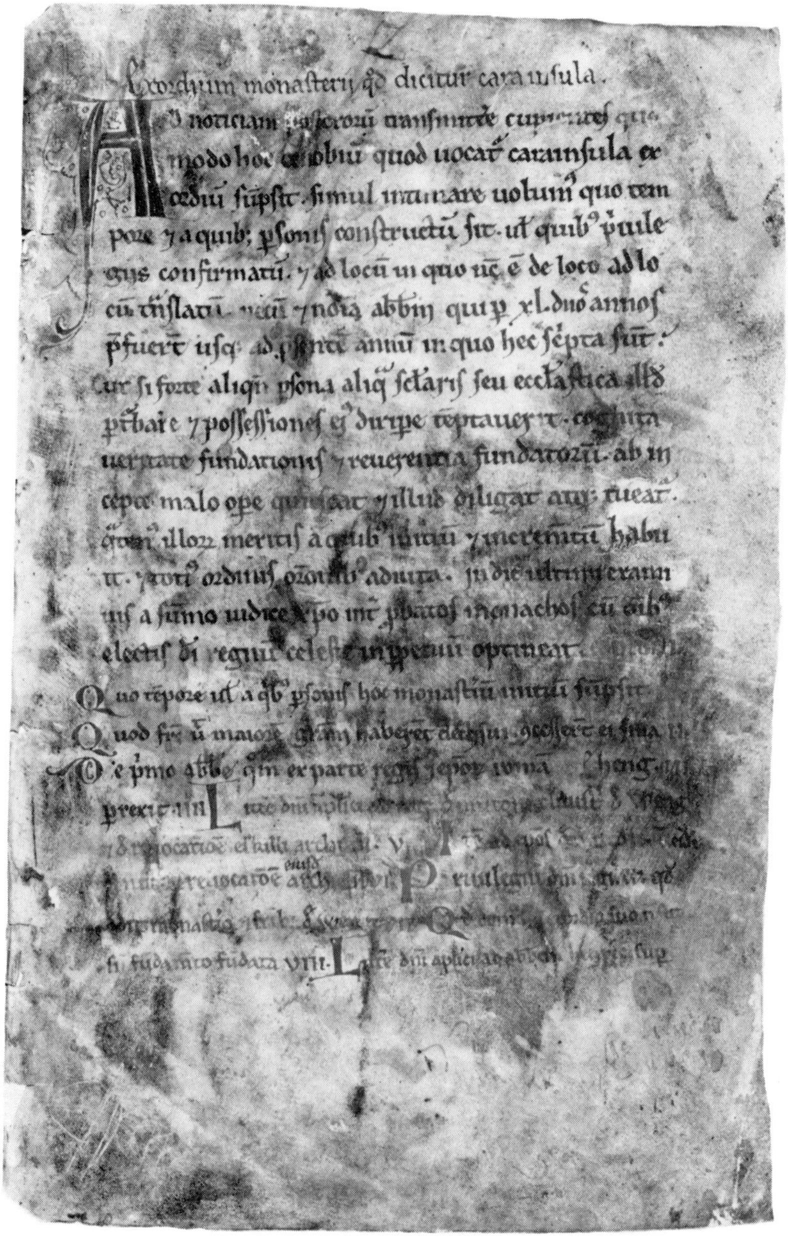

Plate 2. The beginning of the Øm Book (Exordium monasterii quod dicitur cara insula), Royal Library, MS E don. var. 135, 1r. (Det kongelige Bibliotek)

Plate 3a. The Øm area from the north, with Mossø in the distance.
(Øm Kloster Museum)

Plate 3b. Veng church. First Benedictine abbey, then Cistercian (1166-7)
before the monks went on to Kalvø and finally to Øm in 1172.
(Øm Kloster Museum)

Plate 4. The abbey church and east wing. (Nationalmuseet)

Plate 5. Junction of the abbey church's north wall in the choir and the northeastern choir pillar as seen from east southeast. (Nationalmuseet)

Plate 6. Bishop Sven's grave in the choir as seen from the east. (Nationalmuseet)

Plate 7. Canal built by the monks, east of the abbey complex. (Øm Kloster Museum)